Ontological Entanglements, Agency and Ethics in International Relations

While the relevance of ontological commitments for epistemology and methodology in International Relations have been the subject of growing debate for several years, the implications for ethics and political agency of embracing an ontology of entanglement have remained unexplored. This work focuses on the importance of addressing the ontological and epistemological assumptions of the discipline of International Relations.

There is increased awareness of the limits of abstract principles as ways of adjudicating real life political and ethical choices regarding International Intervention and international development for both practitioners and scholars. The work challenges IR prevailing ontological imaginaries rooted upon Newtonian physics. It argues that non-substantialist ontological positions nurture a political ethos that privileges 'modest' engagements of practical solidarity. Such ethos weights political choices with regard to the consequences and distributive effects they may produce in the context where they are made rather than based upon their universal normative aspirations. While the book is firmly rooted in metatheory, Zanotti also highlights the easiness with which political failures are dismissed as unintended consequences and argues that the current crisis in Syria, and genocides in Srebrenica and Rwanda have shown that advocating abstract ethical principles, be they the Responsibility to Protect, impartiality, or following rules can lead to disaster and can foster violent and exclusionary practices. She also exemplifies how an alternative ethos can be practiced through the example of an international NGO in Haiti.

Highlighting the need for critically re-thinking the way we conceptualize political agency and validate ethics, this work will be of interest to scholars of International Relations theory, ethics and critical security studies.

Laura Zanotti is Associate Professor at Virginia Tech, USA. Prior to joining academia, Zanotti worked in peacekeeping and peacebuilding at the United Nations.

Interventions

Edited by Jenny Edkins
Aberystwyth University and Nick Vaughan-Williams,
University of Warwick

The Series provides a forum for innovative and interdisciplinary work that engages with alternative critical, post-structural, feminist, postcolonial, psychoanalytic and cultural approaches to international relations and global politics. In our first 5 years we have published 60 volumes.

We aim to advance understanding of the key areas in which scholars working within broad critical post-structural traditions have chosen to make their interventions, and to present innovative analyses of important topics. Titles in the series engage with critical thinkers in philosophy, sociology, politics and other disciplines and provide situated historical, empirical and textual studies in international politics.

We are very happy to discuss your ideas at any stage of the project: just contact us for advice or proposal guidelines. Proposals should be submitted directly to the Series Editors:

- *Jenny Edkins (jennyedkins@hotmail.com) and*
- *Nick Vaughan-Williams (N.Vaughan-Williams@Warwick.ac.uk)*

> *As Michel Foucault has famously stated, "knowledge is not made for understanding; it is made for cutting" In this spirit The Edkins – Vaughan-Williams Interventions series solicits cutting edge, critical works that challenge mainstream understandings in international relations. It is the best place to contribute post disciplinary works that think rather than merely recognize and affirm the world recycled in IR's traditional geopolitical imaginary.'*
>
> *Michael J. Shapiro, University of Hawai'i at Manoa, USA*

On the Persistence of the Japanese 'History Problem'
Historicism and the International Politics of History
Hitomi Koyama

Ontological Entanglements, Agency and Ethics in International Relations
Exploring the Crossroads
Laura Zanotti

For a full list of available titles please visit www.routledge.com/series/INT

Ontological Entanglements, Agency and Ethics in International Relations

Exploring the Crossroads

Laura Zanotti

Routledge
Taylor & Francis Group
LONDON AND NEW YORK

First published 2019
by Routledge
2 Park Square, Milton Park, Abingdon, Oxon OX14 4RN

and by Routledge
711 Third Avenue, New York, NY 10017

Routledge is an imprint of the Taylor & Francis Group, an informa business

British Library Cataloguing-in-Publication Data
A catalogue record for this book is available from the British Library

Library of Congress Cataloging-in-Publication Data
Names: Zanotti, Laura, author.
Title: Ontological entanglements, agency and ethics in international relations : exploring the crossroads / Laura Zanotti.
Description: Abingdon, Oxon ; New York, NY : Routledge, 2018. | Series: Interventions | Includes bibliographical references and index.
Identifiers: LCCN 2018009401 | ISBN 9780415786355 (hbk) | ISBN 9781315227764 (ebk)
Subjects: LCSH: International relations—Philosophy. | International relations—Moral and ethical aspects.
Classification: LCC JZ1305 .Z37 2018 | DDC 172/.4—dc23
LC record available at https://lccn.loc.gov/2018009401

ISBN: 978-0-415-78635-5 (hbk)
ISBN: 978-1-31522-776-4 (ebk)

Typeset in Times New Roman
by Apex CoVantage, LLC

MIX
Paper from responsible sources
FSC® C013056
FSC www.fsc.org

Printed and bound in Great Britain by
TJ International Ltd, Padstow, Cornwall

To Giovanni, who creates food as a work of art.
To Riccardo, who wants to be buried with his tool box.

Contents

Acknowledgements

The argument of this book has been shaped by many conversations. Edward Weisband has been a mentor, a friend and source of comfort in dark moments. I am indebted to Francois Debrix, Janell Watson, Scott Nelson, Lydia Patton and Mario Khreiche, as well as to other members of the ASPECT working group for their comments on sections of this work. Tim Luke, Karen Hult and Ilja Luciak in the Department of Political Science at Virginia Tech have been in many ways supportive of my scholarly work during the years. I am grateful to Jason Weidner for having pointed me to the work of Karen Barad and to Sandy Thatcher for introducing me to the work of Peg O'Connor and, of course, for publishing my first book. I owe Nick Onuf for his (as always) challenging remarks on sections of this book. Conversations with Fritz Kratochwil helped me to gain confidence that this was an inquiry worth pursuing. The questions and comments from the graduate students of the seminar "Topics in Security Studies. The Political Ethics of International Security" in the fall of 2016 helped me to clarify and sharpen my argument. Conversations with my former UN colleague Francesco Manca have contributed to shape my reflections on that organization, though we do not always agree. I am indebted to Max Stephenson in many ways: for having shared many reflections on agency, for being a partner in scholarly work and in attempts to make a difference in the world, and for being a loyal friend. Paola Iannucci shared with me her knowledge of the work of Gianrico Carofiglio as well as copies of his books. I am also thankful to Anthony Szczurek and Augusta Nannerini for their editorial revisions and to Jenny Edkins and the Intervention Series Editorial Team for patiently waiting for this book. My son Giovanni has survived a busy mother and the difficulties of making logistics work. Riccardo made me laugh and rescued me from failing appliances, plumbing disasters and the challenges of everyday life. My lifetime friends in Italy have been in many ways a source of support when I was about to give up. My parents provided the feeling of security that made it possible for me to take risks to pursue my dream. Of course, the limitations and shortcomings of what is written here remain my sole responsibility.

Introduction

> Politics is the terrain of competing ontologies. Politics is about competing visions of how the world is and how it should be. Every ontology is political. If there were no ontological differences there would be no politics.
>
> (Wight 2006: 2)

> Failure to be explicit in one's ontology merely results in the passive secretion of an *implicit* one.
>
> (Bhaskar 1998: 642)

Ontological starting points shape the way we imagine how the world is and how we fit in it, the way "things" relate one another, what we consider valid knowledge and how we may be able to bring about change. Ontologies, as Colin Wight (2006) argues, are deeply political. And so is the problem of truth (Foucault 1984). Conceptualizations of who we are and how we relate to the world are relevant for the way we theorize how we make a difference in it. Starting points are important. As metaethical philosopher Peg O' Connor aptly put it, "Start in the wrong place and you will quickly become mired in philosophical 'problems' that are unsolvable" (O'Connor 2008: ix).[1] This book explores how ontological assumptions shape the way we understand agency and justify ethical and political decisions in the realm of international and world politics. It does not make a claim about quantum ontology as the "true" alternative to Newtonian physics. Instead, it makes an argument about the political relevance of ontological imaginaries. While not constituting a homogenous theoretical framework, ontological starting points constitute a shared common sense – a system of references that legitimizes theoretical and political positions.[2]

The prevalent ontological imaginary within the discipline of International Relations (IR) (and more broadly of Western political thought) by and large relies upon the Cartesian dualism of mind and matter, and the ontological assumptions of Newtonian physics. The Cartesian tradition views matter as homogenous and inert, or *res extensa*, or amenable to be molded to serve the purpose of rational thought, *res cogitans*. In this ontological imaginary, the human subject is ontologically separated and detached from matter. Leibnitz' picture of the subject as monad endowed with *potentia* also shapes how we imagine the way we relate to the world.[3] In this framework, agency is conceptualized as the manifestation of the *potentia* of the rational free subject, as *his* ability to shape the natural world and society through planning rationalities – an imaginary that is in turn deeply intertwined with representations of masculinity and with the attributes of sovereignty. Newtonian physics sees the world as made up of entities with stable characteristics and standing in a relation of externality to one another.

This view of the word, which I term *substantialist*, is characterized by ontological closure. Substantialist ontological assumptions deeply shape the way we imagine agency, ethics, valid knowledge and hence how we design and assess policy. The commitment to substantialism straddles many schools of thought, including liberalism, some versions of structuralism and Marxism, as well as some critical IR scholarship such as versions of governmentality studies. Substantialist starting points favor understandings of knowledge as a search of regularities that connect entities with given physical properties, such as in positivism, and/or as explanations of all that exists through overarching organizing principles as in some versions of structuralism. Furthermore, substantialist positions embrace ontological dualism and portray humans' ontological status as detached from matter and other beings. Humans are the masters of a world that is inert, homogenous, causally simple, amenable to be understood through abstractions and shaped through planning rationalities. As subjects, we are imagined as ontologically endowed with freedom and reason. Freedom is portrayed as the independence from others and the ability to shape the world and other people's deeds according to one's will. Or, alternatively, we are portrayed as the "alienated" victims of an oppressive power that jeopardizes our ontologically given pristine freedom.

As Diana Coole and Samantha Frost noted, "Presumptions about agency and causation implicit in prevailing paradigms have structured our modern sense of domains and dimensions of the ethical and the political as such" (2010: 6). Politically, ontological assumptions about the separability of what exists and the linearity and regularity of causal relations nurture an ethics based upon the presupposition that universal guidelines for action can be identified regardless of circumstances. The Kantian categorical imperative relies upon such presuppositions and justifies action through universal prescriptions. Substantialist ontological assumptions also constitute the foundations of research programs aimed at devising overarching theories that can explain everything with few principles (the positivist principle of parsimony) and that rely on the assumption that representing phenomena through abstract indicators and theoretical constants valid across situations is the soundest way of gauging what happens in the world, both physical and social. Kenneth Waltz's idea of good theorizing in IR reflects this view (Waltz 1979). These assumptions bear important practical and political implications because they legitimize initiatives predicated upon the presupposition that the international arena is a Newtonian space where the same conditions and causal regularities obtain. In making decisions about international intervention and in justifying them politically, states and international organizations alike rely upon abstract norms and principles while paying little attention to the means through which action is carried out and to its distributive effects. In other words, *practices* are of little relevance for ethical adjudication.

The relevance of ontological commitments for epistemology and methodology in IR has been the subject of a growing debate over the past 15 years. This includes Patrick Thaddeus Jackson's book on the status of IR theory, and its relevance for politics and ethics is the topic of an ongoing debate in the discipline (2011).[4] Colin Wight (2006) and Jonathan Joseph (2010) have highlighted the deeply political nature of ontological claims and the inseparability of ontological and epistemological assumptions. Heikki Patomäki (2002) has examined the relevance of such reflections for questioning universal normativity as a central justification of international politics and advocated conducting inquiries in search for singularity and difference. Milja Kurki (2008) has questioned notions of causation as law regularity, and Friedrich Kratochwil (2008) has advocated thinking of causality in the social sciences as a cluster of conditions coming together under specific circumstances rather than linear cause-effect relations. Emilian Kavalski has also critically explored the Newtonian roots of the IR ontological imaginary and the challenge of complexity theories to such understanding of causality (Kavalski 2015).

Scholars from different orientations have challenged prevailing conceptualizations of the subject and Kantian justifications of moral choices based upon universal normativity (Amoureux and Steele 2014; Connolly 2013; Kennedy 2004, 2006; Kuperman 2008; Mac Ginty and Williams 2009; Onuf 2009; Zanotti 2011). In contrast to Kantian positions, Jacques Derrida (1992) frames ethics as a sphere that "exceeds the law" in a way that situates ethical decision-making in the sphere of uncertainty and personal responsibility. Foundations of ethics based upon the presupposition of separability and closure of meaning have also been questioned by Wittengsteinian feminist philosophers such as Alessandra Tanesini (2004) and Peg O'Connor (2008), as well as by proponents of an "ethics of care" such as Fiona Robinson (2011). James Der Derian (2009) has advocated the need for embracing quantum conceptualizations of reality and for adopting a theoretical framework (which he calls virtual theory) that "begins with the premise . . . that reality has always be inflected by the virtual" (786–787), and Alexander Wendt (2015) has mobilized quantum ontologies as a central topic within IR. Diana Coole and Samantha Frost's (2010) explore the implications of new materialism for agency and politics, while Jane Bennett invites IR scholars to go beyond juridical models of moral responsibility in favor of a broader consideration for what she refers to as an "agency of assemblages," where agentic capacities are distributed across human and non-human actors (2010: 3). Recently, the debate on the relevance of complexity theories, non-dualistic ontologies and posthumanist reflections for the discipline of IR has intensified (Cudworth and Hobden 2011 Kavalski 2015; Malette and Stoett 2018; Pentinnen 2018; Cudworth, Hobden and Kavalski 2018). In the meantime, Mark Salter explored the increasing relevance of non-human actants for understanding IR (Salter 2015). This body of scholarship signals an increasing interest in quantum physics, complexity theories and human/non-human entanglements, and in the relevance of such reflections for the discipline of IR. However, the implications of entangled ontological imaginaries for re-imaging ethics and (human) agency in IR remain by and large unexplored. This book represents a step in this direction.

In an interconnected world, "not only it is harder to get things done when there is no agreement, but deciding which ethics should apply in what contexts and whether there is any universal rule, are themselves ethical dilemmas" (Shapcott 2010: 4). Is ethics grounded upon the recognition of universal laws that should guide everybody's behavior at all times, as the Kantian, deontological tradition would have it, or do ethical decisions always exceed the law, and occupy instead the space of undecidability as Derrida (1992) would have it? Is morality based upon duties that hold regardless of circumstances or are means to ends and possible consequences central components to ethical decision making? Substantialist and entangled ontological imaginaries nurture different answers to these questions.

Quantum ontologies, I argue, invite us to re-think how the world is, how we fit in it, how we get to know it and how we can bring about change in it. Therefore, they pave the way for re-imagining political agency and the justification of ethical decisions. A quantum world looks much less homogenous than the Newtonian/Cartesian universe, and causality looks less linear and more complex. Ontologies of entanglement do not start with substances but with phenomena – i.e. with clusters of relations within which "what is" acquires its shape. As a result, they nurture a different imaginary on political agency from Newtonian physics. As humans, we do not stand in relations of externality to matter, to each other and to the practices we inhabit and enact. As Karen Barad (2007) would have it, we are "of the world" not "above the world."

Quantum ontologies start from a state of connectedness rather than separation. In a book that contributed to bringing quantum theories to the field of IR, Wendt (2015) suggests that while atomism tends to promote individualism and competition, an ontology of entanglement may nurture cooperation and open new avenues for agency. I generally embrace Wendt's argument. However, as I will demonstrate in Chapter 3, while Wendt embraces a quantum ontology, his position remains firmly rooted within an idealist tradition that ultimately reproduces ontological dualism while reframing the centrality of "free will" in quantum terms. Wendt's strong anti-materialist thesis maintains that "consciousness" imbues all that exists. For Wendt, we are walking quantum waves and hence ontological closure happens through acts of volition that make the quantum brain's waves collapse. Differently from Wendt's, feminist quantum physicist Karen Barad's (2007) position is anti-substantialist and materialist. Barad's ontology does not start from *entities* but *phenomena* – i.e. entanglements of human and non-human. What is acquires ontological closure in the context of experimental apparatuses. In fact, while Barad paves the way for a radical practice-oriented conceptualization of agency, Wendt remains committed to an idealistic starting point that posits the primacy of the Cartesian *res cogitans* as the ontological characteristic of reality "all the way down." Differently from Wendt's, whose version of quantum ontologies reproduces a metaphysics centered upon consciousness as the substance that imbues the universe, I rely upon quantum ontologies to affirm the ontological and ethical primacy of practices. In doing so, I have no aspiration to construct an alternative metaphysics of the world, or to make "truth" statements about the nature of the universe. I am less interested in devising an alternative metaphysics to Newton's than in outlining the political potential of a quantum ontological imaginary for reshaping our political ethos.

Embracing an entangled ontological imaginary blurs the divide between materialism and idealism and emphasizes the relevance of ontological starting points. In reading Niels Bohr's model of quantum physics through Michel Foucault and Judith Butler, Barad sees us enmeshed in a world of ontological indeterminacy – an entanglement of relations without *relata*. Matter is performative, and ontological closure only occurs in the context of specific apparatuses of observation. Because there are no entities before entanglements, ontological indeterminacy is resolved through intra-actions. By radically questioning the very notion of separability that underlines images of individuality, rationality and universal normativity, Barad's intra-agential realism paves the way for devising an ontological and epistemological horizon where ethical and political decision-making embraces uncertainty and complexity. As actors, we cannot control all chains of events that produce any given outcome. However, we do take part in processes of shaping reality by operating intra-agential cuts differently. In this radical relational ontology, ontological closure happens in the practices through which we engage with the world. These practices are thick and layered, can never be completely described from an external standpoint and cannot be overdetermined by abstractions and calculations.

While Karen Barad criticizes Michel Foucault for ignoring the non-human in his inquiries, their respective positions are in many regards attuned with each other, nurturing a similar ethos. While Foucault did not concern himself with ontological questions, he did embrace a radical non-substantialism both in his research methods and in his political position. Foucault viewed scholarly, as well as ethical and political, activities as endeavors aimed at questioning "universals" – i.e. the necessity of social arrangements that are given to us as inevitable. For Foucault, social "entities" (including concepts like madness, subjectivity and statehood) take shape in the context of specific historical contingencies, the configurations of which do not follow the laws of necessity and must be explored in their specificity. Foucault's inquiries consistently aimed at de-bunking ontologies of the social that start from entities or assume overarching regularities and principles that explain and govern all that exist. Foucault has defined the ethos of modernity as an ethos where critical inquiry, practices of life and political agency are deeply interrelated. (Foucault 1984). Knowledge, for Foucault, is imbricated with apparatuses of social control, the normalization of behavior and the organization of space. Meaning only takes shape in the context of a web of relations (as, for instance, in the "archive"), and subjectivity is molded within the diverse and material social practices that articulate relations of power.

Similarly, because what is acquires ontological determinacy only within apparatuses of observation, for Barad, ontologies and epistemologies are not separate. They are entangled in processes of mattering of matter that experimental apparatuses contribute to shape. I maintain that both "apparatuses" or *dispositifs* – i.e.

the instruments and social arrangements we deploy to know what we know and to "intervene" in the world have morphogenetic properties and operate ontological cuts. Thus the notion of "apparatus" is central for reframing the way we imagine how we fit in the world. As actors, we are entangled with, constituted and transformed by the very processes we aim to shape. In a universe of entanglements, the classical notion of agency-as-power prevalent in IR – i.e. as the ability to make others do what they would otherwise not have done – comes under question. Instead of conceiving of subjects as monads endowed with *potentia*, subjectivity is re-imagined as entangled with, but not determined by, the specific situations of our existence. Humans are not detached or self-contained. We do not act upon the world by applying forces of push and pull, but instead produce ontological effects we only partially control within the material and entangled reality of which we are part and by which we are in turn shaped. The apparatuses through which we engage with the world bring ontological indeterminacy to (provisional) ontological closure. Both the liberal assumptions that we are ontologically free and reasonable beings, and the Marxist notion of alienation by which such ontological freedom is crushed by the capitalist economic order come under question. As quantum subjects, we are relational beings (unequally) immersed in a world endowed with morphogenetic properties which we contribute to shape.

I contrast a non-substantialist reading of Foucault's position with regards to power and subjectivity with prevalent interpretations of his work that portray power as a substance that oppresses otherwise "free" subjects. Contra these interpretations, Foucault repeatedly emphasized that he was interested in inquiring *how* power is articulated, not *what* power *is*. In fact, genealogy and eventalization, two pillars of Foucault's approach to the study of social phenomena, diagnose how historical contingencies come together to constitute knowledge formations and social arrangements. Foucault's non-substantialist position on the conduct of social inquiries plays a central role in his political ethos, never aimed at establishing an alternative metaphysics or political order. In this regard, Foucault strongly rejected the Marxist intellectuals'aspiration to give overarching prescriptions aimed at bringing about an alternative immanent social order as potentially harboring the specter of totalitarianism (Foucault and Fontana 1979; Foucault 1984). As I will show in Chapter 7, Foucault's non-substantialist ethos is centered upon three "how" questions: "How are we constituted as subjects of knowledge? How are we constituted as subjects who exercise or submit to power relations? How are we constituted as moral subjects of our own actions?" (1984: 11). This book explores the relevance of quantum ontological imaginaries for these three trajectories of analysis.

In summary, while Foucault focuses on the social and Barad has extended her considerations to the non-human, they both radically embraced a non-substantialist onto-epistemology. Both Barad and Foucault begin from relations instead of entities and regard practices as the place where reality is shaped and ontological closure happens; they both question taken for granted substantialist attributes of subjectivity and reality; they recognize the deeply political relevance and imbrication of ontologies and epistemologies. Both Foucault and Barad challenge prevailing ways how we make truth statements, the notion of objectivity as well as how, as subjects, we interact with the world of which we are part. For both, objectivity and truth statements are performative and imbricated in practices; ontological closure is never final; agency is not a force exerted on external entities. Both for Foucault and Barad, the apparatuses through which we engage with reality are central in *shaping* its form, while not imposing one's will on its course.

Embracing ontological openness means that we cannot reduce how we view relations of cause and effect simply to forces of push and pull; we cannot assume that the world is constituted by atomist entities, whether material or social. As a result, as I will argue over the course of this book, knowledge is not a strict "reflection" of the external world. It is not necessarily premised upon the search of universal laws and abstract principles that explain everything, but rather upon the ability to diagnose what is the case in specific situations. Entangled ontologies have central implications for the way we justify ethical and political decisions. In recognizing that our world is entangled, ethical decisions must take into account the morphogenetic properties of practices and the importance of careful evaluations of complexities. Political and ethical choices are uncertain and situated engagements, the soundness of which cannot be adjudicated mainly based upon abstract normativity. As Amoureux and Steele (2014) have also argued, such political choices demand instead a careful, prudent and competent diagnosis of the situations within which they are cast.

This entangled ethos radically differs from idealist voluntarism. Seven decades ago, E. H. Carr (1946) advocated the need for conceptualizing political agency and ethics in a way that addresses both the limits of the idealist illusion regarding the possibility to transform reality through acts of will, as well as the realist persuasion about the inescapable subordination of actors to external conditions. Both of these positions, Carr pointed out, lead to self-defeating outcomes and stifle political imagination because they focus on general abstractions, failing to take into consideration what conditions and political opportunities actually obtain in specific historical configurations. Quantum ontologies do not imply that all possibilities are always open or that reality is available to be molded by humans. Practices are at the same time the space where ontological properties are defined, the horizon where knowledge is possible and the space where we *become* who we are.

Quantum ontologies debunk assumptions regarding the ontological properties of the human subject as the starting point for theorizing ethics and affirm the ethical potential of deconstruction. As subjects, we are ontologically shaped and defined in our intra-actions within practices, or, to use Barad's vocabulary, within phenomena. *Subjectification* takes the place of an imaginary that privileges humans as ontologically endowed with characteristics of rationality, freedom and *potentia*. Subjectification is the process through which we become who we are. For Foucault, freedom is not an ontological attribute of the subject, but the result of relational engagements through which the subject shapes herself "as a work of art." Foucault's use of the metaphor of the "work of art" is central for understanding his ethos. A sculpture or a painting is tangible and physical. Each is created by engaging with what is and opening novel forms of materialization. Freedom is not the starting point of Foucault's ethos, and his aspiration is not a struggle aimed at the liberation of a pristine "true self" oppressed by external forces. In the many debates with Marxist scholars of his time, Foucault argued that he did not see political engagements as a way of bringing about an immanent idealized and utopian social order that reverses all that exist, but as a life practice of questioning and interrogating that opens new possibilities into what is otherwise assumed to be unchangeable and ontologically closed (Foucault and Fontana 1979; Foucault 1984). Foucault's political ethos does not aspire at reversing whatever organizing principle of social order one imagines to be in place nor does it assume the ability of planning rationalities to re-shape what is. Political agency for Foucault is rooted above all in valuing creativity, alertness and contestation. It is exemplified by the Greek philosophers' *parrēsia* – a life practice that interrogates what is made to appear as inevitable and natural. In this ethos sound decisions do not rely upon prescriptions that hold true across situations. Valid ways of making decisions must be rooted upon careful diagnostics of what obtains in the specific contingencies within which we act. Similarly, instead of relying upon universal normative prescriptions, in an entangled ontological imaginary, ethical decisions result from attitudes of curiosity and from questioning the necessity of what is. This ethos also requisites assuming radical responsibility for the effects that result from our actions and suggests a prudent use of universal prescriptions as well as of the justification of failure as "unintended consequences."

A reflection on ontological imaginaries is relevant for a critical assessment of international intervention. Development programs and peacekeeping interventions rely upon substantialist assumptions, such as the linearity of relations of causality, the homogenous nature of political realities and the existence of constant and standard conditions across place, space and time. The ontological starting points of Newtonian physics and the Cartesian separation of *res cogitans* and *res extensa* are central for shaping the way how international interventions, including peacekeeping, peacebuilding and international development have been conceived, justified and implemented. International interventions by and large presuppose that post-conflict societies are similar to each other and that what is at stake in different places can be grasped through technical knowledge and modified through standardized benchmarks of performance. Post-conflict societies are imagined as *tabula rasa* – a homogenous space containing inert matter upon which internationally crafted institutional shells can be implanted in order to pacify societies and ameliorate the human condition. International interventions devise standardized ways of addressing conflicts that give little consideration to the forces at play in specific places. As I have shown elsewhere, institutional shells exported to conflict societies in order to make peace are designed along the blueprints of what (somehow) worked in other places, in different contexts and material conditions. Databases that attempt to assess practices of government through standardized indicators, such as the World Bank database on governance indicators, are examples of this approach to studying and steering social phenomena. The Standardization and Association Process for former Yugoslavian republics aspiring to join the European Union has also relied upon such methods (Zanotti 2011).

However, the obsession with standardized measurements and abstract indicators goes hand in hand with the disregard for the specific forces at play in particular spaces and places. Political programs that are based upon assumptions that recipient societies are "flat" and homogenous, that planning rationalities may control social change and that the main justification of political decisions relies upon abstract norms have led to self-defeating outcomes. Jean Marie Guehénno, former under secretary general for peacekeeping operations, noted more than a decade ago that representing the world in this way has become near illusions. In fact, for Guehénno,

> The interdependent world looks more and more like the weather system described by chaos theory; influenced by millions of variables, its causality does not follow a linear model, and consequences are not proportionate to causes. . . . The idea that an individual or a human community could determine long-term goals and develop a strategy to attain them may become increasingly unrealistic.
>
> (2001: 83–95)

In my work, I have highlighted the shortcomings of pro-democracy peacekeeping operations that attempt to implant "democratic institutions" in post-conflict situations by transferring institutional shells as solutions to conflict. When such plans do not work, their failure is mostly attributed to "unintended consequences," or to the lack of moral qualities or "maturity" of recipient societies. Ontologies of entanglement invite us to reconsider how we fit in the world and, hence, ground our ethical choices upon the primacy of practices. Practices have morphogenetic properties, while consequences of political choices can never be completely determined by the logic of planning rationalities. However, what obtains in specific circumstances must be carefully assessed in order to devise the possible effects of our deeds. In a quantum world, what is is at the same time sticky and endowed with morphogenetic properties. In this framework, the future is not already inscribed in the present and causality is non-linear. Practices are not the residual of theories: they are the actions through which ontological closure occurs within complex processes that include, but are not limited to, knowledge and aspirations.

In this perspective, the aspiration to universality coupled with the attempt to resolve the Cartesian anxiety through the insistence on stable foundations constitute starting points that lead to unresolvable impasses. They also potentially nurture endeavors that may result in unethical consequences. Assumptions of ontological closure stifle creative political transformation and harbor the specter of totalitarianism. In this ethos, following rules is not good enough. In fact, in an entangled universe made of relations without *relata*, where practices have morphogenetic properties, ethics requires paying attention to what is the case in specific situations and to the inclusions/exclusions the ontological cuts we operate entail. Hence valid justifications of ethical choices are not grounded mainly upon universals but upon careful analysis of the particular. This ethos relies on ways of inquiry that allow us to make "good bets" (to borrow Friedrich Kratochwil's terminology) in the specific situation where we have to operate and upon exerting sound judgment competently.

In summary, the following are the six starting points for an entangled ontological imaginary and ethos:

1 There are no entities but phenomena.
2 There exists no separation between ontological and epistemological statements; they all contribute to generating ontological effects.
3 Ontological closure occurs through practices.
4 Causality can only be explored and analyzed as clusters of factors.
5 Universal ethical prescriptions are insufficient to make good decision because they do not take into consideration the context of their application.
6 Ethics is a practice and the ethical quality of any given action cannot be adjudicated based upon abstractions.

In this book, I explore how these starting points are relevant for devising an ethos that is not rooted upon universal prescriptions but instead upon radical assumption of responsibility and careful assessment of the entanglements that obtain in specific practices. In building upon Barad's concept of intra-agential agency, I call this position an *intra-agential ethos*. Because it pays attention to practices, an intra-agential ethos raises the bar for adjudicating the ethical validity of our actions. And because it does not start with the assumption of causal closure, intra-agential ethos opens up possibilities for creative engagements to bring about transformation in what exist. Ontologies of entanglement favor reframing ethics not as a matter of following rules but as a game of discovery and responsibly pushing the limits of what we assume is the case. An intra-agential ethos also calls for remaining responsibly engaged and alert to the distributive effects our actions may trigger, as well as humble in accepting the limits of our ability to shape the world.

Organization of the book

This book starts by exploring substantialist ontological imaginaries in the context of long-standing debates in IR. The first chapter addresses the classical debate between Kenneth Waltz, Robert Cox and Richard Ashley, as well as the position of a number of IR critical scholars including, but not limited to, Giorgio Agamben (1998) Michael Hardt and Antonio Negri (2000), as well as Martha Finnemore's (1996) brand of constructivism. It argues that substantialist starting points shape not only Kenneth Waltz's brand of structuralism but also critical and constructivist positions, and that such ontological imaginaries are methodologically conservative and stifle possibilities for political agency.

Chapter 2 investigates the relevance of explorations of causality for ontological imaginaries and political agency. It addresses in particular the contributions of Colin Wight (2006), Milja Kurki (2008) and Heikki Patomäki (2002) to reconceptualize causality beyond mechanistic relations of push and pull. It shows that these scholars in different ways embrace a complex and layered conceptualization of causality, challenge ontological individualism, affirm the morphogenetic properties of practices and present a version of structuralism that opens up its causal closure and tames teleological views of history. However, critical realism remains committed to a dualistic ontology. Because of this ontological starting point, while arguing for embracing contestability as its central ethical orientation, critical realism does not bring the reconceptualization of the way we fit in the world (and hence agency) to its full potential.

Chapter 3 is central for devising the implications of quantum ontological imaginaries for agency and ethics. It debates the position of two proponents of quantum ontologies – i.e. feminist physicist Karen Barad (2007) and IR theorist Alexander Wendt (2015). I argue while both Barad and Wendt embrace relational ontologies and reconceptualize what exist in a way that questions the foundational principles of Newtonian physics, the way they make their respective arguments relies on very different sets of questions and starting points. While Barad challenges substantialism by emphasizing the ontological relevance of practices as well as the entanglements of the human and the non-human, Wendt aims at explaining human consciousness and free will in quantum terms. In contrast to Wendt's limited challenge to extant understandings of agency and ethics as centered on human intentions, for Karen Barad, the apparatuses we deploy to engage with the world are central for entailing inclusions/exclusions. This position challenges the distinction mental/material, emphasizes the centrality of practices and the ontological effects of our agency and raises the bar for adjudication of ethical decisions. This chapter also introduces the argument that Barad onto-epistemology and ethos deeply resonate with Michel Foucault position.

Chapter 4 puts in conversation postmodernist and Foucauldian critiques of the subject with Barad's ontological imaginary. It challenges imagining agency as force exerted on others by monadic subjects endowed with *potentia*, along the lines of a Newtonian ontological imaginary. It maintains that by devising an ethos that does not start from assumptions regarding substantive qualities of the subject, an intra-agential ontological imaginary affirms the ethical potential of deconstruction and the relevance of responsibility instead of abstract normativity.

Chapter 5 further challenges the possibility of adjudicating ethical choices based upon universal and abstract normativity. It argues that this way of framing ethical decisions relies upon an ontological imaginary that sees the world as homogenous and casually linear, where similar conditions obtain across circumstances. Contra an imaginary that regards norms as "entities" endowed with stable meaning which exert causal power in linear ways, this chapter mobilizes Foucault's *Archeology* to argue that meaning only takes shape relationally as part of material entanglements and that norms do not function as mass forces. It also explores the relevance of circulation of emotions and of professional epistemes in shaping "ideas" and ethical and political choices. It concludes by advocating justifications of agency based upon careful considerations of the conditions that obtain in practice and of the apparatuses we deploy to achieve certain ends as an alternative to abstract universal norms.

Chapter 6 engages with the connections between epistemology and ethics and with the ongoing debate on the practical and political relevance of IR. It argues that reflecting on what we consider valid knowledge is an ethically and politically relevant exercise. It relies on Karen Barad's position on the non-separability of ontology and epistemology to challenge conceptualizations of knowledge as a detached individual exercise of *representing*. In line with Wittgensteinian feminist philosopher Alessandra Tanesini (2004) and philosopher of science Ian Hacking (1983), this chapter proposes to regard knowledge as a tool. It engages with E. H. Carr as well as Friedrich Kratochwil's reflections on the political relevance of the science of IR and affirms the relevance of ways of conducting inquiries in IR that instead of trying to find parsimonious laws of the whole offer instruments for assessing the complex causal entanglements that obtain in specific situations. Epistemologies are part of ethics and must not be embraced lightly. They are constituted within the entanglements that obtain and at the same time exceed and transform those entanglements. Knowledge is not above or before, but part of ethics and agency.

Chapter 7 fully develops my position on intra-agential ethos. It engages with Wittgensteinian feminist philosopher Peg O' Connor, Foucault, William Connolly and, of course, Barad to argue that instead of relying on abstractions an intra-agential ethos embraces imagination, contestation and creativity as key ethical virtues, but also values prudence and radical assumption of responsibility for the inclusions/exclusion the apparatuses we put in place entail. In an entangled ontological imaginary, ethics is not an affair of "the mind" but a way of life and conduct. With regard to international politics, such ethos questions assumptions that the world is homogenous and organized according to mechanistic laws, as well as the assumption that planning rationalities are a valid way of solving political problems across situations. It also advocates justifying international intervention in a way that cares for the effects of our actions on its recipients first and questions the justification of lack of consideration for practical entanglements and means to end as "unintended consequences."

While no practical example can exhaustively portray all aspects of the argument of this book, Chapters 8 and 9 exemplify the shortcomings of abstract normativity, as well as how a practice ethos can be performed. In Chapter 8, I explore how dwelling on abstract normative formulations and adopting bureaucratic thinking has led to humanitarian and political disaster, and ineffective ways of conducting peacekeeping operations. In Chapter 9, I argue the life and work of a medical doctor active in Haiti and in other poor places of the world offers an example of how the ethos theorized in previous chapters can be practiced. Dr. Paul Farmer's approach to providing medical care to the poor starts from an understanding of disease as a bio-social phenomenon. While Farmer acknowledges the importance of structural factors (specifically structural violence) in limiting the options of poor people, he also strives to challenge these constraints at the microlevel through initiatives carefully rooted upon the assessment of the conditions that come to bear in the life of the poor his organization serves.

My conclusions briefly wrap up the theoretical argument and the practical examples. I re-affirm the need for an ethics founded on competent assessments of the means for action and of what is possible under specific circumstances, while also gauging the political consequences and distributional effects of proposed decisions. I also advocate the need for remaining engaged in micropolitical endeavors and of critically challenging accepted truths. If adopted at all level of decision making, this attitude also would make it more difficult to relinquish responsibility for the consequences of our acts, and for disengaging from politics. Intra-agential agency recognizes our interconnectedness, a degree of openness of what is and at the same time the impossibility to determine what will be. It fosters a call for creative, modest and responsible political engagements.

Notes

1 Starting points differ from foundations. Foundations establish the bedrocks upon which a correct argument relies and offer a "truthful" account of the nature of entities "out there." Starting points are not intended to provide universally valid bedrocks or "first philosophies," but possible beginnings for (maybe unbeaten) research paths.

2 This definition is loosely built upon Stefano Guzzini's definition of security imaginaries. See Guzzini 2013.

3 Interestingly, in his book on the quantum brain, Alexander Wendt embraces Leibnitz' image (Wendt 2015). I will address this point in another part of the book.

4 See, for instance, the *European Journal of International Relations* (2013), 19(3); *Millennium: Journal of International Studies* (2015), 43(3) and *Millennium, Journal of International Studies*, 41, no.3 (2013).

Bibliography

Amoureux, Jack L., and Brent J. Steele. 2014. "Competence and Just War." *International Relations* 28 1: 67–87.

Barad, Karen. 2007. *Meeting the Universe Halfway: Quantum Physics and the Entanglement of Matter and Meaning*. Durham and London: Duke University Press.

Bennett, Jane. 2010. *Vibrant Matter: A Political Ecology of Things*. Durham and London: Duke University Press.

Bhaskar, Roy.1998. "Dialectical Critical Realism and Ethics." In *Critical Realism: Essential Readings*. Centre for Critical Realism, eds. Margaret Archer, Roy Bhaskar, Andrew Collier, Tony Lawson and Alana Norrie. London and New York: Routledge, 641–687.

Carr, Edward H. 1946. *The Twenty Years' Crisis, 1919–1939: An Introduction to the Study of International Relations*. London and New York: Palgrave Macmillan.

Connolly, William. 2013. *The Fragility of Things: Self-Organizing Processes, Neoliberal Fantasies, and Democratic Activism*. Durham and London: Duke University Press.

Coole, Diana H., and Samantha Frost. 2010. *New Materialisms: Ontology, Agency, and Politics*. Durham and London: Duke University Press.

Cudworth, Erika and Stephen Hobden. 2011. *Posthuman International Relations. Complexity, Ecologism and Global Politics*. London and New York: Zed Books.

Cudworth, Erika, Stephen Hobden and Emilian Kavalski. 2018. *Posthuman Dialogues in International Relations*. London and New York: Routledge.

Derian, James Der. 2009. *Critical Practices in International Theory: Selected Essays*. London and New York: Routledge.

Derrida, Jaques. 1992. "Force of Law: The 'Mystical Foundation of Authority.'" In *Deconstruction and the Possibility of Justice*, eds. Drucilla Cornell et al., 3–67. London and New York: Routledge.

Finnemore, Martha. 1996. "Constructing Norms of Humanitarian Intervention." In *The Culture of National Security: Norms and Identity in World Politics*, ed. Peter J. Katzestein, 153–185. New York: Columbia University Press.

Foucault, Michel. 1984. "What Is Enlightenment?"("Qu'est que les Lumières?"). In *The Foucault Reader*, ed. Rabinow, Paul, 32–50. New York: Pantheon Books.

Foucault, Michel, and Carlo Fontana. 1979. "Truth and Power: An Interview With Michel Foucault." *Critique of Anthropology* 4.1: 131–137. https://doi-org.ezproxy.lib.vt.edu/10.1177/0308275X7900401311

Frost, Samantha. 2010. "Hobbes's Politically Subversive Messianism." *Theory & Event* 13.1. Baltimore: Johns Hopkins University Press.

Guehénno, Jean Marie. 2001. "The Impact of Globalization on Strategy." In *Turbulent Peace: The Challenges of Managing International Conflict*, eds. Chester A. Crocker, Fen Osler Hampson and Pamela Aall, 83–95. Washington, DC: United States Institute for Peace.

Guzzini, Stefano. 2013. *The Return of Geopolitics in Europe? Social Mechanisms and Foreign Policy Identity Crises*. Cambridge: Cambridge University Press.

Jackson, Patrick Thaddeus. 2011. *The Conduct of Inquiry in International Relations: Philosophy of Science and Its Implications for the Study of World Politics*. London and New York: Routledge.

Joseph, Jonathan. 2010. "The International as Emergent: Challenging Old and New Orthodoxies in International Relations Theory." In *Scientific Realism and International Relations*, eds. Jonathan Joseph and Colin Wight, 51–68. London and New York: Palgrave Macmillan.

Hardt, Michael, and Antonio Negri. 2000. *Empire*. Cambridge: Harvard University Press.

Hacking, Ian. 1983. *Representing and Intervening: Introductory Topics in the Philosophy of Natural Science*. Cambridge: Cambridge University Press.

Kavalski, Emilian. 2015. "Inside/Outside and Around: Observing the Complexity of Global Life." In *World Politics at the Edge of Chaos: Reflections on Complexity and Global Life*. New York: SUNY.

Kennedy, David. 2004 *The Dark Sides of Virtue: Reassessing International Humanitarianism*. Princeton, NJ: Princeton University Press.

Kennedy, David. 2006. *Of War and Law*. Princeton, NJ: Princeton University Press.

Kratochwil, Friedrich. 2008. "Constructivism: What It Is (Not) and How It Matters." In *Approaches and Methodologies in the Social Sciences: A Pluralist Perspective*, eds. Donatella Della Porta and Michael Keating, 80–98. Cambridge: Cambridge University Press.

Kuperman, Alan J. 2008. "The Moral Hazard of Humanitarian Intervention: Lessons From the Balkans." In *International Studies Quarterly*. New York: Wiley-Blackwell.

Kurki, Milja. 2008. *Causation in International Relations: Reclaiming Causal Analysis*. Cambridge: Cambridge University Press.

Mac Ginty, Roger, and Andrew J. Williams. 2009. *Conflict and Development*. London and New York: Routledge.

Malette, Sebastien, and Peter Stoett. 2018. "Posthumanist International Relations and Ecopolitics." In *Posthuman Dialogues in International Relations*, eds. Cudworth Erika, Stephen Hobden and Emilian Kavalski. London and New York: Routledge.

O'Connor, Peg. 2008. *Morality and Our Complicated Form of Life: Feminist Wittgensteinian Metaethics*. University Park, PA: Penn State University Press.

Onuf, Nicholas. 2009. "Structure, What Structure?" *International Relations* 23.2: 183–199.

Patomäki, Heikki. 2002. *After International Relations: Critical Realism and the (Re)Construction of World Politics*. London and New York: Routledge.

Pentinnen, Elina. 2018. "Potential of Posthumanist Onto-Epistemologies for the Study of International Relations." In *Posthuman Dialogues in International Relations*, eds. Cudworth Erika, Stephen Hobden and Emilian Kavalski. London and New York: Routledge.

Robinson, Fiona. 2011. *The Ethics of Care: A Feminist Approach to Human Security*. Philadelphia: Temple University Press.

Joseph, Rouse. 2002. *How Scientific Practices Matter: Reclaiming Philosophical Naturalism*. Chicago: University of Chicago Press.

Shapcott, Richard. 2010. *International Ethics : A Critical Introduction*. Cambridge: Polity.

Salter, Mark B. 2015. "Introduction. Circuits and Motion." In *Making Things International Vol 1.*, ed. Mark B. Salter, vii–xxii. Minneapolis: University of Minnesota Press.

Tanesini, Alessandra. 2004. *Wittgenstein: A Feminist Interpretation*. Cambridge: Polity.

Waltz, Kenneth N. 1979. *Theory of International Politics*. Reading, MA: Addison Wesley.

Wendt, Alexander. 2015. *Quantum Mind and Social Science: Unifying Physical and Social Ontology*. Cambridge: Cambridge University Press.

Wight, Colin. 2006. *Agents, Structures and International Relations: Politics and Ontology*. Cambridge: Cambridge University Press.

Zanotti, Laura. 2011. *Governing Disorder. UN Peace Operations, International Security, and Democratization in the Post-Cold War Era*. University Park, Pennsylvania: The Pennsylvania State University Press.

1 Questioning substantialism in unsuspected places

Anarchy, empire and the power of ideas

> The majority of IR theories are substantialist – they presume that entities precede interaction, or that entities are already entities before they enter into social relations with other entities . . . This analytical or ontological commitment to substances cuts across conventional divisions in the field, including theories in all major paradigms of IR.
>
> (Jackson and Nexon 1999: 293)

IR theories and prevalent understandings of ethics and political agency more broadly are rooted within substantialist ontological starting points. This imaginary assumes a world composed of stable entities, atomistic separateness of agents and linear relations of causality. In line with the Cartesian distinction between *res cogitans* and *res extensa*, this imaginary also maintains a radical divide between mind and matter. While *res cogitans* is rational, active and creative, *res extensa* is flat and inert. The Enlightenment's ontology fully embraced Greek atomism, by which reality is constituted by material entities endowed with defined characteristics (atoms). This resulted in the development of paradigms that understand reality based upon a mechanical model. For Newton, the world is made of bodies, "built from infinitely small, infinitely tough, and never changing parts, which themselves are taken to require no further explanation" (Giulini 2005: 5). Because it posits these "point masses" as its starting points, "Newtonian mechanics is able to reduce the motion of complex configurations of such point masses to their simple laws of motion" (ibid). Mechanical models constitute a powerful ontological imaginary. As Giulini points out, "If one adopts the viewpoint of naïve atomism, one might even conjecture that all physical phenomena to be eventually reducible to the laws of mechanics" (2005: 6).

In contrast to Aristotelian notions where qualitative characteristics of what exists have a key role in explaining reality, mechanistic interpretations see causality as a matter of quantifiable relations of push and pull among hard bodies. These deterministic laws are believed capable of explaining all that happens in nature. The epistemological position resulting from this ontological imaginary is that science is a form of knowledge that grasps law regularities, which are in turn representable through abstractions and mathematical models. It also affirms the validity of a particular way of knowing in fields other than physics, including biology, sociology, psychology and political sciences.

Clifford Geertz (1973), Heiiki Patomäki (2002) and Michelle Le Doeuf (1989) have all argued metaphors are relevant for establishing horizons of intelligibility. The world Newton depicted in his *Philosophiae Naturalis Principia Mathematica* remains the prevalent ontological imaginary of IR theories across schools of thought (1687). Agents, be they states or subjects, are portrayed as *monads* endowed with *potentia*. Power (or *potentia*), in line with a mechanistic imaginary, is by and large understood through analogy with "mass." Substantialism shapes conceptualizations regarding ways to achieve knowledge as well as notions of subjectivity, causality and understandings of how we fit in the world as actors. In turn, these starting points shape the ways we conceptualize agency and ethics, the ways we validate our political actions and how we imagine possibilities for political change. For instance, understanding causality as a matter of law regularities endorses the notion of the world as a homogenous and flat space where the same conditions obtain. Such an understanding supports the idea that political decisions may be taken based upon universal prescriptions, that standardized solutions may be offered to complex problems and that success can be evaluated through standard benchmarking. Furthermore, by focusing on abstractions rather than practices, substantialist ontological imaginaries promote ways of justifying political action that may end up diverting responsibility for the practical and material consequences such actions entail.

Justifications of international interventions based upon abstract principles or aspirations have been exposed for inadequacy to act as the foundations upon which to respond to unfolding world crises. For instance, Brent Steele and Jack Amoureux (2014) have demonstrated that the Bush administration's disastrous decision to intervene in Iraq was based upon principled abstractions that excluded *competent* considerations of conditions on the ground and of the means to achieve a stated end. As I will show in Chapter 8, the US intervention in Iraq, the unfolding crisis in Syria and the genocides in Srebrenica and Rwanda have all demonstrated adopting abstract, supposedly universal, principles as justification for action has opened the way for disasters.

In the new millennium, risk and complexity have entered the vocabulary used by the United Nations to describe the security challenges it faces and its role as an international security organization (Zanotti 2010). In this vein, former under secretary general for peacekeeping operations Jean Marie Guehénno challenged the validity of planning rationalities to understand and steer international dynamics. For Guehénno (2001), the world looks like a dynamic weather system, one characterized by millions of variables that combine according to non-linear relations of causality. These critiques notwithstanding, justifications for international interventions mostly rely upon abstract principles and on the correlative assumption that desired outcomes will result from aspirational goals. In the meantime, the categorization of political failure as an "unintended consequence" results in diverting responsibility for the effects of decisions based upon unsound premises.

In the pages that follow, I will address the substantialist assumptions of different streams of structuralism in IR, from Waltz's neorealism to some versions of governmentality theories, as well as the substantialist implant of constructivist positions about the causal power of ideas, and I will sketch the implications of these positions for conceptualizing political agency and ethics. First, Waltz's neorealist versions of structural substantialism portrays the status quo as stable and immutable, a totality that can be understood through its organizing principle (anarchy), the law regularities that obtain under that principle and the quantity of power of its parts (i.e. states' military capabilities). In the meantime, rigid versions of Marxism and governmentality imagine power as a totalizing might that limits and dispossesses otherwise free subjects. And constructivist-substantialist imaginaries envision ideas as forces that act like billiard balls on a pool table. This imaginary obfuscates the layered, thick and entangled constitution of meaning within practices. In different ways, all of these schools of thought share an image of the social world in which entities are endowed with qualities and properties pre-existing relations, interacting according to the laws of physical mechanics. In this ontological imaginary, questions about agency focus on how much force entities may be able to exert on other entities. I maintain that regardless of their stated political aspirations, these positions embrace causal determinism and therefore stifle possibilities for rearticulating political agency.

Before I proceed, I need to outline a few caveats. My goal here is not to demonstrate the "truth" of quantum metaphysics as opposed to the "fallacy" of the Newtonian one. Such an undertaking does not fulfill the scope of this book nor does it match my set of skills. My goal instead is to explore unstated assumptions about "reality" and how selecting entangled ontological starting points would nurture a different ethos – one that focuses on practices rather than abstractions. My goal is also not to offer a critique of all substantialist positions in IR (that would be too big of a task just for one book), nor to address the nuances and subtleties of the entirety of the theoretical production by the scholars I criticize. While my approach may seem vulnerable to criticisms of using straw persons, in my defense, I maintain that the examples I have chosen are meant to assess the similar ethico-political implications of substantialist ontologies in IR and to detect substantialism in unsuspected places.

Revisiting a long-standing debate in IR: substantialism, neorealism and their critics

In the introduction of his by now classical work debating the work of Kenneth Waltz, Robert Keohane (1986) emphasizes the necessity for a careful scrutiny of the assumptions within and proposed conditions of applicability for, any theory. Interestingly, Keohane argues that it is precisely because theories of world politics are not like the ones of Newtonian physics, that they require careful scrutiny so theorists do not remain "prisoners of unstated assumptions" (1986: 4–5). Are causes and relations, established by theory, Keohane asks, supposed to obtain under every circumstance? Or are they to be assessed in context? Is theory oriented towards representing universal truths or contextual ones? (1986: 5). I argue the debate in Keohane's book reflects the difference in ontological and epistemological orientation between methods of inquiry that embrace substantialism regarding entities, search for regularities and explain social dynamics through a few overarching principles that govern the relations of "things" and scholarship that focuses on unsettling taken-for-granted conceptualizations of "reality" in diagnosing how what is comes to being and focus on discovering differences instead of sameness.

For Waltz (1979), scientific theorizing in IR is about devising an overarching principle (i.e. anarchy) able to explain all major forces at play within the international system. Waltz portrays states as Newtonian "point masses," whose agency is imagined as proportional to the amount of power (i.e. mass) they possess. Like the Newtonian universe, the international system is imagined as flat and closed. The most stable condition of this system is the condition of equilibrium, where the "masses" of powerful states balance each other, like weights on a scale. The organizing principle of the system, anarchy, rewards states of different "weights" that position themselves in such a way as to achieve at least temporary stability. On this ontological horizon, the forces that can exert the stronger push or pull on others (i.e. the states with the stronger military capability) are the ones endowed with more agency. Theorizing state behavior is driven by assumptions about what function preference the state would maximize, with all states imagined as black boxes, only differing in degrees of power they are willing and able to exercise. For Waltz, theorizing is about finding the organizing principle of the system that can explain the law regularities that occur within it. The broader the principle, the sounder the theory is. In fact, Waltz's theory of IR, like mechanistic physics, aspires to explaining all that happens in a given system according to a few basic principles and deterministic laws.

The ideological effects of neorealism's theoretical implant have been the subjects of a long-standing debate that is worthy of summary here. I argue the main trajectories of that debate are still relevant today and can be read along the lines of the differences between substantialist and non-substantialist approaches to the study of social phenomena. Neorealism's ideological function, both Cox (1986) and Ashley (1986) argue, is strictly connected to its claim to objectivity, primarily as a way of conducting social sciences that mimic strict positivist methodology. Cox and Ashley criticize Waltz for embracing parsimony as the best indicator of theoretical validity. Cox summarizes such methodology as follows: beginning with assumptions regarding entities and their qualities; aspiring at finding stable principles for devising interactions among entities; aiming at explaining recurrent patterns more than change; embracing, at least at the aspirational level, the idea of unity of knowledge and methods across disciplinary lines; and relying upon representationalist conceptualizations of knowledge that consider truth as a progressively accurate reflection of what is "out there." This approach to theorizing in the social sciences, and in IR in particular, lends itself to gross oversimplifications of complex phenomena that in turn lead to ideological reinforcement of contingent social and political configurations by representing them as natural. Kenneth Waltz's a-historical approach is not value neutral, but politically conservative because it posits as natural the permanence of the institutions and power relations that exist in the present. The commitment to ontological substantialism is central for this ideological move. In Cox's words,

> The frequent claim of problem- solving theories is to be value-free. It is methodologically value-free insofar as it treats the variables it considers as *objects* (as the chemist treats the molecules or the physicist forces and motion); but it is value-bound by virtue of the fact that it implicitly accepts the prevailing order as its own framework.
>
> (1986: 209, emphasis added)

Determinism is rooted upon a commitment to "fundamental and unchanging substrata of changing and accidental manifestation or phenomena" (1986: 211). Indeed, the concern with "a continuing process of historical change" and the critical scrutiny of what we take as reality or natural processes are the two main trajectories that, for Cox, differentiate critical from problem-solving theories (1986: 210). He identifies the main limits and ideological functions of neorealism within its commitments to substantialism and causal regularity, as follows:

1. A commitment to *individualist substantialism* – i.e. to the nature of man [sic], a power seeking monad.
2. A commitment to the *nature* of states, which differ in capabilities and strength but embrace a similar understanding of national interest.
3. And a belief in the *immutable nature of the state* system and its *organizing principle* as "anarchy" which in turn places "rational constraints" upon the pursuit of national interest.

(1986: 212)

In summary, Waltz's determinism is rooted upon an unquestioned conceptualization of social phenomena along the lines of the laws of Newtonian physics that imagine matter as inert, made of separate atoms and connected through causal relations of push and pull. These substantialist assumptions allow for a very limited view of rationality and ethics and stifle political imagination. Rationality is defined as an actor's "appropriate response to a postulated anarchic system" (Cox 1986: 212), and morality is only effective when it "is enforced by physical power" (1986: 213). Cox emphasizes the centrality of practices as the starting points both for theorizing and for exercising political agency. Beginning with practices, instead of abstract theorizing and assumptions about the homogenous and flat ontological character of what exists is Cox's methodological alternative to oversimplified models, whether it is Waltz's structuralism or Marxist IR. In this regard, Cox distinguishes a kind of Marxism, and structuralism more broadly, that "reasons historically and seeks to explain, as well as promote, changes in social relations", from "structural Marxism," which shares with neorealism an "a-historical, essentialist epistemology" (1986: 214–215). Both neorealism and structural Marxism are problematic because they aim at discovering the laws of motion of history, instead of attempting to understand what goes on in practice. In other words, I argue, they embrace the presuppositions of law regularities of Newtonian physics and transfer its methods of inquiry to the social sciences. While neorealism's conservatism originates from its posting of an eternal *status quo*, structural Marxism stifles political imagination by embracing "an ideology underpinning revolution by revealing the certainty of a particular future" (Cox 1986: 248).

Cox's brand of structuralism does not assume direct, constant or unchangeable relations of causation from the structure on the parts, nor does it presuppose given qualities of actors (in particular their rationality) or any overarching organizing/explanatory principles of historical unfolding. Cox instead explores how *clusters of causes* come to define and shape a given historical opening. His approach is grounded within a relational ontology, where what is is the result of the coming together of clusters of causal forces. For Cox, a critical theoretical approach "is not reductionist in the sense of making one single factor or set of factors the explanation of all changes. It is grounded in the notion of reciprocal relationship among basic forces shaping social and political practice" (1986: 246). For instance, the notion of "class struggle" that is central to Marxist thought is a heuristic tool for inquiry rather than a one-size-fits-all organizing concept for explaining all functioning of power, the scripts of domination or the inescapable forces that govern history. Methodologically, Cox's view of inquiry in the social sciences demonstrates family resemblances with Foucault's genealogy – i.e. the study of the making of social objects and of the contingent convergence of trajectories that led to their formation. Furthermore, while not theorizing the notion of "emergence" that is so central to critical realism, Cox embraces the idea that social interactions open the way to processes the outcomes of which may not be totally planned for or expected in advance. This is, for Cox, the key contribution of Marxism and structuralism more broadly, a contribution that has however been lost along the way in favor of universalizing abstractions that explain all that exists with a few overarching principles that organize the whole and with a few substantial characteristics of its parts.

Ashley's critique of Waltz specifically addresses the stifling implications of neorealism and structural Marxism onto-epistemological assumptions for theorizing human agency. Ashley clearly outlines the family resemblance of Waltz's position with substantialist structuralism and ontological atomistic individualism. For Ashley, the shortcomings of both structural Marxism (i.e. a brand of Marxism focused on finding "scientific," abstract laws of history, which he sees represented in particular by Althusser) and Waltz's structuralism, are rooted in their shared rejection of practices in favor of an aspiration to be "truly scientific." In this vein, these schools of thought "claim to grasp a structural totality that constrains, disposes, and finally limits political practice" while establishing an orthodoxy and consensus about the categories that constitute the "dominant structures of the totality" (Ashley 1986: 257).[1] These interpretations of structuralism and Marxism more specifically "abolished the role of practice in the constitution of history" and "produced an ahistorical and depoliticized understanding of politics in which human agency does not have any place" (Ashley 1986: 256). As Ashley aptly observes, regardless of the particular political aspirations, these ways of theorizing present "a totalizing anti-historical structure, which defeats the Marxian project for change" (1986: 256).

Ashley insightfully highlights the convergence of substantialism about entities with a conceptualization of the world as governed by law regularities. Neorealism's commitment to statism is a version of a neoliberal ontological commitment to individualism. Statism assumes that states are unitary actors, along the lines of the liberal images of the "individual" conceptualized as an atom, a monad endowed with *potentia*. The "state-as-actor" assumption is a metaphysical commitment "where the state is *ontologically prior* to the international system" (1986: 270–271). For Ashley, neorealism and positivism share four ontological and epistemological commitments: (1) the commitment to knowledge as correct representation of a reality out there, endowed with causal relations independent from human subjectivity; (2) the commitment to the idea that anything called science must enable predictions of phenomena; (3) the commitment to the idea that science is value neutral; and (4) the commitment to the idea that science's verification resides on concepts' correspondence to a field of external experience (1986: 281). Most of these commitments, I argue, are in line with the ontological determinist views of causality and knowledge inherent to Newtonian mechanics. These commitments methodologically orient scholarly inquiries towards what Ashley calls an "actor model" – i.e. to an ontology where there is no co-constitution between the actor and its environment – an epistemology where questions of how actors have been historically constructed are irrelevant. The resulting inquiries only explore the "efficiency of means," and far from being "value neutral," they are politically conservative because they universalize the *status quo* (1986: 285).

In summary, the ontological and epistemological assumptions of apparently anodyne substantialist ontologies and representationalist epistemologies are conducive to a politically conservative ethos. Ultimately, substantialism, including its structuralist version, naturalizes and oversimplifies complex processes, imagining that the social is regulated by a few overarching organizing principles similar to Newtonian laws of nature. While substantialism selectively looks at a few "variables" and relies on arbitrary assumptions about "entities" and their connections to one another, critical theory is methodologically rooted in the exploration of how things are constructed, how processes change, and of how what is develops through complex, non-linear interactions. The latter kind of scholarship shares methodological family resemblance with Foucault's preference for conducting social sciences, "starting from the decision that universals do not exist" (2008: 3). It aims at understanding how what is is shaped in practice through partially open processes, instead of ascertaining a supposedly true nature of things or the overarching laws of the universe. Contra substantialist frameworks, Milja Kurki insightfully argues that while structures tend to stabilize the effects of agents' actions the latter also produce morphogenetic effects (2008: 212). Actors are not independent from pre-existing social contexts but deeply related to one another through such contexts. As a result, for Kurki, states cannot be conceived as black boxes (as in Waltz's) and the international system cannot be understood as "closed system from which state behavior can be deduced" (2008: 259). Even

Wallerstein's version of Marxism, Kurki notes, "has a a-historicist and mono causal connotations, and because of his concentration on the 'abstract structure of capitalism', does not necessarily provide nuanced explanation of specific contexts" (2008: 258). In a similar vein, Jonathan Joseph (2010) is critical in his discussion of oversimplified versions of Marxism offering explanations of all that happens in society along the lines of a single logic deriving from the capitalist mode of production. While Marxism still provides a valid framework for understanding social relations, it needs to develop a "sufficiently complex, differentiated, stratified and emergent conception of the international" (2010: 67). More recently, Didier Bigo, William Walters, Michael Shapiro, and R.J.B Walker have all emphasized in their respective contributions to Phillippe Bonditti (2017) edited book that the discipline of IR must resist reifying its field of inquiry through overgeneralizing categories and metaphysical assumptions. Collectively, these scholars acknowledged the contribution of Michel Foucault to a praxis-oriented way of inquiry in IR. This way of inquiry, I argue is attuned to a non-substantialist ontology and central for re-thinking ethics.

Ontologies of entanglement, as I will argue in the rest of this book, pave the path for devising ways of conducting inquiries in social sciences and for justifying political agency that are not straightjacketed by assumptions regarding the immutable nature of what is or by the aspiration to reverse what is believed to constitute the overarching organizing principle of the whole. In line with this ontological imaginary, micropolitical engagements offer real possibilities for bringing about political change (Connolly 2013), even if they are not necessarily aimed at establishing an immanent alternative order or the reasons for political choices cannot be justified according to criteria of universal validity. Ultimately, entangled ontologies also open the door for revisiting the notion of valid knowledge and subjectivity and for revealing the ethical potential of deconstruction.

Substantializing governmentality? Oppressive power, alienated subjects and the struggle of the multitude[2]

In this section, I argue that some versions of governmentality theory, despite adopting a Foucauldian language, remain trapped in the very substantialist ontology they are supposedly out to criticize and that this ontological position stifles the possibility of re-imagining political agency beyond liberal constraints. Over the last 20 years, governmentality theory has gained considerable traction as a tool for critically exploring techniques of government within and beyond the state.[3] Foucault defined governmentality as the "conduct of conduct" and used it as an analytical tool to study the transformations that made modern modalities of government possible. In contrast with governance scholarship that is largely confident in the instruments of liberal government and Western democracies (or at least in their inherent potential to be perfected), governmentality theories de-naturalize these practices and by and large criticize them. Governmentality explores government beyond its institutional aspects and studies how discursive dimensions of power are manifested in political imaginaries and political rationalities that guide praxis, the connections between instruments of knowledge and technologies of power, the entrenchment of governmental practices in apparently anodyne administrative provisions and the unintended consequences of these endeavors.[4] Scholars have demonstrated that practices that "governance frameworks" portrayed as natural, democratic and benevolent may actually be part of oppressive modalities of power and embody ethnocentric aspirations. They focus on exploring apparently natural *dispostifs*, or apparatuses invented to govern the social and shape subjectivities. Foucault's Panopticon is a *dispositif* of this kind (1977).

While there are important variations in the way IR scholars use governmentality, I identify two broad trajectories.[5] One body of scholarship uses governmentality as a *heuristic* tool to explore practices of local and international government and assess their effects in the contexts where they are deployed. The other trajectory adopts governmentality as a *descriptive* tool with which to theorize the globally oppressive features of the organizing principle of the international system.

Scholars in the heuristic camp tend to conduct inquiries based upon practices of government and resistance. These scholars rely on ethnographic inquiries, emphasize the multifarious ways government works (including its oppressive trajectories) and the ways uneven interactions of governmental strategies and resistance are contingently enacted. Several important examples include Didier Bigo's building on Pierre Bourdieu, encouraging a research methodology that privileges a relational approach and focuses on practice (2011), William Walters advocating considering governmentality as a research program instead of as a depiction of discrete systems of power (2012) and Michael Merlingen criticizing the downplaying of resistance and the use of governmentality interchangeably with liberalism (2006). Other scholars engage in contextualized analyses of governmental tactics and resistance efforts. Oded Löwenheim has shown how responsibilization has become a governance instrument, whether it is the use of travel warnings for travelers or performance indicators for developing states (2007). Wendy Larner and William Walters have questioned addressing globalization as the ontological dimension of the present and instead advocate less substantialized accounts that focus on studying the particular discourses, processes and practices through which globalization is constructed as a space and a political economy (2004); Ronnie Lipschutz and James Rowe have explored how localized practices of resistance may engage and transform power relations (2005), and my own work has looked at deployment of disciplinary and governmental tools for reforming governments in peacekeeping operations and how these practices are hijacked and resisted by their intended targets (2008, 2011).

On the other side, scholars using governmentality as a *descriptive* tool focus instead on one particular trajectory of global liberalism – that is, on the convergence of knowledge of life processes (or biopolitics) and violence. They theorize global liberalism as an extremely effective formation, a coherent and powerful Leviathan, where biopolitical tools and violence are integrated to serve dominant classes' or states' political agendas. Giorgio Agamben (1998), Michael Hardt and Antonio Negri (2000) and Sergei Prozorov (2007) all embrace this position.[6]

The distinction between governmentality as a *heuristic* tool versus governmentality as a *descriptive* tool is central to the debate over the relevance of substantialist assumptions for imagining political agency. I argue that, notwithstanding their critique of liberalism, scholars who use governmentality as a descriptive tool rely on the same substantialist ontological assumptions as the liberal order they criticize and so move away from Foucault's emphasis on historical practices in order to privilege abstract theorizations. By using governmentality as a description of "liberalism" or "capitalism" instead of as a methodology of inquiry on power's contingent modalities and technologies, these scholars tend to reify a substantialist and atomist ontology that ultimately reinforces a liberal conceptualization of subjects and power as standing in a relation of externality and stifles the possibility of re-imagining political agency on different grounds. "Descriptive governmentality" constructs a critique of the liberal international order based upon an ontological framework that presupposes that power and subjects are entities possessing qualities that pre-exist relations. Power is imagined as a mighty totality, subjects as monads endowed with *potentia*. As a result, the *problematique* of political agency is portrayed as a quest for the liberation of a subject who is ontologically gifted with a freedom that power will inevitably oppress. In this way, the conceptualization of political agency remains confined within the liberal struggle of "freedom" and "oppression" imagined as opposite entities pitted one against another. Even researchers who adopt a Foucauldian vocabulary end up falling into what Didier Bigo (2011) says are the "traps" of political science and IR theorizing – i.e. essentialization and ahistoricism.[7]

Scholars who use governmentality as a descriptive tool tell a story where biopolitical, disciplinary and governmental techniques have converged into what is commonly thought of as global liberalism. They explore the oppressive trajectories of the liberal international regime and its violent dispositions, while emphasizing the general effectiveness of its scripts. While adopting a Foucauldian vocabulary, a descriptive governmentality trajectory moves away from Foucault's commitment to relationality. In representing liberalism mainly as an oppressive force driven by repressive intent, descriptive scholars substantialize power along the blueprint of a mighty Leviathan that can be understood based upon its capacity to impose on others. Depicting liberalism in this way oversimplifies the complex and multifarious political rationalities and instruments of government at play in the context of liberalism, substantializes subjects and entities which are endowed with specific characteristics and obfuscates the many ways how power games are indeed hijacked and twisted in practices of political engagements and resistance.[8]

One strand of thought in descriptive governmentality has emphasized the state's role in enacting oppressive modalities of rule. By coupling biopolitical and governmental techniques of control with the power to declare "states of exception," states contribute to the obliteration of the possibility of political life (Agamben 1998). Agamben adopts the Nazi concentration camp as the paradigm for understanding global liberalism and uses governmentality and biopolitics to theorize that liberal power is a coherently effective and homogenous apparatus of domination – a powerful Leviathan in which sovereignty and biopolitics are joined together to produce violent and totalizing effects. In his narrative, the subject (imagined as originally ontologically free) is continuously exposed to the possibility of being stripped of her political rights and reduced to bare life – one excluded from the juridical order.

Differently from Foucault, who engages in a historical critique of sovereignty and analyzes its formation as resulting from the convergence of a number of trajectories, Agamben poses the problem of sovereignty in apolitical and juridico-philosophical terms by caricaturing extremes contexts. Agamben does indeed acknowledge that

> one of the most persistent features of Foucault's work is its decisive abandonment of the traditional approach to the problem of power, which is based on juridico-institutional models . . . in favor of an unprejudiced analysis of the concrete ways in which power penetrates subjects' very bodies and form of life.
>
> (1998: 8)

At the same time, however, Agamben takes issue with the claim that Foucault deliberately chooses not to develop a theory of power and undertakes the task to build such a theory based upon a question Foucault left open in his latter writings; that is the way in modern states procedures of individualization (or biopolitical knowledge and control) converge with procedures of totalization:

> Yet the point at which these two faces of power converge remains strangely unclear in Foucault's work, so much so that it has even been claimed that Foucault has consistently refused to elaborate a unitary theory of power.
>
> (1998: 5)

Agamben fails to connect Foucault's refusal to theorize power as an entity to Foucault's radical anti-substantialism and in this way he misses his central onto-epistemological contribution. Agamben's detachment from Foucault's historical method results in a theory of liberalism that is centered on a *description* of one of its trajectories – that is, the convergence between individualization and totalization. In this way, Agamben creates an abstract and monolithic picture of liberal power and portrays it as a mighty, unitary and totalizing entity, analogous to the Nazi concentration camp. In this narrative, modern power is a mass-like, homogenous and nefarious entity that works across space and time with consistent modalities, and so produces the same outcomes in a world that is in turn imagined as similarly homogenous and inert.

In this same vein, Hardt and Negri portray liberalism as a mighty, oppressive totality. In working with a theoretical apparatus that merges Marxist explanations of social dynamics in terms of class struggle and Foucauldian concepts like biopolitics and governmentality, Hardt and Negri depict international liberal power and associated capitalist production as hyperbolic expressions of sovereign power, now made mightier by the capacity to inscribe a vast array of actors within a coherent and unified logic of domination. In Hardt and Negri's words,

> Our basic hypothesis is that sovereignty has taken a new form, composed of series of national and supranational organisms united under a single logic of rule. This new global form of sovereignty is what we call Empire. Empire is completely immanent; it has no territorial limits, hence the impossibility of escape.
>
> (2000: 5)[9]

Indeed, for Hardt and Negri,

> the concept of Empire posits a regime that effectively encompasses the spatial totality, or reality that rules over the entire "civilized" world.
>
> (2000: xii)

Empire is at the same time the organizing principle for all that happens in the world, with a mass-like force that oppresses the Multitude – a group with varying political needs and claims. In order to achieve political transformation, the Multitude must eventually constitute itself as a singularity against the mighty totality of Empire. In this framing, the only possible way of bringing about political change is to overturn the organizing principle of the system. Such transformation is portrayed as the opposite confrontation of forces – a confrontation that can only happen when the Multitude's might is greater than the Empire's. While widely adopting a Foucauldian terminology, Hardt and Negri join Agamben in obfuscating Foucault's fundamental non-substantialist commitment. They imagine political agency as a drama of subjectivities aimed at acquiring "quantities" of power imagined as an entity, and their confrontation is imagined as the one of the masses pushing and pulling in different directions. In this political narrative, the image of the subject as monadic, sovereign and endowed with *potentia* shapes how agency and the possibility for political change are depicted. In Hardt and Negri's words,

> The teleology of the multitude is theurgical; it consists in the possibility of directing technologies and production towards its own joy and its own increase of power. . . . Through circulation the multitude constitutes itself as an active subject.
>
> (2000: 396–8)

The moves towards substantialization of both the Empire and the Multitude produces a quite oversimplified, but still rhetorically powerful, portrait of the complexity of world politics and of the multifarious ways that different forces interact. Complexity in the world is reduced to dialectics, where political change is understood as bringing about the ideal conditions that would follow the Empire's fall. Thus the entire theoretical framework of Hardt and Negri is deeply rooted within substantialist understandings of political struggles and of the political as a space where actors interact according to the laws of Newtonian mechanics. Such struggle will eventually lead to the defeat of the malevolent power of Empire and substitute it with an immanent, benevolent and alternative socioeconomic order. In this framework, the victory of the Multitude is contingent upon its ability to unify multiple political quests in one so as its point-mass would be able to counter balance the weight-might of Empire.

Sergei Prozorov's (2007) ontological horizon is very much in line with the tracks of Agamben and Hardt and Negri. For Prozorov liberal biopolitical power is a totalizing project that completely absorbs human existence. While Agamben focuses on the convergence of state power and biopolitics, and Hardt and Negri on global empire and revolution, Prozorov grounds his argument on the liberal ontology of the subject understood as a priori endowed with freedom. For Prozorov, freedom is ontologically "anterior and exterior to any form of positive order" and essentially antagonistic to it (2016: 10). All discourses of power "sacrifice the experience of freedom by turning human existence into a project" (ibid). Prozorov envisages two ways out of the totalizing inscriptions of liberal power. On the one hand, building on Carl Schmitt, Prozorov situates the exit point with the subject-sovereign's decision on exceptions that constitutes the foundation of modern political order (2004).[10] Here sovereignty remains the preeminent metaphor around which the idea of the subject, as well as power and freedom, are constructed in IR theory. On the other hand, Prozorov identifies resistance as a "bottom-up" act by oppressed subjects that totally reject inscriptions of biopolitics (2016).[11] In this perspective, resistance is articulated as the absolute rejection of the diagram of power and its "drawing lines." Political agency is portrayed as a series of struggles to escape power through acts of "dispossession" by which humanity will achieve "the end of the exodus of the subject of freedom from the diagram, the recovery of one's potentiality for being from its biopolitical confinement" (2016: 146). Liberated from all constraints, diagrams and inscriptions, a freed humanity will live in a world of pure possibilities: "Elated by the infinite expanse of possibilities now available to him [sic], he [sic] breaks into a run, eager to return to a life he [sic] never had" (ibid 152).

Agamben and Prozorov, in line with the liberal tradition and its reductionist conceptualization of the problematique of power, subjects and the political, imagine freedom as the subject's fundamental ontological attribute, a godly status that would be perfectly realized in the absence of external constraints, and that is always potentially to be crushed by a power conceptualized along the image of a powerful mass – a Leviathan endowed with totalizing effectiveness. In turn, Hardt and Negri view the making of a unitary subject out of the Multitude as the origin of a political revolution imagined as a drama of entities jointly endowed with a unitary will. Notwithstanding their differences, all of these positions imagine power and subjects as substances standing in relations of externality and endowed with a priori ontological characteristics. In this way, they reduce the many possibilities for political agency to a quest for an immanent condition of perfect freedom and social justice, which can only be achieved through a total rejection of transnational biopolitics and its accompanying scripts. By portraying liberal power as a mighty, nefarious entity along the lines of the Leviathan – or its biopolitical version, that is, the Nazi concentration camp or Empire – Agamben, Hardt, Negri and Prozorov obfuscate the numerous ways resistance may be exerted and so theoretically limit political agency to within a very narrow range of options. Furthermore, they romanticize the political actors they portray as the targets of liberal power and thus homogenize and depoliticize the complexity of political tactics and rationalities labeled as "liberal," as well as the variety of agendas and constituencies that can be found among the opponents of liberal orders.

In summary, while seeming to favor divergent political aspirations and agendas, structural-substantialist positions share an ontology that, in line with the imaginary of Newtonian mechanics, posits agents as monads endowed with substantial characteristics and qualities. These positions also explain the behavior of entities through overarching principles that regulate supposedly closed systems governed by law regularities. Governmentality as a descriptive tool embraces the same liberal substantialist ontology it sets out to criticize and in so doing, it limits the problem of agency to the confines of the liberal problematique of sovereignty and freedom, where agency is imagined mainly as a struggle of free subjects and oppressive power.

In mono-causal, structural-substantialist frameworks, the structure tends to reproduce its stability, thus reorienting actors' political engagements towards preserving the *status quo*. The ways out of this scripted determinism are few. Short of changing the organizing principle of the system, as a conservative structural substantialist like Waltz would have it, totally withdrawing from the script of power, as Prozorov suggests, or constituting the Multitude-as-one to fight the mighty Empire, as Hardt and Negri put it, agents can do very little to change what is (Zanotti 2013). In fact, regardless of their stated diverging political aspirations, these positions are *ontologically* and *methodologically* conservative. By emphasizing the stabilizing effects of the structure, they stifle political imagination and limit options for action. In structuralist frameworks, only changes in the organizing principle of the structure (be it anarchy or capitalism) will achieve meaningful social change. Other forms of agency by and large end up reinforcing whatever the organizing principle of the extant order is. Politically, this brand of structuralism may nurture either a resignation to the *status quo* or, alternatively, totalizing and violent forms of political action that are imagined as steering history towards a given teleology and an immanent alternative social order.

Substantialist constructivism

Sociological institutionalism[12] has made key contributions to the study of international organizations (Barnett and Finnemore 1999; Finnemore 1996, 2003; Finnemore and Sikkink 1998). However, the way most of this scholarship has explored the role of norms in producing political effects has remained deeply entrenched in a Newtonian framework of understanding nature and causal effects.[13]

For example, in studying the universalization of human rights norms, Martha Finnemore traced these ideal formations to processes of de-colonization, by which humanity is no longer considered a culturally dependent category but rather as a quality "inherent to individual human beings" (1996: 173). The rhetorical universalization of human rights explains interventions that apparently are not driven by state interest; the fact that international organizations seem to act in line with these norms is seen as a proof (against realist arguments) of their role as agents. Finnemore explains bilateral humanitarian interventions the same way, in terms of norm-driven behavior that cannot be understood in terms of self-interest (2003). Finnemore's research is organized along the lines of the liberal understanding of individual liberty, as autonomy from external forces, and so aims at establishing what degree of agency (represented as idea-driven independence from state interest) international organizations do have. The inquiry here focuses on to what extent stable relations of causation between norms (the independent variables) and behavior (the dependent variable) can be established. It allows for the tracing back of specific effects (in this case the behavior of international organizations) to a given set of causes (in this case, ideas and norms shared by their employees) along linear relations of causality. If such a link can be established, then it is inferred that international organizations are endowed with a certain degree of autonomy and agency, understood as the capacity for influencing others. It can also be inferred that ideas are considered as causes of institutional behavior. While introducing factors (norms and rules) that were overlooked by realists and not sufficiently explored by liberals, the ontological assumptions, the structure of relations among the units of analysis and the theoretical implant mobilized by Finnemore are the same as in those traditions. The theoretical implant is a positivist one, focusing on exploring relations of causation among "entities" interacting like Jackson and Nexon's billiard balls (1999). International organizations are imagined as rational agents, with ideas and norms treated as transparent.

Positivist models of what happen in the world are rooted within a substantialist understanding of causality as law regularity, of entities as ontologically closed prior to practices and of causes as forces of push and pull that act consistently, regardless of circumstances. As a result, by Finnemore's own admission, the analytical framework she adopts cannot fully explain why linguistically identical normative prescriptions do not necessarily produce the same outcomes in terms of institutional choices. Not willing to relinquish her mechanistic ontology, nor her positivist methodology of inquiry in favor of an analysis of practices within which norms are entangled, Finnemore argues that norms are "permissive," not "efficient," causes. Through this move, she "tames" and "attenuates" the causal power of her independent variables, and makes it possible to retain a substantialist ontology and a positivist methodology, which focuses on the exploration of relations of linear causation among entities that are posited as primary (i.e. the "ideas") and their effects (institutional choices).

Kratochwil and Ruggie's (1986) joint criticism of regime theory well captures the tension between embracing a positivist epistemology and an intersubjective ontology. Kratochwil and Ruggie argue, "Positivist models do not easily apply when norms . . . are a significant element in the phenomena to be explained"

(1986: 757). Thus, instead of treating norms as "variables" that can be alternatively abided or violated by behavior, one should analyze the "communicative dynamics" that characterize the way actors *interpret* norms and interact with others in the process. In summary, for Kratochwil and Ruggie,

> actors not only reproduce normative structures they also change them by their very practice, as underlying conditions change and new constraints or possibilities emerge, or as new claimants make their presence felt.
>
> (1986: 770)

For Kratochwil and Ruggie, the problems of normative formation and the consequent relations to behavior cannot be solved without referring to the instruments offered by interpretive sciences.[14] They reject the substantialization of normative structures, and advocate focusing on relations of continuous transformation of meaning produced in the context of contingent interactions. While Kratocwhil and Ruggie limit their contextual analysis to interpretation and do not engage in a broader exploration of practice, they implicitly critiqued social sciences that embrace Newtonian models regarding relations of causality. In their words,

> The standard positivist model works with an initial condition plus a covering law, on the basis of which it hypothesizes or predicts an occurrence . . . (A probabilistic formulation would, of course, appropriately modify the criteria for refutation, but it would not alter the basic structure of the explanation).
>
> (1986: 767)

In a similar vein, Walters and Haahr (2005) criticize streams of constructivism that treat ideas as "missing independent variables" overlooked by other approaches, while Jennifer Sterling-Folker (2000) argues that constructivist scholars do not significantly depart from functionalist and liberal theoretical implants. In functionalist analyses, an international organization's change in preferences and behavior is conceptualized as a response to environmental inputs (2000).[15] Notwithstanding their claim to the contrary, some constructivists in fact adopt a similar framework, with the only difference being that normative formations are given priority in defining the environment that drives behavioral transformation.

> It is the coupling of pre- given collective interests with external circumstances that distinguishes a functionalist account of institutional innovation and change, because the combination leads almost inevitably to an argument that the function of institutions and social practices is to efficiently achieve particular goals for a collective within a larger context.
>
> (2000: 105)

In summary, while claiming to offer an alternative to functionalism and liberal institutionalism some constructivists remain committed to the same theoretical implant which, on the one hand, substantializes normative formations and, on the other, embraces linear relations of causality regarding the role of international institutions and the relations between context and ideas.

Conclusions

In this chapter, I have argued that ontological substantialism influences a wide swath of IR schools of thought, including neorealism, neoliberalism, post-Marxism and even some versions of constructivism and post-modernism. Ontological substantialism, I have argued, has atomistic and structural versions. Atomistic versions of ontological substantialism explain what happens based upon entities' attributes, while structural versions do so by positing organizing principles of the whole. In some cases, as in Waltz's framework, atomistic and structural inclinations converge in theories that aspire to explaining all that happens in terms of an overarching principle driving the behavior of entities with fixed characteristics. The organizing principle of choice may vary – i.e. Anarchy for Waltz, Empire for Hardt and Negri or the Liberal Biopolitical order for Agamben. However, regardless of political affiliations or schools of thought, that principle is reified as an inescapable deterministic factor that orients the behavior of actors and shapes the outcomes of their deeds. On the other hand, idealist versions of substantialist positions portray the power of ideas along the lines of Newtonian causal models as quantifiable relations among self-contained entities.

Furthermore, I have traced two primary impacts of substantialism for IR political ethos. Simply put, substantialist structuralism stifles possibilities for imagining political agency. By depicting political struggles along the lines of the metaphor of unitary masses opposing each other, and by focusing on organizing principles of the system and linear relations of causality, structural substantialism depicts existing political orders as stable, which in turn limits imagining novel forms of agency and political change. Second, by embracing substantialist starting points, some versions of constructivism depict ideas as substances, interacting according a model of linear causation. This view nurtures ethical justifications that rely on abstract norms of behavior regardless of the practice-rooted meaning of normativity and the different ways normative formation may be entangled with other clusters of causes in political practices. In the following chapter, I will turn to explore alternative conceptualizations of causality in IR theory before moving on to exploring more in-depth the features and ethical possibilities of quantum ontologies.

Notes

1 Ashley's critique of Althusser may be an oversimplification and may not engage directly with his latest work. For the purpose of my argument here, I am not engaging with Althusser specifically. I limit my exploration to the position of Ashley. Actually, Foucault embraced Althusser for making possible a "truly political" reading of Marx (Foucault 1998 (1972): 422).

2 This section and the following one rely upon arguments I have developed in Zanotti 2013 and 2016.

3 Here I embrace William Walters' position that governmentality is to be seen as an analytical toolbox. See Walters 2012. However, I also adopt Michael Merlingen's framework regarding governmentality theory. Merlingen convincingly argues that while many governmentality scholars make a deliberate choice of not referring to their approach as theory, "this diffidence in using the term 'theory' concedes too much to mainstream positivist accounts of what counts as proper theory and what does not" (Merlingen 2006).

4 For an exploration of the relevance of "governmentality" for studying global phenomena see Neuman and Sending 2010.

5 Governmentality was adopted by a variety of scholarly positions in IR, including Marxism, realism, network theories, field theories, feminist theories and some versions of constructivism. The exploration of the subtleties of these variations is beyond the scope of this work and has been conducted by others. See, especially, Walters 2012; Merlingen 2006; Walters & Haahr 2005.

6 See also Dillon & Reid 2009; Duffield 2007.

7 For an analysis of the formation of central concepts in IR, and of the complexities they embody, see R.B.J. Walker 2010. For Walker, imagining new political possibilities is linked to questioning how boundaries (between national and international, between subject and power, etc.) came into being and what kind of tensions, contradictions and aporias are contained in concepts that are used as foundational. The way Walker states the goals of his inquiry well exemplifies a non-substantialist methodology: "I start the analysis with an attempt to resist the familiar privileging of the state, the individual or the system of states as the unquestioned starting point of political analysis. I do so . . . by considering what is at stake when the constitutive uncertainty as to whether the individual, the state or the system of states has ontological structural, historical or ethical priority is usurped by the methodological and doctrinal certainties that have been at work in many forms of contemporary political analysis" (15).

8 For Sergei Prozorov (2004), the intensification of the biopolitical trajectories of international power leads to the inscription of freedom into governmental diagrams; for Michael Hardt and Antonio Negri (2000), it is the reconstruction of a mightier sovereignty in global Empire, while for Mark Duffield (2007) the formation of overarching assemblages of occupation aimed at protecting the life of "insured" population in the rich countries from the circulation of "surplus, uninsured life" migrating from the poor ones. Even scholars such as Mike Dillon and Julian Reid (2009) who in principle question substantialist methodologies, end up reifying liberal power as a homogenous formation that governs by exterminating deviant actors. In this way, they oversimplify the complexities of liberal international governmentality by explaining liberal interventionism based upon the threat of "extermination" – a feature that liberalism shares with illiberal political orders.

9 Walker has insightfully questioned Hardt and Negri's representation of Empire as a totally immanent formation where "all philosophical and political options are organized within" (Walker 2002).

10 Here Prozorov differs from Agamben. While for Agamben the sovereign's decision on exception is the basis for the reduction of political life to bare life, for Prozorov the sovereign's decision on exception constitutes a pristine constitutional moment of political life and the "way out" from the totalizing inscriptions of liberal power.

11 See Prozorov 2007.

12 For a critique of Agamben position see also Lemke 2011.

13 I adopt here Samuel Barkin's (2006) terminology.

14 Here Kratochwil and Ruggie specifically refer to Bernstein (1971), Toulmin (1972), Geertz (1973) and Foucault in Dreyfus and Rabinov (1982).

15 See, for instance, Keohane and Nye's (1977).

Bibliography

Agamben, Giorgio. 1998. *Homo Sacer: Sovereign Power and Bare Life*. Stanford: Stanford University Press.

Amoureux, Jack L., and Brent J. Steele. 2014. "Competence and Just War." *International Relations* 28.1: 67–87.

Ashley, Richard. 1986. "The Poverty of Neorealism." In *Neorealism and Its Critics*, ed. Robert Keohane, 255–300. New York: Columbia University Press.

Barkin, Samuel. 2006. *International Organizations: Theories and Institutions*. London and New York: Palgrave Macmillan.

Barnett, Michael N., and Martha Finnemore. 1999. "The Politics, Power, and Pathologies of International Organizations." *International Organization*: 699–732.

Bernstein, Richard J. 1971. *Praxis and Action: Contemporary Philosophies of Human Activity*. Philadelphia: University of Pennsylvania Press.

Bigo, Didier. 2011. "Pierre Bourdieu and International Relations: Power of Practices, Practices of Power." *International Political Sociology* 5.3: 225–258.

Philippe Bonditti (ed.). 2017. (with Didier Bigo and Fredéric Gros). *Foucault and the Modern International: Sciences and Legacies in the Studies of World Politics*. New York: Palgrave Macmillan.

Connolly, William. 2013. *The Fragility of Things: Self-Organizing Processes, Neoliberal Fantasies, and Democratic Activism*. Durham and London: Duke University Press.

Cox, Robert. 1986. "Social Forces, States, and World Orders: Beyond International Relations Theory". In *Neorealism and Its Critics*, ed. Robert Keohane, 204–249. New York: Columbia University Press.

Dillon, Michael, and Julian Reid. 2009. *The Liberal Way of War: Killing to Make Life Live*. London and New York: Routledge.

Duffield, Mark. 2007. *Development, Security and Unending War: Governing the World of Peoples*. Cambridge: Polity.

Dreyfus, Hubert, and Paul Rabinov. 1982. *Beyond Structuralism and Hermeneutics*. Chicago: University of Chicago Press.

Finnemore, Martha. 1996. "Constructing Norms of Humanitarian Intervention." In *The Culture of National Security. Norms and Identity in World Politics*, ed. Peter J. Katzestein. New York: Columbia University Press.

Finnemore, Martha. 2003. *The Purpose of Intervention: Changing Beliefs About the Use of Force*. Ithaca: Cornell University Press.

Finnemore, Martha, and Kathryn Sikkink. 1998. "International Norm Dynamics and Political Change." *International Organization* 52.4: 887–917.

Foucault, Michel. 1977. *Discipline and Punish: The Birth of the Prison*. New York: Pantheon Books.

———. 1998. "Return to History." In *Aesthetics, Method and Epistemology*, eds. James Faubion and Paul Rabinow, 419–432. New York: New Press.

Foucault, Michel, Michel Senellart and Collège de France. 2008. *The Birth of Biopolitics: Lectures at the Collège de France, 1978–79*. New York: Palgrave Macmillan.

Geertz, Clifford. 1973. *The Interpretation of Cultures: Selected Essays*. New York: Basic Books.

Giulini, Domenico. 2005. *Special Relativity: A First Encounter*. Oxford: Oxford University Press.

Guehénno, Jean Marie. 2001. "The Impact of Globalization on Strategy." In *Turbulent Peace: The Challenges of Managing International Conflict*, eds. Chester A. Crocker,

Fen Osler Hampson and Pamela Aall, 83–95. Washington, DC: United States Institute for Peace.

Hardt, Michael, and Antonio Negri. 2000. *Empire*. Cambridge: Harvard University Press.

Jackson, Peter Thaddeus, and Daniel H. Nexon. 1999. "Relations Before States." *European Journal of International Relations* 5.3: 291–332.

Joseph, Jonathan. 2010. "Is Waltz a Realist?" *International Relations* 24.4: 478–493.

Keohane, Robert. 1986. *Neorealism and Its Critics*. New York: Columbia University Press.

Keohane, Robert, and Joseph Nye. 1977. *Power and Interdependence: World Politics in Transition*. New York: Little and Brown.

Kratochwil, Fredrich, and John G. Ruggie. 1986. "International Organization: A State of the Art on an Art of the State." *International Organization* 40.4: 753–775.

Kurki, Milja. 2008. *Causation in International Relations: Reclaiming Causal Analysis*. Cambridge: Cambridge University Press.

Larner, Wendy, and William Walters. 2004. "Globalization as Governmentality." *Alternatives: Global, Local, Political* 29.5: November–December.

Le Dœuff, Michele. 1989. *The Philosophical Imaginary*. London and New York: Continuum.

Lemke, Thomas. 2011. *Biopolitics. An Advance Introduction*. New York: New York University Press.

Lipschutz, Ronnie D., and James K. Rowe. 2005. *Globalization, Governmentality and Global Politics: Regulation for the Rest of Us?* London and New York: Routledge.

Löwenheim, Oded. 2007. "The Responsibility to Responsibilize: Foreign Offices and the Issuing of Travel Warnings." *International Political Sociology* 1.3: 203–221.

Merlingen, Michael. 2006. "Foucault and World Politics: Promises and Challenges of Extending Governmentality Theory to the European and Beyond." *Millennium: Journal of International Studies* 35.1: 181–196.

Neuman, Iver B. and Sending Ole Jacob. 2010. *Governing the Global Polity: Practice, Mentality, Rationality*. Ann Arbor: University of Michigan Press.

Newton, Isaac., I. Bernard Cohen and Anne M. Whitman. 1999. *The Principia: Mathematical Principles of Natural Philosophy*. Berkeley and Los Angeles: University of California Press.

Patomäki, Heikki. 2002. *After International Relations: Critical Realism and the (Re)Construction of World Politics*. London and New York: Routledge.

Prozorov, Sergei. 2004. "Three Theses on 'Governance' and the Political." *Journal of* International Relations and Development 7.3: 267–293.

———. 2007. *Foucault, Freedom, and Sovereignty*. Burlington: Ashgate.

———. 2016. "Ex Nihilo in Mundum: A Reply to Paipais." *Millennium: Journal of International Studies* 45.1: 72–79.

Sterling-Folker, Jennifer. 2000. "Competing Paradigms or Birds of a Feather? Constructivism and Neoliberal Institutionalism Compared." *International Studies Quarterly* 44.1: 97–119.

Toulmin, Stephen. 1972. *Human Understanding*. London: Oxford University Press.

Walker, R. B. J. 2002. "On the Immanence/Imminence of Empire." *Millennium: Journal of International Studies* 31: 337–345, 344.

———. 2010. *After the Globe, Before the World*. London and New York: Routledge.

Walters, William. 2012. *Governmentality: Critical Encounters*. London and New York: Routledge.

Walters, William, and Jens Henrik Haahr. 2005. "Governmentality and Political Studies." *European Political Studies* 4.3: 288–300.

Waltz, Kenneth N. 1979. *Theory of International Politics*. Reading, MA: Addison Wesley.

Zanotti, Laura. 2008. "Normalizing Democracy and Human Rights: Discipline, Resistance and Carceralization in Croatia's Euro-Atlantic Integration." *Journal of International Relations and Development* 11.3: 222–250.

———. 2010. "UN integrated Peacekeeping Operations and NGOs: Reflections on Governmental Rationalities and Contestation in the Age of Risk." *International Peacekeeping* 17.1:17–31.

———. 2013. "Governmentality, Ontology, Methodology: Re-Thinking Political Agency in the Global World." *Alternatives: Global, Local, Political* 38.4: 288–304.

———. 2016. "Constructivism, Archaeology, and Humanitarian Intervention: A Reflection on Method." In *The Ashgate Research Companion to Modern Theory, Modern Power, World Politics: Critical Investigations*, eds. Scott Nelson and Nevzat Soguk, 347–360. London: Ashgate.

2 Re-thinking causality and structures

The critical realist position

In the previous chapter, I have explored substantialist ontological imaginaries in several IR schools of thought. I have argued substantialist-ontological imaginaries portray causality as relations of push and pull among entities endowed with fixed characteristics. Substantialist onto-epistemological inquiries focus on finding regularities (i.e. laws) and explaining what happens through a few concepts that encompass the functioning of everything. The more general these principles are, the more elegant the theories, in compliance with the standards of parsimony. In the pages that follow, I explore critical realist critiques of causality and their implications for re-thinking epistemology, agency and ethics. In particular, I will engage with the work of Milja Kurki (2008), Heikki Patomäki (2002) and Colin Wight (2006). These scholars, while maintaining different foci, convincingly challenge conceptualizations of causality as law regularity, emphasize focusing on clusters of causes instead of isolated variables and reframe the notion of structure in practical and nuanced ways. They reject structuralist determinism, positivist reduction of causes to law regularity as well as the constructivist/postmodernist reduction of all knowledge to mental constructions. These important achievements notwithstanding, critical realism's ontological imaginary does not challenge the Cartesian dualistic ontology that reproduces a representation of matter as *res extensa*. As I will show next, quantum ontologies challenge the very notion of reality as an externality endowed with fixed qualities, thus pushing the critique of substantialism a step forward. Entangled ontologies, I will argue, pave the way for re-imagining how the world is, how we fit in the it and how we produce morphogenetic effects. Building upon Karen Barad (2007), I call this approach *practice ontology*. In this view, reality is not constituted of entities, but of *entangled phenomena*, in the context of which specific ontological "cuts" happen as the result of the intra-action of what is (be it "nature" or "the social") and the apparatuses through which we engage with it.

Causes, agents, structures: reshaping the debate[1]

The problem of causation is deeply embedded with ontological assumptions and has important implications for how we see the world. As Heikki Patomäki argues, questions "concerning the existence of social entities and causal explanations are indeed, very closely related" (2002: 72). In a now classical book, Martin Hollis and Steve Smith (1991) explore how different ways of theorizing conceptualize knowledge and in causation. The different IR theorizations they explore also rely on different assumptions regarding ontology. In fact, notions of causality are central for imagining how we may fit in the world we inhabit and how we get to know and transform it. Hence, the way we understand causality has a bearing upon how we validate ethical decisions. Critical realists question portraying causality as relations of push and pull, as in Newtonian mechanics, as well as positivist ways of conducting social analysis (Patomäki 2002; Kurki 2008). More broadly, critical realists reject explanations of social phenomena in terms of *singular* causal forces, in favor of careful considerations for the complexity of the *causal clusters* that concur to shape what happens. They also challenge the assumption that societies are closed systems and the possibility of predicting social processes based mainly upon abstractions and logical deductions. Critical realists favor instead considering how different causal forces (local and global, visible and invisible) contribute to shape any given situation.

Milja Kurki (2008) in particular, has critiqued in two ways the way twentieth-century natural sciences, along with IR, conceptualized relations of causality first by taking into consideration "the *ontological* aspect of the problem of causation" and, second, by disentangling the "notion of cause from the notion of efficient cause" (2008: 10, emphasis in original). Kurki attributes the conceptualization of relations of causality as relations of push and pull to David Hume. While such attribution has been questioned, an in-depth analysis of Hume's philosophical position is beyond the scope of my present inquiry.[2] I take Kurki's criticism as directed generally towards mechanistic conceptualizations of causality that reduce it to law regularity. These conceptualizations, Kurki argues, entail that "casual relations are tied to regular patterns of occurrences," and science is about studying such regularities, that such regularities are observable and deterministic, and that causes are "efficient causes that push and pull" (2008: 6). By focusing on "variables and their relations these approaches reproduce an atomistic ontology that represent social phenomena as quantifiable and predictable" (2008: 6).[3]

In order to devise an alternative conceptualization of causality, Kurki returns to Aristotle. For Aristotle, *aition* (cause) did not have the closed meaning it gained with Hume. In fact, *aition* for Aristotle is "anything that contributes in any way to producing or maintaining of a certain reality" (Kurki 2008: 220). Aristotelian causality is four-folded: material and formal causes are intrinsic to being, while efficient and final causes are external to it. Material causes refer to the "passive potentiality of matter," while formal causes refer to "that which shapes or defines matter" (Kurki 2008: 221). Efficient causes activate what is only *potentially* real. They do not make things what they are, but only make potentials become real. Therefore, for Kurki "efficient causality is fundamentally embedded within and in relation to other types of causes and cannot in itself explain anything" (2008: 222). These different types of causes interact in different ways to form a "holistic" conceptualization of causality. In this framework, complex interrelations among causes and careful considerations for the multifarious trajectories that converge in any single situation must be taken into account in order to garner a complexity-sensitive understanding of social processes. This view of causality strongly rejects monologic accounts that explain all that happens in terms of abstract structures or relations of push and pull among "things" that produce predictable effects regardless of the particular context of their application.

In relying upon Roy Bhaskar, Kurki argues that science presumes that "objects can generate certain processes in particular conditions" but these conditions remain contingent (2008: 201). In a similar vein, Patomäki proposes to make "Humean invariance" more complex by searching for "conditional regularities" rather than "universal" ones (2002: 75). Thus scientific explanations are not primarily concerned with searching for universal patterns, but with identifying how different causal forces interact. This view considers *clusters of causes* instead of isolated variables as the object of scientific inquiry.[4] In this regard, Patomäki embraces Mackie's (1976) position, focusing on contingent and case-specific clusters of conditions rather than on linear, reproducible, relations among entities. For Patomäki, causes are INUS – i.e. "Insufficient but Non-redundant elements of a complex that is itself Unnecessary but Sufficient to produce an effect." As Friedrich Kratochwil (2008) also argues, Mackie's description of what caused a fire in a house well exemplifies this conceptualization of causality:

> For example, the source of the fire was an electric coffee machine that was not switched off. However, it would have not caused a fire, had the window not been open and had the curtain, moved by the wind, not touched the hot plate (since I had not placed the coffee pot there but had left it in the sink). But even the curtain would not have been able to cause further damage had the initial flames not reached a pile of old papers atop the cupboard, and had the sprinkler system actually worked instead of being deactivated by a faulty sensor. In other words, instead of arguing with necessary and sufficient conditions, we are only able to make much more contingent claims.
>
> (Kratochwil 2008: 95–96)

In this understanding of causality, events should be understood as the result of conditions coming together under specific circumstances rather than deriving from isolated linear cause-effect relations. These clusters of conditions may be described *ex-post facto*, but cannot necessarily be modeled through abstract laws of societal functioning.

Critical realist claims about causality focus specifically on the social world, which they see as a complex but ultimately open system, yet ontologically different and distinct in its functioning from the "natural world." Thus "various kinds of social structures, concrete and abstract, global and local, constantly impinge on actors and interact and counteract in complex ways" (Kurki 2008: 215). In this vein, Colin Wight (2006) observes that "empirical invariance" and reproducibility function well when *ceteris paribus* (i.e. all other conditions being the same) conditions exist, such as in experimental situations set in laboratories. Here the inputs that may intervene to determine a given result may be controlled. However, the social is not a closed system, therefore rarely do the same conditions manifest across time and space. As Wight asserts, "The ability to predict outcomes in open systems is beyond all sciences" (2006: 52). In open systems, science is not about *predicting* outcomes, but about assessing what kind of causal factors come to bear and *how* and *why* they do so.

Critical realists' epistemological and ethical positions are firmly rooted upon the joint assumption of ontological realism and epistemological relativism. Critical realists maintain that while there is a reality independent from human agency and observation, such reality is amenable to multiple, though not equally plausible, explanations. Patomäki outlines the three fundamental tenets of critical realism: ontological realism (i.e. the belief that there is reality out there independent from the observer), epistemological relativism (i.e. there are different plausible interpretations of such reality) and judgmental rationalism (i.e. that it is possible to give good, yet provisional and contestable, reasons for the validity of a judgment). For Patomäki, the world is differentiated, layered and structured (2002: 78). It also has emergent properties, which means it is open to change. Patomäki radically rejects what he calls the "ampliative approach" – i.e. a way of conducting inquiry that starts from established assumptions and aims at determining secure propositions. Instead, he embraces "iconic modeling" as an alternative method of inquiry. While ampliative models focus on law regularities, iconic models facilitate the understanding of complex relations of causality in a way that ampliative methods do not. Iconic models are both heuristic and predictive tools. In Patomäki's words,

> Iconic models are based on idealisations and abstractions, and they always involve metaphors, metonyms and analogies. Although they are interpretative and based on implicit and explicit conventions and language, these conventions are also *projective*: the model describes and posits existential hypotheses about entities and their relations.
>
> (2002: 79)

Patomäki's position on ethics is also driven by a radical commitment to situational evaluations and is firmly rooted in critical realism's acceptance of ontological realism and epistemological pluralism. While reality can be theoretically explained, it is not theoretically driven. This position contains an implicit critique of voluntarism and idealism and constitutes the ontological background for Patomäki's political ethos. Oversimplifications lead to oversimplified political solutions. Positivist assumptions of monotonity (that the social world is constituted of qualitatively invariant objects) are not only theoretically flawed but also politically dangerous. (2002: 134–135). Openness to challenge is not simply a scholarly virtue but also an ethical one (2002: 149). In quoting Hannah Arendt, Patomäki argues that "at least we can learn from Rousseau and Robespierre that absolute goodness [truth] is hardly any less dangerous than absolute evil [untruth and deceit]." (Arendt 1973: 82 in Patomäki 2002: 143). Thus detaching "normative discourse from concrete realities" may end up "making normative discourse monological and potentially violent by ignoring or excluding the ethico-political concerns of different others" (2002: 158). Instead of setting the ground for justifying ethical behavior as in Kantian positions, normative universalism in this view harbors a risk of totalitarianism. Thus, critical realism paves the path for ethically and politically relevant ways of conducting inquiries in IR that on the one hand are open to multiple interpretations and on the other offer plausible grounds for making competent political decisions based upon a careful assessment of what is the case.[5]

Critical realist positions about causality and pluralist epistemologies also have an important bearing on the classical debate on agents and structures. Margaret Archer (1995) uses the notion of morphogenesis to question both structuralism and individualism. For her,

> the "morpho" element is an acknowledgement that society has no pre-set form or preferred state: the "genetic" part is a recognition that it takes its shape from, and is formed by, agents, originating from the intended and unintended consequences of their activities.
>
> (1995: 5)

The notion of emergence is central to finding a middle ground between realist determinism and the possibility of explaining change.[6] In this view, interactive processes produce transformations and generate possibilities that exceed the *status quo* and may have bearings that go beyond localized manifestations. In an emergent world, the direction and outcomes of practical interactions cannot be fully planned or predicted in advance and may have non-local effects.

In the light of these considerations, Wight repositions the agent-structure debate from the *theoretical* to the *empirical* sphere. For him, whether agents or structures determine a particular outcome is an empirical question: "No general transhistorical or purely philosophical resolution of these problems is possible" (2006: 102). Accordingly, attempts to resolve it in the abstract inevitably lead to solutions that that are all agential or all structural (2006: 101). In this framework, the solution to questions about agency can only be adjudicated after careful consideration of specific contexts and circumstances. The problematique of agency, in other words, is firmly re-stated as a problem that can only be assessed and adjudicated in the context of practices.

For critical realists, I argue, structures resemble Foucault's "events." Structures are historical formations that result from the contingent convergence of distinct trajectories, not stable arrangements governed by general laws that determine how societies function, evolve and change. In fact, contra understandings that portray structure as the virtually inescapable organizing principle of the whole and see actors as endowed with fixed characteristics, critical realists tend to offer a layered understanding of the multiplicity of forces that may come to play in specific circumstances and of their effects. This brand of structuralism calls for a definition of how structure affects particular phenomena instead of reifying universal organizing principles or laws of history. While analyses should include considerations of invisible broad forces and causal clusters alongside local ones, the effects of these forces must be assessed in their specific local articulations.

For example, Patomäki explores how organized practices of governance or the capitalist world economy may produce local effects. Practically relevant social science must explore specifically *how* these broader practices produce effects in specific circumstances.[7] In Patomäki's words, "any explanatory iconic model of *concrete outcomes* has to articulate a unified account of the *complex of relevant and efficient causes at work* in a well specified area of time" (2002: 106, emphasis in original). This position is in fact attuned to the Foucauldian notion that, while power has "stickiness," it can only be understood as a matter of multiple articulations, not as an entity that produces the same effects across time and space.

Patomäki also recognizes the imbrication of theorizing, ethics and politics. Iconic models operate choices about which relations of causality are relevant in specific circumstances. In this way, they also produce political effects. Indeed, for Patomäki, as well as for Foucault, the production of truth is performative, not reflective.[8] The choice between different theories and explanatory models is "a matter of the ethical responsibility of the actors involved," instead of the result of cognitive processes. This does not mean that theories can bring into reality any arrangement one may wish. In fact, an accurate analysis of the forces at stake in specific situations is key for making sound political decisions.[9] Social sciences may contribute to "re-signify practices in their temporal dimension" (2002: 160) and "to ascertaining what is ethico-politically good and how to reach that good – if it is achievable at all" (2002: 160). In this regard, scientific inquiry and political engagements are closely related enterprises. Because the production of truth and the political are interconnected, social sciences play a special role in establishing the meaning of political actions and ethical choices.[10] While Patomäki does not specifically take his reflection this far, I suggest in this framework social sciences can produce morphogenetic effects. Contra his own distinction between ontology and epistemology, Patomäki's position with regard to knowledge points towards a reunification of these spheres.

In summary, in the layered and textured causal horizon proposed by critical realists sound political decisions are grounded more in the careful examination of the causal contexts that obtain in specific situations than on abstract prescriptions based upon the assumption that law regularity obtains across time, places and spaces. The failure to do so may lead to potentially disastrous practical outcomes. In a world of emergence, political action always takes place in conditions of uncertainty regarding to the effects it triggers. The possibility that universal norms, principles or totalizing planning rationalities may offer valid grounds for making sound decisions is slim. This situation was acknowledged in 2001 by former Under-Secretary General for UN Peacekeeping Operations Jean Marie Guehénno who identified the need to revise the conceptualizations of causality upon which decisions regarding peacebuilding are taken and to let go of the hubris underlying the persuasion that we can control outcomes and steer history.[11]

Kurki's critique of democratic peace theories also well exemplifies the political dangers of portraying social phenomena as law regularities. Faulty methodological starting points favor the creation of a consensus about causal relations between democracy and peace. A concomitance of occurrences, Kurki argues, does not imply that democratic regimes cause peaceful relations among states, as many other factors may cause that outcome. As I have shown in my own work, similar assumptions informed the design of programs of peacekeeping as democratization and state building interventions (Zanotti 2011). Peacekeeping strategies based on transplanting institutional models of "democracy and state building" with the assumption that these will in turn trigger "peace and development," fail to take into consideration the clusters of conditions obtained locally and regard the places where international peacekeeping was deployed as homogenous, inert *res extensa*, amenable to being molded according to abstract planning rationalities. I will return to the (ir)relevance of abstract models and planning rationalities for the practice of international intervention in Chapter 8.

To summarize, the social world for critical realists is an open system, complex and dynamic (Kurki 2008: 204). It can not be understood in terms of law regularities, and linear relations of causality. Thus predictions may not be made based upon models such as "when A, then B" (Kurki 2008: 204). Critical realists privilege a notion of social sciences that focuses on diagnosing *how* social "realities" come to being, a position attuned to Foucault's preference for ways of conducting inquiries "starting from the decision that universals do not exist" (Foucault 2004: 3). In this perspective, structures look more like "contexts" than systems strictly regulated by overarching principles and laws of history. Such contexts possess causal power, but do not necessarily wield all that happens towards the conservation of the *status quo* or a given teleology of history. In fact, for critical realists, every causal story is holistic, and outcomes must be assessed in the context of complex causal clusters.

Importantly, in this view, our stories of observation do not have any ontological effects on the world out there. Kurki well illustrates this point:

> Causes can be conceived to have real "natural necessitating" ontological existence outside of our stories or observations, and it has been seen that the goal of causal explanation is to build conceptual systems that provide accounts of the various kinds of ontological causal forces in the world, accounts that are fallible, yet of a kind that provide evidential and conceptual reasons for their adoption.
>
> (2008: 240)

The radical divide between observer and observed joined with the assumption that there is a given reality "out there" – one we cannot fully grasp, is also a central tenet of Patomäki's position. The possibility of multiple descriptions of reality is rooted upon the incompleteness of our ability to know the world and completely grasp what clusters of causes obtain in specific situations. This epistemological incompleteness is also a key political value, the recognition of which leads to tolerance rather than oversimplified assertions of causal relations that may lead to extremism and totalitarianism.

This strong separation between ontology and epistemology constitutes in my view the limit of critical realism. Notwithstanding its important contribution to the study of social sciences, ultimately this body of scholarship focuses more on questioning the applicability of linear and simplified conceptualizations of causality to social sciences than on exploring how an alternative ontological imaginary may pave the way for a radical reconceptualization of agency and ethics. I argue that Wendt and Barad's quantum onto-epistemology has pushed critical realism's holism a step forward. It traced the pathway for re-imaging causality and our being in the world as agents in a way that starts from the presupposition of connectedness instead of atomistic separation. Alexander Wendt (2015) specifically mobilizes quantum ontology to address the agent-structure debate. For Wendt, separate from theories of "structuration" or "mutual constitutions," the agent-structure relation (as a quantum entanglement) is not "a process of causal interaction over time, but a non-local, synchronic state from which both are emergent" (2015: 260). In this way, both the notion of structure and the notion of agent are redefined. For him, "as superpositions social structures are only potentialities rather than actualities, but this is equally the case for agents. Their superposed states are co-emergent, and if they become real realities they do so together in localized practices" (2015: 265). In Wendt's words, "What is going on is that agents are themselves emergent from interaction, and that the causal power of the structures in which they are embedded is not that of efficient causation" (2015: 266). In this way, Wendt offers an ontological background for Wight's empirical repositioning of the agent-structure problem.

I argue Karen Barad's (2007) position partially differs from Wendt's (as we will see in the next chapter) and is particularly relevant for re-thinking how we fit in the world. Differently from Patomäki, who assumes a reality "out there" and bases ethics upon epistemological pluralism, Barad characterizes the world as *ontological indeterminacy*. Such indeterminacy (such as the agent-structure problem for Wight and Wendt) can only be contingently resolved in the intra-action between the observer and the observed. In relying upon Niels Bohr's model of physics, Barad argues, "Things do not have inherently determinate boundaries or properties and words do not have inherently determinate meanings" (2007: 138). Objectivity is not predicated upon a "distance" from reality, but upon engaging with reality through experimental apparatuses that produce intra-agential ontological cuts in what exists. For Barad, far from falling into relativism this position offers a way to "hold on to the possibility of objective knowledge" (2007: 138). This reworking of causality as *intra-activity*, goes beyond the notion of complex systems. In Barad's words, "Emergence, in an agential-realist account, is dependent not merely on the non-linearity of relations but on their intra-active nature (i.e. on non-separability and nontrivial topological dynamics as well)" (2007: 393). Hence reality is not an externality, endowed with properties we may discover, but an "externality within." Matter is not inert, but something within which we are entangled by way of intra-agential activities. In other words, the world is made by *phenomena* that cannot be controlled by agents, but of which agents are part and within which they operate ontological cuts that "close" a range of possibilities. What is comes into existence as an effect of these ontological cuts. In this framework, the fundamental commitment of both Newtonian physics and Cartesian epistemology to a "representationalist triadic structure of words, knowers, and things" comes into question (2007: 138). This ontology, Barad notes, "entails a reworking of the notion of causality and agency" (2007: 393). I will explore this topic in-depth in the next chapter.

Conclusions

Critical realist explorations of causality have important implications for how we validate knowledge, for how we conceptualize agency and for how we justify ethical and political engagements. By re-thinking causality in terms of clusters, rather than invariant relations among entities, and by reframing the agent-structure question as an empirical one, critical realists make a vital contribution to re-thinking agency in a way that is not bound by the stifling assumptions of substantialist structuralism or validated mainly through an a priori recognition of universal norms of behavior valid across circumstances. However, while successfully challenging the limitations of mechanistic views of causality for understanding social phenomena and for political decision making, critical realists remain committed to the duality of mind and matter that characterize Cartesian philosophy and mechanical physics. While warning against oversimplified narratives that justify action based upon abstract norms and universal principles, critical realism falls short of bringing the centrality of practices to their full potential. In starting from quantum ontological entanglements, Barad not only argues that causal relations are more complex than in Humean conceptualizations. She also offers a pathway for re-imagining how we fit in the world and for putting practices at the center of our reflections about ontology, epistemology and the ways ethical decisions may be justified. Barad's ethos is firmly rooted upon a radical imbrication of ontology and epistemology, and not, as critical realists maintain, on their separation. Thus, as we shall see, entangled ontologies, and in particular Barad's intra-agential ethos, raise the bar for adjudicating the validity of political decision making. Because it asserts the ontological relevance of practices, Barad's intra agential ethos brings into focus our deep ethical responsibility for the ontological cuts we produce and operate in the practices we partake with. It also expands possibilities for political agency. I will explore these concepts further in the rest of this book.

Notes

1 An earlier version of this argument has appeared in the *International Studies Review*. See Zanotti 2017.

2 Friedrich Kratochwil in particular has questioned Kurki's view of Hume's conceptualization of causality (Kratochwil 2011). Furthermore, Hollis and Smith (1991) see the Newtonian position with regard to causality as very different from the Humean one, inasmuch the first accepts the existence of invisible forces, the latter only the existence of observable patterns. However, for the purpose of my argument, it suffices to note that both embrace causality as linear constant relations among entities.

3 My point here is not to discard quantitative methods as inevitably socially conservative. On the contrary, I tend to agree with J. Samuel Barkin and Laura Sjoberg (2015), who argue that quantitative methods may offer useful tools to answer questions with origins in socially critical positions. My critique is directed at ways of theorizing that do not question how social objects and conceptualizations are formed and take for granted reified conceptualizations of what is.
4 This position is attuned to Foucault's eventalization as a meaningful way of doing social sciences.
5 This position echoes E. H. Carr's, who warns about the danger of basing political decisions upon abstract aspirations without a careful consideration of their practical feasibility and conditions of application. I will return to Carr's position in Chapter 6.
6 The notion of emergence has been adopted as part of a reflection on agency by sociologist Margaret Archer (1995, 2000) and more recently by Pierpaolo Donati (2011). Patomäki more specifically incorporates this concept within IR theory.
7 Patomäki engages both Roy Bhaskar and Anthony Giddens, but he distances himself both from "Bhaskar naturalist metaphors" and from Giddens' focus on "rules and resources" (2002: 99). In defining critical realism's social ontology, Patomäki acknowledges a debt to hermeneutics (and more specifically of Peter Winch and Hang-Georg Gadamer), the Frankfurt School, Michel Foucault and Ludwig Wittgenstein's late work (2002: 99–100).
8 Speaking from a constructivist standpoint, Nicholas Onuf (2009) also argues model making (or theorizing) is a way of exchanging views about the world intersubjectively and to institutionalize these views. This may contribute to social change by promoting alternative forms of institutionalization. In fact, for Onuf, the real source of trouble about Waltz's structuralism is not the model itself but the notion of correspondence to such a model of the world.
9 For Patomäki, while epistemological relativism recognizes that all beliefs are socially produced, not all beliefs are equally plausible. As an example, if one believed s/he could fly and jumped out a window, s/he would be found to be utterly wrong. Similarly, social phenomena produce practical consequences that cannot be manipulated at will.
10 This conceptualization of the relations between truth and purposive political action shows family resemblances with feminist Wittgensteinian philosopher Alessandra Tanesini (2004) as well as with Fiona Robinson's (2011) "ethics of care." For Tanesini, truth statements are not the only way we connect to other human beings. Indeed, in acting and living we make many claims whose content is not cognition (i.e. "truth") but are demands for or expression of recognition.
11 In Guehénno worlds, "The interdependent world looks more and more like the weather system described by chaos theory; influenced by millions of variables, its causality does not follow a linear model, and consequences are not proportionate to causes. . . . The idea that an individual or a human community could determine long-term goals and develop a strategy to attain them may become increasingly unrealistic." (2001: 91).

Bibliography

Archer, Margaret Scotford. 1995. *Realist Social Theory: The Morphogenetic Approach*. Cambridge, UK: Cambridge University Press.

———. 2000. *Being Human: The Problem of Agency*. Cambridge, UK: Cambridge University Press.

Arendt, Hannah. 1973. *The Origins of Totalitarianism*. New York: Houghton Mifflin.

Barad, Karen. 2007. *Meeting the Universe Half Way: Quantum Physics and the Entanglement of Matter and Meaning*. Durham and London: Duke University Press.

Barkin, J. Samuel, and Laura Sjoberg. 2015. "Calculating Critique: Thinking Outside the Methods Matching Game." *Millennium: Journal of International Studies* 43.3: 852–871.

Donati, Pierpaolo. 2011. *Relational Sociology: A New Paradigm for the Social Sciences*. London and New York: Routledge.

Foucault, Michel. 2004. "An Interview With Michel Foucault by Chalres Ruas." In *Death and the Labyrinth: The World of Raymond Roussel*. New York: Continuum.

Guehénno, Jean Marie. 2001. "The Impact of Globalization on Strategy." In *Turbulent Peace: The Challenges of Managing International Conflict*, eds. Chester A. Crocker, Fen Osler Hampson and Pamela Aall, 83–95. Washington, DC: United States Institute for Peace.

Hollis, Martin, and Steve Smith. 1991. *Explaining and Understanding International Relations*. London: Oxford University Press.

Kratochwil, Friedrich. 2008. "Constructivism: What It Is (Not) and How It Matters." In *Approaches and Methodologies in the Social Sciences: A Pluralist Perspective*, eds. Donatella Della Porta and Michael Keating, 80–98. Cambridge: Cambridge University Press.

———. 2011a. "The Human Perspective in International Relations." In *The Puzzles of Politics: Inquiries Into the Genesis and Transformation of International Relations*, ed. Friedrich Kratochwil, 15–37. Abingdon: Routledge.

———. 2011b. *The Puzzles of Politics: Inquiries Into the Genesis and Transformation of International Relations*. Abingdon: Routledge.

Kurki, Milja. 2008. *Causation in International Relations. Reclaiming Causal Analysis*. Cambridge: Cambridge University Press.

Mackie, John Leslie. 1976. "Causes and Conditions." In *The Nature of Causation*, ed. Myles Brand, 308–344. Urbana: University of Illinois Press.

Onuf, Nicholas. 2009. "Structure, What Structure?" *International Relations* 23.2: 183–199.

Patomäki, Heikki. 2002. *After International Relations: Critical Realism and the (Re)Construction of World Politics*. London and New York: Routledge.

Robinson, Fiona. 2011. *The Ethics of Care: A Feminist Approach to Human Security*. Philadelphia: Temple University Press.

Tanesini, Alessandra. 2004. *Wittgenstein: A Feminist Interpretation*. Cambridge: Polity.

Wendt, Alexander. 2015. *Quantum Mind and Social Science: Unifying Physical and Social Ontology*. Cambridge: Cambridge University Press.

Wight, Colin. 2006. *Agents, Structures and International Relations: Politics and Ontology*. Cambridge: Cambridge University Press.

Zanotti, Laura. 2011. *Governing Disorder: UN Peace Operations, International Security, and Democratization in the Post-Cold War Era*. University Park, PA: Penn State University Press.

———. 2017. "Reorienting IR: Ontological Entanglement, Agency and Ethics." *International Studies Review*. https://doi.org/10.1093/isr/viw044.

3 Quantum entanglements

Intra-agential agency and the ethos of practice

Introduction

In Chapter 1, I argued IR theories and, more broadly, prevalent understandings of ethics and political agency are rooted in a substantialist ontology that assumes stable entities, atomistic separatedness of agents and unilinear relations of causality. These understandings of the world and the place we occupy in it are shaped by the Cartesian separation between *res cogitans* (mind) and *res extensa* (matter), Newtonian physical assumptions of matter as inert and conceptualizations of causality as linear relations of push and pull. Regardless of their stated political preferences, these positions are *methodologically* conservative and therefore conducive to stifling political imagination.

I have argued that in structuralist versions of substantialist ontologies, political change is imagined as resulting from "revolutionary moments" aimed at construing new "totalities" free of all oppressive power. In this framework, any political action short of changing the overarching organizing principle that orients the behavior of the components of the system has conservative political effects. On the other hand, atomistic versions of substantialism imagine agents as detached monads endowed with the power to trigger linear relations of causality according to abstract aspirations and the recognition of universal rules of behavior. These approaches lead to oversimplified understandings of practices and ease the way to relinquishing responsibility for the consequences that these initiatives trigger in the first place. Unintended consequences are considered the inevitable "residual" of otherwise rational choices considered as valid because justified by abstract or universal prescriptions.

In Chapter 2, I have explored the relevance of critical realism's reflection on causality for re-thinking how IR may build better narratives about the social. The relevance of critical realism's contribution notwithstanding, I argued that while it challenges mechanistic relations of causality, critical realism remains rooted within the Cartesian separation of mind and matter, *res cogitans* and *res extensa*. Critical realism paves the way for an ethos of practice, as it warns against both oversimplified explanations of social phenomena and the dangers of justifications of ethics and political agency based upon abstract normativity. Because it considers reality as separate from agency, critical realism's ethos is based upon the distinction between ontology and epistemology and emphasizes the ethical centrality of pluralism. However, because it starts from ontological dualism, critical realism falls short of outlining the ontological significance of practices and hence the potential of micropolitical initiatives and the centrality of the notion of responsibility in adjudicating the validity of action.

In this chapter, I argue that quantum ontologies, and intra-agential realism in particular, radically challenge ontological dualism and thus bring an ethos of practice to its full potential. As Diana Coole and Samantha Frost have argued, developments in the natural sciences do in fact "gradually transform the popular imaginary about our material world and its possibilities" (2010: 5). Quantum physics begins with relations, not entities. It affirms an ontology of entanglement that allows for re-imagining how we fit in the world and how we may justify ethical decisions. Entangled ontologies affirm the ontological centrality of practices. In order to make my argument, I will contrast the different implications of the positions of two proponents of the relevance of quantum theories for the social sciences, Alexander Wendt (2015) and Karen Barad (2007). I argue both of these authors successfully challenge substantialist ontologies and Newtonian understandings of causality as linear relations of push and pull. However, Wendt and Barad's different starting points have diverging implications for ways of adjudicating ethical and political decisions. Wendt's (2015) quantum ontology is aimed at establishing the ground for explaining consciousness and free will and is framed as a critique of materialism. For Wendt, ontological closure happens as a result of the collapse of brain quantum waves by acts of free will. This position, I argue, reproduces extant conceptualizations of subjectivity as a "mental thing" and confines the ethical and political implications of ontologies of entanglements to liberal problematiques of will, speech acts and intentions. In this way, Wendt does not move away from a reliance on voluntaristic and anthropocentric views of agency. In contrast, Barad puts practices at the center of her ontological reflection, and in doing so, she opens the way for redefining ethics as responsibility for the practical effects (the "ontological cuts" in Barad's language) we contribute to producing (but do not determine). Ontological closure occurs as a result of human/non-human intra-actions made possible within the apparatuses (or *dispositifs*) we deploy to measure phenomena. The primary ontological referents for Barad are entangled phenomena, not entities.

Ultimately, I am arguing that Wendt's version of quantum entanglements, in line with idealist versions of constructivism, reinforces liberal assumptions regarding humans' ability to direct phenomena through acts of free will. By contrast, for Barad humans are entangled in a world within which we have agency, but we do not control.

Barad's ontological imaginary paves the way for an ethos of modesty and constant engagement, and invites a responsible consideration for the effects of inclusion/exclusion entailed in the practices within which we take part. By emphasizing the ontological effects we produce by living in the world, an ethos of entanglement calls for a radical assumption of responsibility for the way we live and the choices we make.

I define positions like Barad's as *practice materialism* – i.e. a way of thinking about the world that centers any ontological reflections on complex practices instead of "mental statuses." In line with Foucault, I consider practices as inclusive of knowledge, power, material arrangements of space, administrative procedures, etc. Normative statements are both constitutive of and constituted by such practices. In particular, Barad's particular model of quantum ontology opens a horizon where ethical and political decisions should be adjudicated not based upon abstract normativity, but upon a thorough analysis of what conditions obtain and a reflection on what kind of *apparatus* we are using to understand and change them. With regard to justifications made for international interventions, the adjudication of validity must include questions about the means to reach any given end goal. Such questions include who would carry out the intervention, with what instruments, at what costs and resulting in what kind of world being brought into existence. I will return to these topics at another point in the book. In the pages that follow, however, I will start to develop my argument by addressing the positions of Wendt and Barad separately first. Furthermore, I will elaborate on the centrality of the apparatus in producing ontological effects both for Barad and for Foucault and on the relevance of this concept for their political ethos.

The quantum brain, consciousness and free will

> Because theory, scientific or otherwise, moves mainly by analogy, a seeing as comprehension of the less intelligible by the more (the earth is a magnet, the heart is a pump, light is a wave, the brain is a computer . . .) when its course shifts, the conceits in which it expresses itself shift with it.
>
> (Clifford Geertz 1973: 22)

Alexander Wendt's recent book asks us to understand the human brain as a quantum phenomenon (2015). For him, humans are walking quantum waves in a state of indeterminacy that is interrupted by acts of free will. As such, his ontology attempts to overcome the Cartesian divide between *res cogitans* and *res extensa* by redefining matter as "minded." In relying upon the "vitalist" philosophical tradition, Wendt questions the metaphysical assumption of modern physics that matter is "dead" and critiques the limits of classical physics' understanding of what matter is as well as the associated causal relations that obtain in the world.

Importantly, Wendt's first theoretical move is to embrace the CCP (causal closure and completeness of physics principle), which means that "the social (and all other) sciences are subject to physics constraints: no entities, relationships or processes posited in their inquiries should be inconsistent with the laws of physics" (2015: 7). However, in Wendt's formulation, the "P" in "CCP" refers to *quantum* physics, not *Newtonian* physics, that sees matter as inert. With this starting point, Wendt endeavors to explain the "anomaly'" of consciousness in quantum terms. Contra Newtonian physics, and in line with what he calls "neutral monism," Wendt argues we must think of matter as intrinsically *minded*. Neutral monism is a position by which, in Wendt's words, "mind and matter constitute a duality, not a dualism, one that . . . emerges from an underlying reality that is neither causal nor material" (2015: 31). Hence, the reality explained by quantum physics opens and broadens what is conceivable as possible (2015: 32). Therefore, Wendt holds that a quantum ontology secures human agency a place in the universe, explains structures' effects in terms of non-local causation and challenges liberal notions of subjectivity as ontologically and pre-socially determined in favor of a relational view of how we connect to the rest of the world (ibid).

Wendt also offers a convincing account of the basic challenges quantum physics poses to Newtonian substantialism and model of causation. First, in a quantum universe, particles cannot be empirically identified until they are measured. Second, quantum physics challenges atomism's basic assumptions that large objects are reducible to the properties and interactions of smaller ones. It also challenges the assumption that objects have definite properties and that they are fully separable – i.e. "that their identity is constituted solely by their internal structure and spatio-temporal location rather than by their relationship to other objects" (2015: 61). Classical ontological assumptions have important epistemological implications. In fact, they lead to the view that phenomena can only be understood by dissecting them into parts and that social outcomes can only be explained as the result of the interactions of independent individuals (or variables) (2015: 61). Since entanglements are "universal phenomena," Wendt argues, the principle of separability is nowhere correct (2015: 62). In summary, quantum ontologies challenge the substantialist presupposition that objects have a priori defined properties (i.e. the principle of separability) in favor of a relational understanding of what is. Furthermore, Newtonian physics is causally deterministic – i.e. it stipulates that there is no randomness in nature and that the future will be the result of relations of causation that exist in the present. In such a framework, the fact that we cannot predict the future is an *epistemological* issue (i.e. we cannot know all causal relations that obtain), not an *ontological* one. In contrast to Newtonian mechanics determinism, quantum physics frames scientific predictions in *probabilistic* terms. Newtonian physics regards causation as a force transmitted from one body to another. In this framework, causation is mechanical and local; it implies a temporal sequencing between cause and effect, and excludes non-local factors. Quantum physics also challenges the assumption that space and time are containers, independent from other forces in the universe. Without going into the details on how this may happen, the position implies that within a quantum ontology, even space and time acquire ontological determinacy only relationally. Finally, quantum physics challenges the possibility of a subject-object distinction – i.e. that there is a reality out there that we can get to observe and know from a position of externality.

The latter is in my view one of the most important outcomes of a quantum-entangled ontology. By blurring the subject-object distinction, this position requires a radical reconsideration of how we fit in the world as actors coupled with a radical reflection on the ontological (see ethical and political) effects of what we consider valid knowledge and the way we can achieve it. We are not external bystanders but intimately entangled with and part of the phenomena we "observe." In turn, observation is performative and does not leave its object untouched. In pursuing knowledge, we contribute to bringing about ontological possibilities by operating ontological "cuts." This position has important implications for reformulating ethics as *a practice*. Decisions must consider the entanglements of the apparatuses we deploy. As I will contend in the next section, in pushing this position to its full implications, Barad argues that ontologies and epistemologies are inseparable. In fact, the apparatuses we put in place to "observe" reality produce ontological cuts in a world of indeterminacy.

However, notwithstanding the fact that they both share the persuasion that quantum ontologies are very relevant for social sciences, Wendt and Barad's theoretical moves are quite divergent. Wendt embraces non-local causation as the starting point for developing a theory of consciousness and human free will in quantum terms.[1] Differently from Wendt, as I will show at another point in this chapter, instead of attempting to demonstrate the existence of an entity (consciousness), Barad establishes an ontology that repositions the human within a web of practices that are neither mental nor material, but entangled intra-actions among the human and the non-human mediated by apparatuses.

Wendt sets the debate on consciousness within a field of problematization where the Cartesian divide between *res cogitans* and res extensa is redefined. Because he is driven by the aspiration to demonstrate materialism's inability to explain consciousness, Wendt extends the notion of subjectivity to matter. Panpsychism is the link between quantum physics and social phenomena: it rejects the mind-body dualism that, in Wendt's view, has characterized the Western philosophical tradition – i.e. the assumption that matter "is wholly material; that it is a substance, hard and tangible; and that it is passive and reactive" (2015: 111–112). In a panpsychist view, experience is inherent in the deep structure of matter, and so underlying reality is *neither material nor mental*. This is a central point of Wendt's theorization that in my view remains undeveloped, since he ultimately contradicts this point. Wendt argues that the traditional framing of the mind-body problem is spurious and that the need to posit two substances demonstrates that dualism is a response to materialism's failure to explain consciousness. However, by maintaining that "mind is neither reducible to matter nor emergent from it, but *in* matter all the way down" (2015: 112, emphasis in original), Wendt ultimately embraces the dualism he criticizes and makes a substantialist move by redefining the substance of what is as consciuousness. Wendt's theorization begins with the assumption that there is something out there capable of being called "consciousness" – a sort of universal connectivity that permeates all that exist in different degrees and that is in need for an explanation. This position is at the same time idealist and substantialist. In fact, Wendt de facto posits one of the two Cartesian *res* as a substance endowed with certain characteristics that imbues reality. As a result, Wendt ends up with "mind" swallowing up all that exists as a manifestation of various "degrees of consciousness." Ultimately, while Wendt deploys a quantum conceptual apparatus and challenges the classical conceptualization of matter as *res extensa*, by focusing on "consciousness all the way down," he actually ends up reproducing the Cartesian hierarchy between mind and matter.

Furthermore, in discussing human agency, Wendt embraces the classical notion of "will" as its central trajectory. Wendt embraces Schopenhauer's definition of "will" as well as the Aristotelian understanding of layered causality to argue that in quantum physics, individuality does not have a privileged ontological status. However, he also argues, "In quantum coherence the whole exists merely as a potentiality (a wave function), and as such is not 'real' in the usual sense. It only becomes real in its expression (collapse) which actualizes it into something classical" (2015: 141). *Will* is the force that objectifies and brings about ontological closure. In Wendt's words, "Conceived as a collapsing wave functions, the choices we make, our actual agency is not generated by an underlying (efficient) causal order at all, but is precisely a rupture or 'perforation' of that order" (2015: 188). In this way, Wendt re-establishes the privileged ontological status of individuality that he had previously toned down. Interestingly, he conceptualizes the essential features of psyche and subjectivity as "Cognition, Experience and Will," three components endowed with ontologically distinct characteristics. These three components provide the ground upon which Wendt justifies how human consciousness is different from the non-human, as a matter of degrees (2015: 115). In fact,

> Cognition and Experience are passive and reactive in the sense that they reflect rather than create reality; their direction of fit to the world is one of world to mind. Will, in contrast, is active and purposeful, a drive that imposes itself upon, and thus changes the world.
>
> (2015: 116)

In summary, Wendt *defines* human consciousness through traditional attributes that supposedly differentiate the human from other species, thus preserving the deep anthropocentrism of the Western philosophical tradition. In addition, the definition of "will as power" reproduces the traditional attributes of masculinity, while "cognition" and "experience" echo traditional feminine attributes of passivity.

The inherent tension between embracing quantum ontology and remaining rooted in anthropocentrism and substantialism is present also in Wendt's conceptualizations of how humans relate to their environment. Wendt starts from the position that quantum coherence is the physical basis of both life and mind (2015: 132) and embraces ontological monism – i.e. the position that from a quantum perspective "human life is essentially on a continuum with, rather than qualitatively different from, other organisms" (2015: 131). He affirms that this position bears important ethical implications when he writes

> Quantum decision theory suggests that the same is true of human beings: who we are at a given moment cannot be separated from our context. And given that our contexts are vastly more complex, subtle and varied than those in

> physics, that means that compared to subatomic particles, our behavior will be vastly more complex, subtle and varied as well.
>
> (2015: 168)

The important conclusion that he draws from this argument is a critique of rational choice theory. He argues that rationality is contextual, and the entanglements of quantum physics suggest that the default position for human beings is not necessarily conflict but cooperation. Nevertheless, the ultimately substantialist flavor of Wendt's position is evident in his subsequent specification of how we relate to our environment, which leads him to re-affirm monism. Wendt argues experiences are "the inside manifestation of what on the outside appears as the collapse of wave functions into particles" (2015: 141). Wendt identifies this collapse of wave functions as "quantum coherence" which he defines as a "*physical but not material force*" (2015: 144 emphasis in original). In order to be sustained, for Wendt, quantum coherence needs to be *shielded from the outside*. As he acknowledges,

> This suggest a picture of organisms reminiscent of Leibnitz' monads, each living in, and making choices based on, its own, inaccessible bubble of experience – though unlike his model, organisms here have "windows" that allow them to interact with the world.
>
> (2015: 142)

Here Wendt resurrects monadism with a twist: instead of being totally isolated, the quantum monads "have windows."

Wendt states that he shares with critical materialism the aim to "rethink matter into a less 'material' and more active force," as well as a "non-anthropocentric, post-humanist view of reality, which would deny to human beings a privileged ontological position" (2015: 146). However, in his very brief engagement with critical materialism, he criticizes this position for not dealing with the problematique of consciousness. By way of remedy, he reconstructs in quantum terms the distinction between *res cogitans* and *res extensa*:

> My proposal implies a sharp distinction between life and non-life, both substantively and normatively. While in my panpsychist view, matter at the quantum level is latent with life, it only *becomes* life when organized into quantum coherent wholes. When there is no quantum coherence, as in thermostats or computers, matter is dead, and as such does not have agency or other intentional properties- causal power but not agency.
>
> (2015: 147)

Not surprisingly, Wendt's ontological reflections remain centered on human minds. Will, and only will, emerges as the force that produces effects in the world. Wendt's theoretical implant is based upon ontological assumptions regarding what individuals *are* (walking wave functions and monads-as-windows), what the *essence* of the universe and social life *is* (consciousness) and how agency can be exerted through "will." In the next to last page of his book, Wendt defines "consciousness as an aspect of matter at the elementary level (panpsychism), which is amplified upward by quantum coherence in the brain" (2015: 292). In his conclusions, Wendt clearly states that the most important achievement of this work is to bring subjectivity back. In his words,

> The most important epistemological implication of this book is that subjectivity, i.e. conscious subjectivity should be "brought back in" to the social sciences. That challenges positivist and interpretivist camps alike, both of whom have tended to run away from subjectivity as something either that is not relevant to science or as a Cartesian anxiety.
>
> (2015: 286)

However, I contend that while Wendt started from the desire to question the mind-matter divide, the Cartesian anxiety remains in full force in his redefinition of the *substance* that imbues the universe – i.e. "mind all the way down." Wendt's redescription of the difference between consciousness and matter in quantum terms mirrors the Cartesian duality and hierarchy between *res cogitans* and *res extensa*, and his description of subjectivity embraces traditional ontological substantialist assumptions with the addition of the "window." Furthermore, Wendt's vocabulary echoes the masculine connotation of traditional conceptualizations of "will as power" that "imposes" itself on others.

Notwithstanding Wendt's declaration to the contrary, social sciences, particularly post-positivist social sciences, have not left out subjectivity, but instead probed substantialist and metaphysical definitions of subjectivity against the effects of social processes. It is the metaphysical foundation of subjectivity that has been put under question.[2] And it is exactly a metaphysical conceptualization of subjectivity that Wendt ends up reinforcing through a quantum conceptual apparatus. By positing consciousness as an "ontological fiat," Wendt takes out of the picture all the material, murky, entangled ways of how we come to be subjectified.[3] While questioning the mind-matter divide, Wendt does not qualify "matter" in any manner except as a *lesser level of consciousness*. By de facto taking the notion of practice out of the picture in favor of a representation that differentiates what is along the line of degrees of consciousness, Wendt offers an abstract and idealist theory of everything. As a result, while he mentions that his framework calls for an ethics of responsibility, such responsibility encompasses mainly ideas. For him, "social scientists are collapsing wave functions" and therefore, our research is "responsible, at the microlevel, for helping to create, sustain and/or transform that reality" (2015: 287).

Ultimately, while Wendt re-describes the process of exerting free will in terms of quantum physics and in doing so questions atomistic understandings of the subject in favor of a relational one, his position is a quantum reformulation of the constructivist view that we are socially co-constituted through language and ideas. By confining his theorization to human consciousness, speech acts and free will, Wendt de facto redeploys the classical Cartesian divide between *res cogitans* and *res extensa*, just reframed in a matter of degrees. Thus Wendt's version of quantum ontology in social sciences remains rooted in a tradition that affirms individual subjectivity, volition and intention as central to all theorization. The focus on consciousness and speech acts leaves the material dimension of human existence and the practices through which (besides volition) political effects are produced unexplored, ultimately confining these practical dimensions to irrelevance. Because he limits his exploration to the problem of "consciousness" and because of his idiosyncratic position towards materialism, Wendt does not fully embrace the ontological implications of his own critique of classical conceptualizations of matter. In fact, he portrays an oversimplified version of materialism for which he defines a position that conceptualizes matter as "dead." In doing so, he simply re-articulates the mutual Newtonian and Cartesian focus on "dead" matter and ignores versions of Marxist, postmodernist and critical materialist positions that center their analyses in *practices*. In summary, by reconceptualizing matter in non-Newtonian terms, Wendt effectively points out the shortcomings of ethics and politics implied by Newtonian physics and opens the way for conceiving of decision making beyond the strictures of rational choice theories. However, in the end, because of his idiosyncratic position towards materialism, his overall analysis remains limited to the problematique of "mind" and "consciousness" and presents the same problematic aspects of the tradition he challenges with regard to the justification of political agency and ethos in idealistic terms.

It is precisely the focus on *practice* that in my view distinguishes Barad's work from Wendt's. Barad develops an open ontology centered on the notion of phenomena and apparatuses of observation, rather than an ontology that explains all of reality through a unifying concept. She asks how, through intra-active processes in which we are agents, what is comes into being. Ontological cuts as well as boundaries do not exist *a priori* but are enacted pragmatically. While Wendt focuses on linguistic exchanges, Barad focuses on practices and processes through which we engage with the world and other human beings. For Wendt, ontological closure happens in language; instead, Barad mobilizes the Foucauldian notion of apparatus and in doing so she puts practices at the center of her ontological reflections. While Wendt's argument focuses on brain waves and individuals, Barad's apparatuses and practices encompass both human and non-human agents. In contrast, Wendt's considerations are limited to human interaction of a constructivist kind – i.e. speech acts. Barad proposes an alternative picture of the universe as unfolding in continuous processes of materialization through human/non-human entanglements. I now turn to examining her position.

Entangled practices, apparatuses and the ethics of responsibility

Metaphors, as we have seen, are relevant for establishing horizons of intelligibility. While both Wendt and Barad rely on quantum ontologies, the language and metaphors they use to construct these ontologies are very different and hence arrive at different implications for human agency. In contrast to Wendt, who bases his argument on the findings of quantum psychology, Barad focuses her onto-epistemological argument on the apparatus. Barad's emphasis on apparatuses focuses attention to the fact that as humans we are constituted within a web of relations and that these relations are material and practical, not only mental. In this framework, the fundamental commitments of both Newtonian physics and Cartesian epistemology to a "representationalist triadic structure of words, knowers, and things" come under question (2007: 138).

Barad sees the world as characterized by *ontological indeterminacy*. Differently from Wendt, she does not posit any overarching substance that inhabits all of reality: ontological indeterminacy pertains both to the "material" and to "the social." Also, differently from critical realism, and in relying upon Niels Bohr's physics, Barad argues such indeterminacy can only be contingently resolved in the intra-action between the observer and the observed, the human and the non-human. Phenomena, Barad argues, "Are ontologically pre-existing relations: relations without pre-existing *relata*" (2007: 139 emphasis in original). In Barad's words, "Phenomena do not only mark the epistemological inseparability of observer and observed, or results of measurements; rather, *phenomena are the ontological inseparability entanglement of intra acting agencies*" (2007: 139 emphasis in original). Phenomena, not entities, are the primary ontological referents. For Barad, while interaction presupposes the existence of independent entities (i.e. an atomistic ontology), intra-action maintains that "the boundaries and properties of the components of phenomena become determinate" only in the context of intra-actions (2007: 139). Thus Barad introduces *intra-agential agency* as a way of describing how ontological effects come to being.

Barad rejects assumptions that portray matter as "passive, immutable and mute," as well as the "representationalist belief in the power of words to mirror pre-existing phenomena" (2007: 133). In following Bohr's quantum physics, Barad argues the properties of a phenomenon's components emerge differently in various experimental situations. In fact, matter is not passive but reveals itself to us in these continuously unfolding intra-active processes. Barad criticizes positions (such as Patomäki 2002) that rely on ontological realism and epistemological relativism as untenable because they reproduce a substantialist conceptualization of reality. A posthumanist position shifts the attention from representation to "mattering practices" thus bringing to the forefront questions about "ontology, materiality and agency" (2007: 135). Because for Barad, "things do not have inherently determinate boundaries or properties and words do not have inherently determinate meanings" (2007: 138), objectivity is not predicated upon "distance" from reality, but by subjecting it to experimental apparatuses that produce intra-agential ontological cuts in what exists. Epistemology and ontology are deeply entangled and hence cannot be separated. Because we are *of* the world, not *above* it, our actions contribute to manifesting ontology, while the world out there shapes our being.

While Barad embraces the Foucauldian notion of apparatus and acknowledges the role of Foucault in challenging some of the tenets of humanism, she argues he did not go far enough in including the non-human in his notion of performativity.[4]

However, I contend that Barad's focus on processes of materialization is methodologically akin to Foucault's preoccupation with the *formation* of social phenomena. Where Barad is interested in processes through which matter materializes, Foucault is interested in processes through which social entities come to being. They both share the conviction that nothing worthwhile discussing exists with definite qualities prior to these processes.[5] In a way that is very attuned with Foucault, Barad argues that political and theoretical claims are not distinct practices. Instead, theorizing is a practice of *engagement* with the world within which we "have our being" (2007: 133).

Furthermore, Barad embraces Foucault's notion of *dispositif*, which argues that apparatuses are not only observation instruments, but are themselves "productive (and part of) phenomena" (2007: 142). Foucault's Panopticon is an example of such an apparatus, and not only a "mental" one. The Panopticon embodies ways of knowing, of exerting social control, of organizing space that in turn reinforce and enable a variety of different social practices through which modern subjectivity has been shaped into what it is. Similarly, Barad argues the apparatus sets the condition of determinability of the properties of entities (2007: 127). This indeterminacy, for Barad (and Bohr) is not a epistemological issue but an ontological one. In other words, it is not that a world endowed with pre-existing qualities is disturbed by our observation. Instead, in Barad's relational ontology, there are no "*determinate objects with determinate properties and corresponding determinate concepts with determinate meanings independent of the necessary conditions needed to resolve the inherent indeterminacies*" (2007: 127 emphasis in original).

A central tenet in her overall argument is that

> measurement apparatus is the condition of possibility for determinate meanings for the concept in question, as well as the condition of possibility for the existence of determinately bounded and propertied (sub) systems, one of which marks the other in the measurement of the property in question.
>
> (2007: 127 emphasis in original)

Apparatuses are what make possible the determination of boundaries and properties of objects (the intra-agential cuts), as well as specific embodiments of concepts in the apparatus (2007: 148).

This position has a direct bearing for how ontology and epistemology intersect and mutually construct each other. Discursive practices and material phenomena are ontologically imbricated while experimental *dispositifs* are not only heuristic but also performative instruments that have a bearing upon resolving ontological indeterminacy. Knowledge is performative, not reflective; matter is not inert. What is and the way we know it cannot be conceptualized separately. Nevertheless, phenomena are not the *result* of human agency. Instead, "the world is a dynamic process of intra-activity and materialization in the enactment of determinate causal structures which determine boundaries, properties, meaning, and patterns of marks on bodies" (2007: 140).

Importantly, apparatuses are not "mere ideations" or "Kantian conceptual frameworks: they are physical arrangements" (2007: 129). This position in fact changes the way we relate to the physical world, and the way we imagine our agency in it. As Barad insightfully puts it, there is no such thing as "absolute freedom in our choice of apparatus, and, on the other hand a strict deterministic causal relationship whereby objects simply "do their things" once the apparatus has been chosen" (2007: 130).

By introducing the notion of *phenomenon* as the primary ontological referent and of *apparatus* as the tool through which ontological cuts within phenomena are set up through intra-agential processes Barad shifts her ontological starting point. *In fact, there is nothing out there besides the practices in which we are entangled.* While Foucault focuses on the social and Barad extends her considerations to the non-human, they both share a non-substantialist onto-epistemology and associated ethos. They explore processes of how what is *comes into being*, rather than the *nature* of things or the organizing principles of systems. Instead of referring to the potentiality of mental faculties, the apparatus refers to material processes of measurement that are the result of layered practices of experimentation. In extending Foucault's radical non-substantialist position to the non-human through Bohr's quantum physics, Barad links a reflection on our being in the world to a reflection on the way we know what we know and the way we act upon it.

Both for Barad and for Foucault, specific arrangements of "things" and particular physical settings do produce ontological effects and enable processes of subjectification as well as possibilities for knowledge. The ontological indeterminacy we are enmeshed with can only be resolved intra-agentially through specific apparatuses through which we engage with what exist. In this ontological imaginary, humans cannot overdetermine outcomes, but can take part in processes of mattering by modifying the apparatuses through which they engage with what is out there.

Far from falling into relativism, this position offers a way to "hold on to the possibility of objective knowledge" (2007: 138). Barad's standpoint on objectivity and political agency is grounded upon this radical, non-substantialist understanding of both the human and the non-human, where the two spheres take part in "mattering practices." Based upon the notion of intra-agential agency, Barad questions maintaining the centrality of language and culture as well as views that reiterate the determinism of matter. The relation between the cultural and the natural (or in other words, that we are of the world) is an "exteriority within", not a "static relationality" that leaves the properties of the terms of the relation unchallenged. The cultural is an "enactment of boundaries", a practice of operating ontological cuts that entails "constitutive exclusions" (2007: 135). And it therefore begs questions of accountability.

In summary, this kind of onto-epistemology challenges human exceptionalism, a view that denies nature "any sense of agency and historicity" (2007: 136). It also offers interesting avenues for reframing both ethics and human agency beyond structuralism, atomism and Wendt's voluntarism. In Barad's words,

> Post-humanism eschews both humanist and structuralist accounts of the subject that position the human as either a pure cause or pure effect . . . post-humanism doesn't presume the separateness of any-"thing," let alone

> the alleged spatial, ontological, and epistemological distinction that sets humans apart.
>
> (2007: 136)

In this framework, *relata* are not prior to relations: "Matter is produced and productive, generated and generative" (2007: 136). Difference has generative effects in the production of other differences and causality is not rooted upon ontologically stable properties of entities. *In fact, "causal structures" are generated by different patterns of differentiation and processes of materialization enacted through practices of knowing and doing. There is no teleological necessity or overarching principle that shapes and orients the development of history.*

Intra-agential agency, I argue, has important implications for what kind of social science may offer useful guidelines for ethical and political decisions. Different apparatuses produce different subjectivities and different "marks on bodies." The modern subject is constituted through such practices, not as the result of abstract ontological qualities, be they free will or wave functions. As a result, the ontological qualities of the subject, imagined as rational and free can no longer be assumed as the starting point for theorizing agency and ethics. Instead, if the apparatus is the (onto-epistemological) space within which ontological closure occurs, and our agency is part of said apparatus, we can only make accurate decisions by providing an as-thorough-as-possible account of how the apparatus is set up and of the ontological cuts it operates. The ground for sound political agency is based upon the possibility of understanding the relations that obtain in the apparatuses of which we are part and that we contribute to setting. By developing inclusions or exclusions, apparatuses affirm ontological effects for which we must take responsibility.

I argue this ethos is attuned to Foucault's. As we shall see more extensively in Chapter 7, for Foucault political agency is an activity by which we engage with and continuously challenge the apparatuses within which our subjectivity is formed. Instead of mobilizing "free will," Foucault points at the ability (which is not exclusively intellectual but deeply practical) to create something different from what exists. This includes exploring how apparatuses in their material configurations are put together. Political agency is exerted by questioning the ontological closures that apparatuses produce and by challenging through alternatives life-practices universal truths and arrangements of things that have been accepted as immutable and "natural" (Foucault 2008b).

It is worthwhile re-emphasizing here that alternatively from Wendt, who makes metaphysical statements about what humans *are* (i.e. walking quantum waves), Barad argues that ontological properties obtain only in the context of relations. It is within intra-action that *what-could-be* becomes *what is*. There is no overarching substance to be explained, no hierarchy of being to be redeployed. Phenomena are the ultimate ontological referents and processes of materialization happen differently within different apparatuses of observation. As I will show in the rest of this book, adopting phenomena and ontological indeterminacy as the starting points of our theorization affirms the possibility of reconceptualizing ethics as a practice. Barad, like Foucault, points at how by coming together in specific (and contingent) ways in specific apparatuses, causal forces produce different ontological effects. Apparatuses set the stage for processes of materialization to happen in a certain way, but do not over determine these processes. For Barad, like Foucault, science and knowledge are performative, and have more to do with giving an account of how the apparatus is set up than with arriving at statements that establish causal regularities or a theory of everything. Regularities can only be established in the context of specific interrogations of nature through particular physical settings in specific conditions. Political and ethical decisions must be rooted upon careful consideration of what these are, and must include assuming responsibilities for the consequences they produce.

Barad's position invokes a radical reconceptualization of human existence in the world. In her version, the notion of entanglement proposed by quantum physics invites us to re-think both what the primary ontological level is – i.e. what the universe is made of – and the notion of causality. It also includes the non-human as relevant to defining the horizon for human agency as well as a referent to be included in ethical considerations. In engaging the world as agents, we do not act as monads endowed with *potentia*, but as entangled phenomena that are part of what exists. We do not act *on* the world but we have agency as part of it. Ontological closure is not the result of *will* that brings consciousness to its actualization, but the result of the entangled practices *within which we have agency*. We do not preordain material dynamics as a result of aspirations dictated by reason, nor do we determine closure of potential wave statuses through speech acts and volition. Instead, we participate in processes of materialization of which we are a part but do not control. In this framework, modest and accurate considerations of what is at stake (or as Barad would put it, of the exclusions and inclusions the ontological cuts we operate in specific practices produce) become necessary steps for validating ethical and political action. In an intra-agential framework, practical processes, rather than abstract principles of reasoning, constitute the basis for ethical decisions. Radical assumption of responsibility for the ontological cuts we entail through practices is central for this ethos. I will continue to explore the impacts of these concepts in the rest of this book.

Conclusions

While Wendt points to a reconsideration of the subject as ontologically connected, these connections are only with other subjects and happen solely through language and brain waves. Free will, as a masculine, impositional force, remains, in line with IR tradition, the ultimate cause of what is. Practical arrangements are not part of Wendt's picture. For him, ontological entanglements occur solely in the mind of subjects while ontological cuts happen when free will is exerted. For Barad, ontological closures occur through use of the apparatus, which in turn embodies the complexity of practices and does not privilege the monadic subject. In the end, Barad's vision entails a broader entanglement than Wendt's, one that encompasses practices and non-humans, and extends the notion of responsibility accordingly. She also points at the importance of complex clusters of causes in actual phenomena. Such causes are not limited to mental wave functions and to intersubjective communications. By radically questioning the very notion of separability that underlines notions of individuality, rationality and universal normativity, Barad traces the ontological and methodological horizon for devising an ethos that embraces uncertainty and complexity, including consideration of specific situations as crucial while taking responsibility for the ontological cuts produced in the practices in which we take part. By focusing on the apparatus, Barad and Foucault argue that reality is not produced mainly as the result of "will," "ideas" or "utterances," but as the effects of layered and complex practices *within which we have agen*cy. These practices are thick and material in the sense that they encompass much more than language and ideas, and open or foreclose opportunities for materialization of specific phenomena.

This position invites a thorough process of evaluation of solutions to international crises. In making decision about international intervention, careful analysis of the materiality of existing conditions and of the means to be employed to achieve goals are necessary, and not only of principled aspirations. For instance, elements such as the cost of war, the administrative arrangements and distribution of power among those who intervene, the consequences of militarization for women and girls, the economies of peacebuilding, and the broader effects of the everyday practices of peacekeepers must be taken into consideration for decision making. All of these factors are not the "residual" of principled aspirations, but they constitute the only possible relevant horizon for ethically sound strategies.

The empty excuse of simply "following the rules" was used by Adolf Eichmann to defend his actions in the Nazi regime. Fighting the Axis of Evil and protecting the Iraqi people from a malevolent dictator were used as rationales by the Bush administration for the Iraq War. And the UN General Assembly resolutions introduced by Saudi Arabia provided the "moral" grounds for undermining the Assad regime in Syria absent a clear understanding of the forces at play, of possible alternatives to militarized solutions or to enticing a rebellion the characteristics and political aspirations of which were and are not clear (UN General Assembly 2013b).[6] As Carr has argued and advocated, in deciding what to do, one's ground of ethos should be the weighing of aspirations against the actual conditions of possibility (1946). Ontologies centered on the material entanglements within which we have agency foster methods for making political decisions that do not rely on the assumption that, by acts of will, what is shall change in the direction we plan for. Instead, an intra agential position fosters a political ethos that recognizes the multiple entanglements constituting practices while emphasizing key *how* questions that are critically relevant to making decisions about the ethical soundness of goals.

Practices do indeed produce ontological effects. Assessing the material apparatuses we set in place and fully including such understandings in political and ethical decision making may help in constructing more apt narratives about international politics, and hence in establishing better ways of making decisions regarding international intervention.

Notes

1 The details of how Wendt elaborates his brain quantum theory are beyond what is relevant to my argument. In fact, I am not interested in questioning the accuracy of Wendt's position. I am not a quantum psychologist, and I cannot speak to this point. What I am interested in debating here are the ethical and political implications of his ontological imaginary.
2 I will return to this notion in the next chapter, where I explore the post-modernist critique of the subject.
3 Kratochwil (2011) in a critical assessment of Wendt's earlier work on the state detected similar issues. Kratowchwil argues that notwithstanding his focus on relations and interaction, Wendt posits one overarching essence, i.e. the state, by "ontological fiat." Kratochwil argues instead in favor of a way of doing science that does not try to achieve a "secure grounding" for everything, but instead provides a way of conducting inquiry that accepts pluralism and where ontology depends on purposes and practices.
4 Thomas Lemke (2015), in engaging with Barad, argues that Foucault's lectures on governmentality implicitly embrace the entanglement of the natural and the human. I agree with Lemke on this.
5 See also Lundborg and Vaughan-Williams (2015: 18), who argue Foucault's scholarship is attuned to new materialisms' assertion of the radical inseparability of language and materiality.
6 Prior to United Nations passage of the Saudi-sponsored resolution concerning human rights violations in Syria in December, the General Assembly on May 17, 2013, had, "strongly condemned the Syrian government's indiscriminate violence against civilian populations and welcomed the establishment of the National Coalition for Syrian Revolutionary and Opposition Forces as interlocutors needed for a political transition" (UN General Assembly 2013a).

Bibliography

Amoureux, Jack L., and Brent J. Steele. 2014. "Competence and Just War." *International Relations* 28.1: 67–87.

Barad, Karen. 2007. *Meeting the Universe Halfway: Quantum Physics and the Entanglement of Matter and Meaning*. Durham and London: Duke University Press.

Carr, Edward H. 1946. *The Twenty Years' Crisis, 1919–1939: An Introduction to the Study of International Relations*. London and New York: Palgrave Macmillan.

Coole, Diana, and Samantha Frost. 2010. *New Materialisms: Ontology, Agency, and Politics*. Durham and London: Duke University Press.

Foucault, Michel. 1998. "Return to History." In *Aesthetics, Method and Epistemology*, eds. James Faubion and Paul Rabinow, 419–432. New York: New Press.

———. 2008a. *The Birth of Biopolitics: Lectures at the Collège de France, 1978–1979*. Basingstoke: Palgrave Macmillan.

———. 2008b. *The Government of Self and Others: Lectures at the Collège de France, 1982–1983*. Basingstoke: Palgrave Macmillan.

Geertz, Clifford. 1973. *The Interpretation of Cultures: Selected Essays*. New York: Basic Books.

Guehénno, Jean Marie. 2001. "The Impact of Globalization on Strategy." In *Turbulent Peace: The Challenges of Managing International Conflict*, eds. Chester A. Crocker, Fen Osler Hampson and Pamela Aall, 83–95. Washington, DC: United States Institute for Peace.

Hacking, Ian. 1983. *Representing and Intervening: Introductory Topics in the Philosophy of Natural Science*. Cambridge: Cambridge University Press.

Kratochwil, Freidrich. 2011. "Constructing an New Orthodoxy? Wendt's 'Social Theory of International Politics' and the Constructivist Challenge." In *The Puzzles of Politics. Inquiries Into the Genesis and Transformations of International Relations*. Abingdon: Routledge.

Kurki, Milja. 2008. *Causation in International Relations: Reclaiming Causal Analysis*. Cambridge Studies in International Relations. Cambridge: Cambridge University Press.

Le Doeuff, Michelle. 1989. *The Philosophical Imaginary*. London: The Athlone Press.

Lemke, Thomas. 2015. "New Materialisms: Foucault and the 'Government of Things.'" *Theory, Culture, and Society* 32.5: 3–25.

Lundborg, Tom, and Nick Vaughan-Williams. 2015. "New Materialisms, Discourse Analysis, and International Relations: A Radical Intertextual Approach." *Review of International Studies* 41: 3–25.

Patomäki, Heikki. 2002. *After International Relations: Critical Realism and the (Re)Construction of World Politics*. London and New York: Routledge.

United Nations General Assembly. 2013a. Resolution 76/262, "The situation in the Syrian Arab Republic," A/RES/67/262. May 15. www.un.org/en/ga/search/view_doc.asp?symbol=A/RES/67/262. Accessed February 16, 2016.

United Nations General Assembly. 2013b. Resolution 68/182, "Situation of human rights in the Syrian Arab Republic," A/RES/68/182. December 18. www.securitycouncilreport.org/cgi-sys/cgiwrap/scrarchives/managed-mt/mt-search.cgi?blog_id=10&tag=A%2FRES%2F68%2F182&limit=20. Accessed February 10, 2016.

Wendt, Alexander. 2015. *Quantum Mind and Social Science: Unifying Physical and Social Ontology*. Cambridge: Cambridge University Press.

4 Entangled agency

Re-thinking subjects and power

> There is massive disagreement about foundations: Is there one for moral judgment? If yes, then what's its nature? Is it universally or absolutely binding on all? How can we know it? And if the answer is negative, then how does morality function in the absence of it? Is it all a colossal error; is there really no foundation but we just act as if there is one?
>
> (O' Connor 2008: ix)

Starting points are important. Conceptualizations of who we are and how we relate to the world are central to the way of theorizing how we make a difference in it. As metaethical philosopher Peg O'Connor aptly puts it, "Start in the wrong place and you will quickly become mired in philosophical 'problems' that are unsolvable" (O'Connor 2008: ix).[1] In a substantialist ontological imaginary, matter is inert and causality linear; subjects are monads endowed with a set of fundamental characteristics such as rationality and freedom; reality is governed by a few overarching principles and knowledge is a reflection of the world. IR theory views of agency, relations of causality and justifications of political decisions are by and large rooted upon a substantialist ontological imaginary. For instance, international intervention mostly relies upon the assumption that reality is homogenous across places and spaces, that it is governed by linear relations of causality and amenable to being molded according to the design of planning rationalities. Thus international intervention has privileged standardized solutions to the problem of peacekeeping and peacebuilding, with very questionable outcomes (Zanotti 2013).

As I have argued in the previous chapter, entangled ontologies portray a different picture of the world from Newtonian physics: they begin from a place of indeterminacy and entanglements, instead of entities. Relations, as Karen Barad (2007) maintains, come prior to *relata*. *Phenomena*, not entities that are constitutive of the universe. While Foucault did not dwell upon ontological debates, and Barad has been critical of his neglect of the non-human, they both share a non-substantialist ontological imaginary. They both begin with relations instead of entities and privilege *practice* as the way to search for meaning and ontological closure. This ontological imaginary is central to re-thinking two main pillars of Western political thought, subjects and power and for re-imagining an ethics that is de-linked from substantialist conceptualizations of either on their own or the relations between them.

In entangled ontologies, subjects are not endowed with fundamental qualities by ontological fiat: subjectivity is an intra-active becoming. In fact, Barad argues identity formation does not follow a "Euclidean grid of identification." Rather, it is a "contingent and contested ongoing material process: 'identities' are mutually constituted and (re)configured through one another in dynamic intra-relationship with the iterative (re)configuring of relations of power" (Barad 2007: 240–241). Both for Foucault and for Barad, ontological closure is never final or necessary. Foucault's excerpt that follows well exemplifies this position:

> For may part, I would like to . . . show how certain things – state and society, sovereign and subjects, etcetera, were actually able to be formed, and the status of which should obviously be questioned. In other words, instead of deducing concrete phenomena from universals, or instead of starting with universals as an obligatory grid of intelligibility for certain concrete practices, I would like to start with these concrete practices and, as it were, pass these universals through the grids of these practices.
>
> (Foucault 2008: 3)

Entangled ontologies challenge the substantialist bedrock of Western political ethos. This includes understanding subjects as monads ontologically endowed with *potentia*, rationality and freedom; the notion of power as a Newtonian mass, its effectiveness understood along the lines of "quantity"; the notion of knowledge as perfectible reflection of an external reality that is separate, ontologically defined and closed and that can be grasped through mathematical regularities; and the belief that space, place and time are flat and homogenous containers of human agency and *potentia*, and therefore any given action can be validated through abstract universal norms valid across situations.

This imaginary constitutes the starting point of political initiatives that unreflectively portray reality as inert *res extensa* where the same conditions by and large obtain. This assumption in turn nurtures the conviction that humans can master and shape social transformations according to the design of planning rationalities and predict and govern the effects of the supposedly linear relations of causality we set in motion. What is overlooked in this framework are the entanglements and morphogenetic processes of practices. As Barad puts it, "The dynamics of intra-activity are explicitly non-linear, causal, and nondeterministic. Enfolding is not an arbitrary, random, or automatic process; it is a matter of iterative agential changes in the nature of production" (2007: 240). Space and time are not

> a preexisting Euclidean container . . . that presents separately constituted bodies with a place to be or a space through which to travel . . . the space-time manifold does not sit still while bodies are made and remade. The relationship between space, time and matter is much more intimate. Spacetime itself is iteratively reconfigured through the ongoing intra- activity of the world.
>
> (2007: 376)

Thus human agency is situated within thick and layered practices within which we become shaped as subjects and garner knowledge. Barad describes this entanglement as follows:

> The particular configuration of that an apparatus takes is not an arbitrary construction of "our" choosing; nor is it the result of forces such as power or culture or history impressing themselves on scientific practices and determining the outcome. "Humans" do not simply assemble different apparatuses for satisfying particular knowledge projects: rather "humans" are themselves specific parts of the world's ongoing reconfiguring. To the degree that laboratory manipulations, observational interventions, concepts and other human practices have a role to play, they do so as part of the material world in its intra-active becoming. "Humans" are part of the world-body space in its dynamic structuration.
>
> (2007: 341)

Because of the radical entanglement that characterizes our being in the world, decisions on setting the apparatuses through which we engage the world are politically and ethically important because they include and exclude, entailing opening or foreclosing possibilities of materialization of matter. Practices of knowledge invoke questions of responsibility. As Barad argues,

> Intra-active practices not only make the world intelligible in specific ways but also foreclose other patterns of mattering. We are accountable for and to not only specific patterns of marks on bodies – that is, the differential patterns of mattering of the world of which we are part but also the exclusions that we participate in enacting.
>
> (2007: 394)

In an entangled universe, reality looks much less homogenous than in a Newtonian/Cartesian universe. An entangled world is not governed by linear relations of causality nor necessarily goes in the direction humans wish or desire. Human agency is not irrelevant, however, because it does contribute to the enfolding of the universe, yet in ways we cannot direct through planning rationalities. For both Foucault and Barad, agency is not a force that simply impresses on reality relations of push and pull. Rather, human agency is embodied in apparatuses that bring about differentiated forms of materialization of matter and the social. Apparatuses shape subjectivity and are also the tools through which humans engage with what is as actors.[2] Agency, in this perspective, is not imagined as a free-floating mass force. By pointing at the ontological effects we inevitably produce in the world within which we have agency, entangled ontologies requisite radical assumption of responsibility and careful and prudent reflections on the forms of materialization of matter we may induce.

In the following pages, I will elaborate on how an intra-agential ontological imaginary helps us to re-imagine ethics beyond substantialist conceptualizations of subjectivity and helps us to enlarge the problematique of political agency beyond the strictures of the oppositional relation of power/oppression. And in this way, entangled ontologies affirm the ethical possibilities of deconstruction.

Entangling subjects, re-imagining agency

Entangled ontologies challenge the way the bedrock of Western political thoughts – i.e. subjects and power – are conceptualized. The substantialist ontological imaginary that depicts subjects as entities pre-existing (or necessary for) political interactions is isomorphic to the substantialization of power as a sovereign totality analogous to mass. As Jeremy Valentine argues, "in numerous ways, the possibility of political transformation hinges on the manner in which the political subject is conceived and the types of evidence used to support such conception" (2002: 36). Post-structuralism offered novel ways to question *how* the foundations of our political imaginary came into being and, further, challenged the idea of the subject as a self-contained being whose primary struggle in existence is with power. In this way, post-structuralism politicizes the political as well as the subject (Finlayson and Valentine 2002; Williams 2002). In Caroline Williams's words,

> For liberal thinkers in particular, this ontology of human essence or nature also gives rise to a notion of free will and individual sovereignty which, in turn, underscores the liberal conception of freedom. Here freedom is understood as the conscious and voluntary *potentia* of the subject acting without external impediments.
>
> (2002: 24)

Furthermore,

> from the social contract theory of Hobbes, Locke and Kant, to its contemporary presentation in the work of John Rawls . . . there is a dominant presupposition that the subject is a self contained, unencumbered, rational, and a priori entity who performs a voluntary act of political contract.
>
> (ibid 23)

Reframing Caroline Williams's assertion that "the reopening of the question of the subject cannot be viewed in isolation from the reexamination of the possible structure of the political" (ibid 10), I argue reconceptualizing the possibility of political agency cannot occur without a careful reflection on the ontological status of power and the subject in IR narratives and as the ontological starting point of Western foundations of ethics and political thought more broadly.

These foundations have increasingly come under question. For instance, Jenny Edkins has insightfully argued that most IR theories embrace a notion of the subjected (and in turn sovereignty) as a pre-existing entity endowed with autonomy and rationality, an entity that is "first born than socialized" (2002: 67). Edkins argued that Lacanian approaches that see "subjectivity and social order as mutually constituted" pave the way for broadening studies of security in a way that, along with Žižek, show the arbitrary constitution of the social order and see the role of the intellectual precisely as a task of challenging the master signifier upon which such order rests (Edkins 2002: 80; Žižek 1993: 2). As I have argued elsewhere (Zanotti 2013), substantialist conceptualizations of power and the subject constitute the bedrock both of liberalism's methodological individualism as well as of rigid versions of Marxism. In the liberal narrative, monadic subjectivity reaches its full potential (i.e. freedom) when unfettered by external influences and in turn is capable to exert power on others according to its will: this assumption is prevalent in IR especially, where representations of subjectivity are isomorphic to representations of sovereignty.[3] In turn, the notion of alienation, which portrays human freedom as crushed by structures of capitalist production, is also rooted upon the image of a subject ontologically endowed with an essence the full expression of which is impeded by external forces. Roland Bleiker questioned substantialist positions that see agency as a reflection of externally imposed circumstances as well as positions that "bestow the human subject . . . with a relatively large sense of autonomy" (2003: 26). Substantialist assumptions of fundamental autonomy (or freedom) would "freeze a specific image of human agency to the detriment of all others" (2003: 26). As he puts it,

> A conceptualization of human agency cannot be based on a parsimonious proposition, a one-sentence statement that captures something like an authentic nature of human agency. There is no essence to human agency, no core that can be brought down to a lowest common denominator that will crystallize one day in a long sought after magic formula. A search for such an elusive centre would freeze a specific image of human agency to the detriment of all others.
>
> (2003: 26)

Entangled ontologies affirm the possibility for re-imagining ethics without grounding it upon the monadic, separate, free and rational subject as its starting point. The need for a redefinition of individual biological beings is supported by recent finding in sciences of the living. For instance, epidemiology has challenged the idea that humans are isolated and stable molecular bodies in favor of views that represent them as open and vulnerable to, for example, pathogens (Lemke 2011; Braun 2007). In the meantime, neuroscientists have shown that children's cells exchanged through the placenta remains living in mothers' brains – a phenomenon called microchimerism. Microchimerism can get very interesting when a mother has multiple pregnancies. "The mother's body accumulates cells from each baby – and potentially functions as a reservoir, transferring cells from the older sibling into the younger one and forming more elaborate microchimeras" (Callier 2015). Furthermore, findings regarding "mirror neurons" that fire when we watch others express emotions may indicate that we are much more interconnected that we imagined (Fadiga et al. 1995; Iacoboni 1999).

In an entangled ontological imaginary, subjects and objects alike "are differentially constituted through specific intra-actions" (Barad 2007: 342). Thus both the liberal assumption that humans are ontologically autonomous as well as the Marxist notion of alienation (in which ontological freedom is oppressed by capitalism) come into question. In a such universe, as Barad demonstrates, subjects are not imagined as *res cogitans* endowed with the power to master *res extensa*. Instead, "there is no *res cogitans* that inhabits a given body with inherent boundaries differentiating self and other. Rather, subjects are differentially constituted through specific intra-actions" (2007: 379). In this, subjects are not completely absorbed nor defined by ideology or by rigid social structures. Again, in Barad's words,

> Agential realism disassembles the notion that structures are Althusserian apparatuses- rigidified social formations of power that foreclose agency and deterministically produce subjects of ideological formations. On the contrary, structures are to be understood as material- discursive phenomena that are iteratively (re) produced and (re) configured through ongoing material-discursive intra-actions.
>
> (2007: 240)

As quantum subjects, we are relational beings, not monads naturally endowed with qualities that power inevitably crushes. In fact, as Finlayson and Valentine, in taking issues with structuralism, aptly put it,

> It is not only the relationship between structure and agents that is 'undecidable.' The structure and agents are too. This means, in distinction to something such as Giddens' notion of structuration, we cannot think of the "agent" as a self possessed entity acting in response to and upon a structure of social action, since what that agent is already part of the structure, which, being indeterminate, is not itself able to determine that subject.
>
> (2002:14)

This point becomes clear if we embrace an entangled ontological imaginary. Ontological closure comes out of the entanglements of phenomena and the apparatuses deployed in order to know, engage and govern what is. In turn, these apparatuses are part of, not external to, the phenomena within which they produce ontological closure. As I have argued earlier, experimental apparatuses of measurement are not simply ways of *knowing* the world. For Barad, the apparatus defines modalities of intra-action that not only make it possible to know what is but also produces effects of inclusion and exclusion – i.e. ontological cuts. Apparatuses are material, practical and thick, and cannot be described from an external standpoint. As humans, we inhabit the apparatuses we deploy and the apparatuses we deploy shape the world.

While not engaging on discussion about ontology, Foucault also assumed a very radical non-substantialist position with regard to the problematique of subjectivity and its relations to power. What Foucault refers to as the historical ontology of the subject is the result of three entangled trajectories: subjectivity, power and ethics. Relevant questions here are as follows: "*How are* we constituted as subjects of knowledge? *How* are we constituted as subjects who exercise or submit to power relations? *How* are we constituted as moral subjects of our own actions?" (Foucault 1984b: 45–46, emphasis added). These *how* questions beg a non-substantialist response. Similarly, the issue of the relation of subject and power is not imbued with any inherent quality (such as oppression or freedom), but rather an open-ended agonism and provocation. In Foucault words,

> At the very heart of the power relationship, and constantly provoking it, are the recalcitrance of the will and the intransigence of freedom. Rather than speaking of an essential freedom it would be better to speak of an "agonism," of a relationship which is at the same time reciprocal incitation and struggle; less of a face-to-face confrontation which paralyzes both sides than a permanent provocation.
>
> (1982: 221–222)

Foucault ethos shifts the starting point of Western political imaginary. *The autonomy of the subject is not the beginning and the foundation of the political; it is a commitment and an end point.* Foucault argues that what distinguishes an Enlightenment-centered historical consciousness is "the principle of critique and a permanent *creation* of ourselves in our autonomy" (1984b: 10, emphasis added). The subject is constituted within relations of power, and it is within such relations that its identity comes into being and its "freedom" is exerted. The exercise of liberty is a *praxis* – an effort by the subject to produce itself. Therefore, "modern man [sic] . . . is not the man who goes off to *discover* himself, his secrets and his hidden truth; he is the man who tries to invent himself. This modernity does not liberate man in his own being. It compels him to face the task of *producing himself*" (Foucault 1984b: 8, emphasis added). It is through questioning what is given as a universal, that the modern subject has the possibility of producing herself "as a work of art" (ibid). There is no pristine "true self" oppressed by external forces, simply waiting to be discovered or liberated. Freedom is an achievement, not an ontological endowment.[4]

Re-thinking power and the political

> The possibilities for liberal forms of freedom may historically depend upon the exercise of discipline.
>
> (Barry, Osborne and Rose 1996: 8)

The earlier passages show that Foucault does not regard social entities, including power and subjects, as substances endowed with attributes prior to their entanglement. Neither can be thought of as fixed, unitary or sovereign entities that are constituted through relations of externality and/or oppression. Instead, power and subjects are formed and transformed in contingent and uneven agonic relations and the modalities of these relations need to be studied in their contingent articulations. Foucault does not formulate a new definition of the subject, or, for that matter, power. Instead, he embraces ontological indeterminacy. Differently from positions that regard subjects as sovereign entities whose boundaries already exist and consider freedom as a pristine condition always potentially threatened by power, Nikolas Rose, relying on Foucault, studies freedom as an articulation of the problematique of liberal governance.[5] In his *Birth of Biopolitics* lectures Foucault describes the emergence of the problematique of how much to govern in order not to hamper the "natural" order of the economy and individual freedom as an exquisitely liberal problematique (2003). Elaborating on this position, Rose argues,

> Freedom . . . is no "natural" property of political subjects, awaiting only the removal of constraints for it to flower forth in forms that will ensure the maximization of economic and social wellbeing. The practices of modern freedom have been constructed out of an arduous, haphazard and contingent concatenation of problematizations, strategies of government and techniques of regulation. This is not to say that our freedom is a sham. It is to say that the agonistic relation between liberty and government is an intrinsic part of what we have come to know as freedom.
>
> (1996: 61–62)

In summary, power and freedom cannot be severed from each other. Yet the historically contingent modalities of their co-constitution must be historically and contingently explored. Both power and freedom are *practices* whose processes of materialization come into being with the deployment of specific apparatuses through which humans engage with, know and govern society.

Re-thinking the subject invites us to re-think "power" and thus the conceptualization of the political as a struggle of freedom/oppression. As we have seen, sovereignty and subjectivity have largely been imagined as isomorphic, opposite force masses. Thus the conceptualization of sovereignty is based upon the foundational image of a unitary, free and rational subject, and the relation between the "subject" and society is conceived as a relation of externality among entities that pits one's sovereignty against the other's in a struggle of freedom and power.

As I have argued earlier, simplified versions of structuralism, regardless of political traditions, rely on the same ontological starting point as methodological individualism. Notwithstanding their adoption of a Foucauldian language, by describing power (or the *Empire*) and subjects (or the *Multitude*) as entities standing in relations of externality, Agamben along with Hardt and Negri, remain embedded in the dominant substantialism of IR theory. In fact, for Hardt and Negri, the emancipation of the *Multitude* is imagined through the possibility of constituting itself as one "subject," a "mass" able to counter-weight *Empire*.[6] Similarly, while neo-Marxists like Ernesto Laclau and Chantal Mouffe insightfully explore the multiple ways of exertion of hegemony, there is also a presupposition that somewhere there is an authentic sphere of subjectivity that is oppressed by the capitalist arrangements of society, and so awaits to be discovered and liberated. The notion of alienation points to an "authentic human condition" that can be made immanent through the reversals of the organizing principles of current social order. Contra these oversimplifications of both human agency and the political, Alessandra Tanesini (2004) questions both Mouffe's (1992) position about the *agonic quality* of the political and Habermas's opposing emphasis on public debates as a way of reaching consensus. Unlike Habermas, political change does not have to be confined to a rational conversation about epistemic standards. It may instead have to start with changing the *social practices* that made those standards possible. Furthermore, Tanesini challenges Mouffe's conceptualization of the political as ontologically limited to an enunciative "we" that excludes the other. She proposes instead that the constitution of meaning is open ended, and that language may become a tool leading to transformation of political relations more broadly.

In conceptualizing power, Foucault distances himself from theoretical traditions where power is understood as *capacity*, as a form of mass that impinges on liberty. In these traditions, as we have seen, in line with a substantialist ontological imaginary, power is imagined as a quantity and a force, usually oppressive, that impedes the full potential of otherwise autonomous agents. The research agenda focuses on analyzing power's effects on individuals imagined as ontologically free, rational and moral. These effects are assessed in terms of the difference between real conditions of oppression and alienation on one hand and a postulated ideal freedom. In turn, freedom is conceptualized along the lines of sovereignty, as the monad's *potentia*. The problematique of emancipation is part of the problematique of legitimacy: illegitimate power is the main obstacle to the achievement of individual autonomy.

As Bleiker aptly puts it, for Foucault, "a *theory* of power is unable to provide the basis for analytical work, for it assumes a prior objectification of the very power dynamics the theory is trying to assess" (2003). Thus for Foucault (as well as for Bleiker), power discourses are not simply "monolithic forces that subsume everything in sight, crush everything in reach" (ibid 29). Foucault moves away from the fixation with sovereignty and legitimacy and provides an elaboration of power as the ubiquitous feature of human interactions (Hindess 1996). For him, the problematique of power and the problematique of the subject cannot be severed from each other; their relationship is isomorphic to Barad's intra-action. For Foucault, analyses of power are not about substances but about processes and speak to "the different modes by which, in our culture, human beings are made subjects" (1982: 208). The political emerges then as a dynamic field of intra-actions that continuously define, redefine and transform both power and subjects. In this perspective, the state has no essential identity prior to practices of government, nor is it a presupposition of analysis but the result of a complex series of administrative and legal processes and activities that need to be explored in light of their specific articulations. Thus "[the state's] unity is not a function of the will of the people' who 'contract' to generate it (as liberals believe) or the needs of capitalism (as Marxists believe) but an *ongoing process*" (Martin 2002: 64). This notion of the state as not pre-existing the practices through which it is constructed also radically challenges the central focus of IR as a discipline dealing with relations among states (Shapiro 2017). As Onuf has argued, these approaches to the study of IR have also challenged assumptions about the relations of states' agency, spatiality and states' ability to exert control on increasingly complex and interconnected processes (Onuf 2017). Foucault's way of inquiry blurs the spatialized-susbtantialist distinction between the national and the international in favor of the study of multifarious practices.

In an intra-agential perspective, power can be re-imagined as reiterative and intra-active enfolding process instead of a mass or a force. As a set of relations brought to bear, power is uneven and unequal, but also unstable, ambiguous and reversible. Hence resistance relates to power not only oppositionally but also transformatively. "Resistance . . . may provoke refinements or modifications of techniques of power- and these in turn, will provide conditions under which new forms of resistance and evasion may be developed" (Hindess 1996: 101). The political is not constituted by pre-existing entities endowed with free will, nor is power imagined as "sovereignty" – i.e. as a mighty Leviathan that inevitably oppresses such freedoms.

While establishing connections between modalities of economic production and techniques of power, Foucault's primary difference with Marxism is that he does not explain power mainly as the economic exploitation of a class over another. While neither neutral nor uneven, the connection between power and the economy is not a matter of functional subordination, nor of formal isomorphism but instead needs to be studied in its historical and contingent articulations (Foucault 2003). Thus, while often being oppressive, power bears the mark of *danger* instead of *domination.* Social relations cannot be explained mainly by referring to one fundamental structure (for instance, the capitalist economy), but through the observation of multifarious and divergent practices. While deeply ingrained within the modalities of functioning of society, power can always be twisted, harassed, and tinkered with. However, because Foucault does not embrace a dialectical vision of history and social transformation, he does not outline a path for achieving an ideal political condition, nor does he identify a clear, linear relation of causality between political action and political effects. Power and resistance are imbricated in and enacted through a series of uneven and unequal strategic relations, the effects of which can only be assessed in the context of *praxis*. As Didier Bigo (2011) puts it, politics is dense and so cannot be described in terms of fixed categories. Foucault's political ethos and research orientation invite historically situated explorations and careful differentiations rather than overarching demonizations of power and it incites reconsidering political agency beyond the dichotomy of oppression/rebellion. This ethos is deeply implicated in the commitment to displace assumptions about the supposedly natural character of what is taken for granted. Thus,

> it's quite true that I don't feel myself capable of effecting "the subversion of all codes," "dislocation of all orders of knowledge," "revolutionary affirmation of violence," "overturning of the contemporary culture," these hopes and

> prospectuses that currently underpin all those brilliant intellectual ventures which I admire all the more because the worth of those who undertake them guarantees an appropriate outcome. My project is far from being of comparable scope. To give some assistance in wearing away certain self-evidences and commonplaces about madness, normality, illness, crime and punishment; . . . to contribute to changing certain things in people's ways of perceiving and doing things; to participate in this difficult displacement of forms of sensibility and thresholds of tolerance – I hardly feel capable of attempting much more than that.
>
> (1991: 83)

Foucault's commitment to questioning universals challenges associated positions that aspire to bring about a totalizing alternative social order, the features of which may be planned in advance, or, alternatively, that embrace the resignation to accept the *status quo* as the only possible and plausible arrangement of social relations. By moving away from a substantialist footing, Foucault opens the way for reconceptualizing the possibility of political agency in *practical*, rather than *a-historical* and *universal* terms. He also detaches the problematique of political agency from the problematique of power and oppression, instead to re-shape it as a game of discovering political possibilities in the context of different apparatuses.

Differently from positions that embrace liberal substantialist ontological assumptions and epistemological frameworks, non-substantialist starting points maintain that nothing simply *is* but rather, reality comes to being what it is as the result of agential practices. Because political power scripts do not pre-exist the practices of their making, along with the specific relations that construct them, relational ontology opens the way for non-idealistic and engrained in *praxis*, analyses of politics and conceptualizations of ethics and agency. In this framework, the opportunity for political agency is rooted in ambiguity and performativity – i.e. on the making and remaking of meaning, subjects, power and political spaces in the context of intra-active relations.

Conclusions

If, in line with Foucault and Barad, power and subject are imagined as intra-active, the political is not limited to a dichotomous struggle between oppression and freedom. Agency exists as a way of life, a reiterative activity of opening or foreclosing different possibilities of materialization of matter, not as a relation of push and pull aimed at imposing force on a mass. We are entangled with, constituted and transformed by the very processes we aim to transform. The choices we make have ontological and morphogenetic effects. Therefore, practices take epistemological and ontological precedence over abstractions. By embracing starting points that challenge substantialist conceptualizations of the pillars of IR theories and more broadly, Western political thought, entangled ontologies affirm the ethical potential of deconstruction. In fact, as we have seen, entangled ontologies foster an ethos that does not start from the ontological attributes of subjectivity and power in order to imagine the political.

Furthermore, ontologies of entanglement nurture an ethos of political engagement through plural and uncertain practices that demand continuous attention to what-happens instead of fixations on what-ought-to-be.[7] Relational ontologies nurture "modest" conceptualizations of political agency and question the overwhelming stability of "mighty totalities," such as the international liberal order or the state. In this framework, political action has more to do with playing with the cards that are dealt to us to produce practical effects in specific contexts than with building idealized "new totalities" where perfect conditions might exist. The political ethos that results from non-substantialist ontological positions privileges relentless engagements and carefully weighs political choices with regard to the consequences and distributive effects they may produce in the context where they are made, rather than justifying action on the ground of universal normative aspirations.[8]

Entangled ontologies place the notion of responsibility at the center of any justification of ethical endeavors. In Barad's words, "We are of the universe-there is no inside, no outside. There is only intra-acting from within and as part of the world in its becoming" (2007:396). In this view, we never get out of ethics, as with every and each single action we contribute to the enfolding of the universe. As Barad puts it,

> With each intra-action, the manifold of entangled relations is reconfigured. And so consequentiality, responsibility and accountability take entirely new valences. There are no singular causes. And there are no individual agents of change. Responsibility is not ours alone. And yet our responsibility is greater than it would be if it were ours alone. Responsibility entails an ongoing responsiveness to the entanglements of self and others.
>
> (2007: 394)

Such awareness raises the bar for the adjudication of ethical validity beyond abstract prescriptions and, at the same time, restricts the possibility of relinquishing responsibility for the consequences of our actions by dubbing them as "unintended consequences." It also broadens what counts as ethically and politically relevant. Ethics is performative, materially entangled, and cannot be suspended. For Barad, "a delicate tissue of ethicality runs through the marrow of being. There is no getting away from ethics, mattering is an integral part of the ontology of the world in its dynamic presencing" (2007: 396).

Notes

1 Starting points differ from foundations. Foundations establish the bedrocks upon which a correct argument relies and offer a "truthful" account of the nature of entities "out there." Starting points are not intended to provide universally valid bedrocks or "first philosophies," but possible beginnings for (maybe unbeaten) research paths.

2 Foucault's *Panopticon* exemplifies the working of apparatuses (*dispostifs*).

3 As we have seen in Chapter 1, individualism also shapes Kenneth Waltz's structuralist account of the international order where states are imagined as unitary mass forces.

4 I will elaborate more extensively on these concepts in Chapter 7.

5 The argument I develop in this section builds upon Zanotti 2013.
6 For an analysis of the relations of Michel Foucault with Marxism, see also Nicholas J. Kiersey (2010).
7 E. H. Carr, in his critique of liberalism, embraced a similar position. For Carr, idealism is guilty of being blind to actual political circumstances and oversimplifying the complex reality of politics in the name of abstract aspirations. Carr warned against the possible self-defating consequences of these positions. See Carr 1946.
8 As an example, David Kennedy argued, whether or not to intervene internationally in defending human rights should be decided with an eye to the distributive effects of such action, instead of based upon "universal" human rights principles that may very well reflect a particular way of framing issues that emerged within the "invisible" college of human rights academic and professionals. See Kennedy 2004.

Bibliography

Barad, Karen. 2007. *Meeting the Universe Halfway: Quantum Physics and the Entanglement of Matter and Meaning*. Durham and London: Duke University Press.

Barry, Andrew, Thomas Osborne and Nikolas Rose. 1996. *Foucault and Political Reason: Liberalism, Neo-Liberalism and Rationalities of Government*. Chicago: University of Chicago Press.

Bigo, Didier. 2011. "Pierre Bourdieu and International Relations: Power of Practices, Practices of Power." *International Political Sociology* 5.3: 225–258.

Bleiker, Roland. 2003. "Discourse and Human Agency." *Contemporary Political Theory* 2: 25–47.

Braun, Bruce. 2007. "Biopolitics and the Molecularization of Life." *Cultural Geographies* 14: 6–28.

Callier, Vivian. 2015. "Baby's Cells Can Manipulate Mom's Body for Decades." *Smithsonian.com*. September 2. www.smithsonianmag.com/science-nature/babys-cells-can-manipulate-moms-body-decades-180956493/. Accessed January 23, 2018.

Carr, Edward Hallett. 1946. *The Twenty Years' Crisis, 1919–1939: An Introduction to the Study of International Relations*. London and New York: Palgrave Macmillan.

Finlayson, Alan, and Jeremy Valentine (eds.). 2002. *Politics and Post-Structuralism: An Introduction*. Edinburgh: Edinburgh University Press.

Foucault, Michel. 1982. "The Subject and Power." In *Michel Foucault: Beyond Structuralism and Hermeneutics*, eds.Hubert L. Dreyfus and Paul Rabinov. Chicago: University of Chicago Press.

———. 1984a. "On the Genealogy of Ethics: An Overview of Work in Progress." In *The Foucault Reader*, ed. Paul Rabinow, 340–372. New York: Pantheon Books.

———. 1984b. "What Is Enlightenment?" In *The Foucault Reader*, ed. Paul Rabinow, 32–50. New York: Pantheon Books.

———. 1991. "Questions of Method." In *The Foucault Effect: Studies in Governmentality*, eds. G. Burchell, C. Gordon and P. Miller, 73–86. Chicago: University of Chicago Press.

———. 2003. *"Society Must Be Defended." Lectures at the Collège de France, 1975–1976*, trans. David Macey. New York: Picador.

———. 2008. *The Birth of Biopolitics: Lectures at the Collège de France, 1978–1979*. Basingstoke: Palgrave Macmillan.

Edkins, Jenny. 2002. "After the Subject of International Security." In *Politics and Post-Structuralism: An Introduction*, eds. Alan Finlayson and Jeremy Valentine, 66–80. Edinburgh: Edinburgh University Press.

Fadiga, Luciano et al. 1995. "Motor facilitation During Action Observation: A Magnetic Stimulation Study." *Journal of Neurophysiology* 73.6: 2608–2611.

Hindess, Barry. 1996. *Discourses of Power: From Hobbes to Foucault.* New York: Wiley-Blackwell.

Iacoboni, Marco et al. 1999. "Cortical Mechanisms of Human Imitation." *Science* 286.5: 2526–2528.

Kennedy, David. 2004. *The Dark Sides of Virtue: Reassessing International Humanitarianism.* Princeton, NJ: Princeton University Press.

Kiersey, Nicholas J. 2010. "Neoliberal Political Economy and the Iraq War: A Contribution to the Debate About Biopolitics." In *Security and Global Governmentality: Globalization, Governance and the State*, eds. Miguel de Larrinaga and Marc G. Doucet, London and New York: Routledge, 61–78.

Lemke, Thomas. 2011. *Biopolitics: An Advanced Introduction.* New York: New York University Press.

Martin, James. 2002. "The State and Sovereign Subjectivity." In *Politics and Post-Structuralism: An Introduction*, eds. Alan Finlayson and Jeremy Valentine, 52–65. Edinburgh: Edinburgh University Press.

Mouffe, Chantal (ed.). 1992. *Dimensions of Radical Democracy: Pluralism, Citizenship, Community.* New York: Verso.

O'Connor, Peg. 2008. *Morality and Our Complicated Form of Life: Feminist Wittgensteinian Metaethics.* University Park, PA: Penn State University Press.

Onuf, Nicholas. 2017. "The Figure of Foucault and the Field of International Relations." In *Foucault and the Modern International: Sciences and Legacies in the Studies of World Politics*, ed. Philippe Bonditti (with Didier Bigo and Fredéric Gros), 15–30. London and New York: Palgrave Macmillan.

Shapiro, Michael J. 2017. "Foucault and Method." In *Foucault and the Modern International: Sciences and Legacies in the Studies of World Politics*, ed. Philippe Bonditti (with Didier Bigo and Fredéric Gros), 115–134. London and New York: Palgrave Macmillan.

Tanesini, Alessandra. 2004. *Wittgenstein: A Feminist Interpretation.* London: Polity.

Valentine, Jeremy. 2002. "Public Reason Without a Public." In *Politics and Post-Structuralism: An Introduction*, eds. Alan Finlayson and Jeremy Valentine,202–218. Edinburgh: Edinburgh University Press.

Waltz, Kenneth N. 1979. *Theory of International Politics.* Reading, MA: Addison Wesley.

Williams, Caroline. 2002. "The Subject and Subjectivity" in In *Politics and Post-Structuralism: An Introduction*, eds. Alan Finlayson and Jeremy Valentine, 23-35. Edinburgh: Edinburgh University Press.

Zanotti, Laura. 2013. "Governmentality, Ontology, Methodology: Re-Thinking Political Agency in the Global World." *Alternatives: Global, Local, Political* 38.4: 288–304.

Žižek, Slavoj. 1993. *Tarrying With the Negative: Kant, Hegel and the Critique of Ideology.* Durham and London: Duke University Press.

5 Entangled norms

Archives, the non-transparency of meaning and ethics

The debate on ethics has mostly been framed as a debate about foundations – i.e. about the source of moral behaviors – and the kind of *prescriptions* that would ensue from different positions about such a source. This way of justifying ethical decision making relies upon a substantialist metaphysics of individualism – i.e. the Cartesian image of the subjects as defined by a detached *cogito*. In line with this ontological imaginary, in the Kantian tradition, ethical choices are driven by principles that all reasonable beings would acknowledge as valid across time, places and situations. For Kant, in order to be universal, ethics must be *formal* and independent from circumstances and consequences. The first and most general way of adjudicating the validity of action is the possibility for its guiding criterion to become a universal law of nature (where nature is imagined along the lines of Newtonian mechanics). In the *Groundworks for the Metaphysics of Morals*, Kant stipulates such principle as follows: "So act in regard to every rational being (thyself and others), that he may always have place in thy maxim as an end in himself." This principle, for Kant, is accordingly essentially identical with this other: "Act upon a maxim which, at the same time, involves its own universal validity for every rational being" (Kant 2016).

Hilary Putnam questioned the Kantian idea that "there is separate and unique moral motivation" derived from the rational and free individual's will to give itself the only law that every other free individual would recognize as valid (2004: 8). Putnam argues, ethics should not be driven, following Kant, by the aspiration to infallibility. Instead, following Dewey, it should offer a methodology to resolve *specific problems* (Putnam 2004: 9 emphasis added). In the meantime, Nicholas Onuf has highlighted the contextual origin of normative formations. Deciding whether or not socially institutionalized practices and the rules that govern them are morally defensible depends on moral principles that are themselves contestable and socially constructed (Onuf 2009: 26).

Richard Shapcott (2010) explored the relevance of different philosophical starting points for adjudicating which criteria should guide ethical decisions and whose responsibility it is to resolve pressing political issues; for instance, who should reduce refugees' suffering, carbon emission, global poverty, sustain the price of humanitarian interventions, etc. The answer to the key question "what do we owe to whom," Shapcott argues, is different for Cosmopolitans, Realists and

Communitarians. While Cosmopolitans ground their position on the assumption that humanity is a single moral community (in virtue of a shared rationality of capacity to suffer), anti-Cosmopolitans ground their justification of ethics upon the primacy of distinct communities (be they defined by the state or by other criteria) and thus emphasize the "relative" and culturally determined nature of morality (Shapcott 2010: 10). While these positions are not clearly demarcated, instead constituting a continuum, they privilege different considerations in adjudicating political and ethical choices.

Ways of validating ethical choices have important practical implications. Cosmopolitan international scholars have praised political de-territorialization, the emergence of the Responsibility to Protect (R2P) as the organizing concept for international intervention, the recognition of universal norms especially with regard to human rights, the expanding role of civil society, and the growing awareness of a "common humanity" (Kaldor 2003; Finnemore 1996). However, universal norms can provide sound guidelines for ethical decision making only if the world is imagined as homogenous and causally linear, and similar conditions occur across circumstances. Ethical universalism pays little attention to the entanglements within which norms acquire meaning and to the apparatuses through which normative claims are deployed. Thus ethical universalism is enmeshed with the potential for offering appeasing rhetoric of self-justification and may elicit unethical choices. "Universal norms" provide a "reassuring" ground for international interventions of every sort by privileging abstract principles over in-depth assessments of the context and means of their deployment and dubbing all shortcomings as "unintended consequences." Former under secretary general for peacekeeping operations Jean Marie Guehénno has argued strategies of international intervention based upon assumptions of causal linearity and invariance amount to *hubris* (2001). Nevertheless, universal norms and bureaucratic routines play a major role in justifying UN decisions regarding the deployment of peacekeeping interventions and their day-to-day operations, as well as in supporting states' decisions to go to war. Relying on abstractions without competently assessing the situation at hand has led to the political disaster of the Iraq War to name just one prominent example (Amoureux and Steele 2014). Justifying action based uniquely on intentions and abstract principles regardless of considerations of means to end and practical consequences also offer grounds for ethical appeasement. The massacres that occurred in Rwanda and Srebrenica in the 1990s provide examples of how, by uncritically following institutionalized rules, UN peacekeepers permitted others to commit atrocities while simultaneously finding a normative base for justifying the decisions that were taken. As I will argue in Chapter 8, the United Nations' justifications for its failure to prevent the Rwanda and Srebrenica genocides testify to the fact that following abstract norms (i.e. the imperative to preserve impartiality) and bureaucratic reasoning (i.e. rules of engagement prescribing not to intervene to disarm any party of the conflict) set the stage for avoiding a careful assessment of what was at stake at the eve of the massacres.[1] These ways of reasoning relieved the responsible parties' consciences for being unaccountable to the people in danger (Zanotti 2014). In summary, justifying ethical choices based on abstract norms may actually relieve international interveners of the responsibility for thoughtfully considering what the appropriate means to achieve certain ends are as well as the morphogenetic properties of intervention.

In the pages that follow, I explore norms as part of *entangled phenomena*, not as entities. I start by mobilizing Foucault's *Archive* in order to challenge assumptions about the fixity and transparency of meaning. Furthermore, I engage with the work of scholars who, while not entertaining ontological debates, have highlighted the centrality of practices for shaping norms and ideas as well as for adjudicating their validity and assessing their political effects. I will conclude by exploring the affinities of these positions with an intra-agential ethos and their implications for adjudicating ethical and political choices in a way that does not rely (mainly) upon abstractions.

The archive and the non-transparency of meaning

As I have argued in Chapter 1, some constructivist scholars embraced the ontological imaginary of Newtonian mechanics and theorized linear relations of causation between international norms (portrayed as independent variables with fixed, intelligible and context-independent prescriptive content), and states' or international organizations' behavior (imagined as a dependent variable), thus substantializing both "norms" and the actors whose behavior norms supposedly cause (Finnemore 1996).

Positions such as Finnemore's, which, as we have seen in Chapter 1, treat norms as "permissive causes," remain firmly rooted within Newtonian conceptualizations of causality. In line with intra-agential ontologies and in following Foucault, I explore instead the possibility of conceptualizing meaning as emerging in the context of entangled practices. In the *Archeology of Knowledge* (1972), Foucault unsettles the possibility of equating meaning with linguistic equivalence and therefore of imagining norms as "things" able to mobilize fix relations of causality.[2] For Foucault, logical equivalence does not exhaust the enunciative function of statements: while in different statements the literal meaning of words may remain constant, what changes are the *relations* of statements to other statements, the different spaces of experience within which they are situated, the problematizations they open and the different practices they mobilize. Thus meaning emerges within a *phenomenon*. For Foucault, the phenomenon within which meaning takes place is the "archive." The archive is not a *container* of separate elements, (analogous to "space" in Newtonian mechanics) where ideas travel as entities endowed with autonomous characteristics and causal power. It is a relational entanglement. Thus while the equivalency of *sentences* can be established based upon their identical logical structures, *statements* are to be understood in the context of *the rules of connection* that link them to other statements *in the context of discursive practices*. Thus

> the identity of a statement is subjected to a second group of conditions and limits: those that are missed are imposed by all the other statements among which it figures, by the domain in which it can be used or applied, by the

> role and functions it can perform. The affirmation that the earth is round or that a species evolve do not constitute the same statement before and after Coperninicus, before and after Darwin; *it is not, for such simple formulations, that the meaning of the words has changed; what changed was the relation of these affirmations to other propositions, their conditions of use and reinvestment, the field of experience, of possible verification of problems to be resolved, to which they can be referred.*
>
> (Foucault 1972: 103 emphasis added)

If norms and what they prescribe are thought of as transparent and context-independent, their regulatory functions can be tested and the connections between prescriptions and praxis probed. An archeological inquiry would focus instead on mapping "discontinuities": the differences between statements situated within different discursive practices. As Dreyfus and Rabinov aptly put it,

> Although speech acts for Foucault . . . have some sort of fixed "information content" or "sentence meaning," whether or not two speech acts mean the same thing (that is determine the same truth conditions) depends not merely upon the words that determine their information content but upon the *context* in which they appear.
>
> (1982: 54)

Thus, instead of focusing on the supposed identity of "meaning" conveyed by the identical linguistic form of sentences and transmitted over time and across situations, a non-substantialist approach aims to find transformations in modalities of connection among statements and their broader relations within the phenomena where they intra-act. The object of inquiry is not the "content" of the archive (i.e. the "meaning" of sentences taken as isolated units), but the modalities of transmission and organization of the statements and their broader entanglements. Inquiries would be about diagnosing the performativity of norms in context, instead of drawing linear relations of cause and effect among ideas and political outcomes.

In a similar vein, anthropologist Ann Laura Stoler (2002) takes issue with approaches to anthropological inquiries that isolate and single out statements and assertions instead of evaluating the entirety of the "archive" (or phenomenon) within which any statement is uttered. For instance, Stoler argues anthropologists often "mine the *content* of government commissions and reports, but rarely attend to their peculiar *form* or *context*" (2002: 90, emphasis in original). Similarly, some constructivist and, more generally, liberal, international organizations (IO) scholars, "mine" UN reports and official documents for their normative content and explore to what extent normative sentences, examined in their linguistic form, influence behavior. Differently, archeological explorations of IOs would not only address the "archival content" (i.e. the normative sentences that can be retrieved in documentation) but also (and most importantly) the way the archive is put together and its entanglement with broader phenomena. For Stoler (in line with Foucault), archives have to be regarded not "as sites of knowledge retrieval, but of knowledge *production*." In other words, analyses should focus on "what forms the archive," on its "taxonomies in making" which signal "critical features of . . . politics and . . . power" (Stoler 2002: 87).

In summary, the archive is not simply an inert container of meaning or structure that fixes and overdetermines it. The archive is instead a performative entanglement – an apparatus through which humans participate in the larger configuration of the world. Meaning is part of a performative process of opening and foreclosing possibilities. Positions that start from entanglements do not obfuscate the divergent effects of norms by treating them as 'weaker' (permissive) causes. Instead, they include an assessment of the ontological cuts certain normative statements produce. In this perspective, differently from positivist epistemologies and substantialist ontologies that trace linear relations of causation between ideas and behavior, and differently from scholars who read the formation of discourses and *savoirs* of international security as totalizing and overdetermining scripts, an archival, non-substantialist approach focuses on detecting epistemic permutations, hybridizations and power's anxieties and so testifies to the entangled trajectories through which meaning is established. As an example, Ann Laura Stoler argues the Colonial Commission of Inquiry's proliferation of paper trails on certain topics is not the expression of a coherent power script, but the *symptom* of power's incertitude and anxiety. In Stoler's words,

> It was not epistemic clarity but epistemic uncertainty that generated the densest debates and the longest paper trails that wound their way through a range of seemingly unrelated subjects. Like imperial formations themselves, colonial truth-claims were provisional and subject to change.
>
> (2009: 43)

In fact, Stoler argues, the terms "'grids of intelligibility' and 'regimes of truth' should be used cautiously, with the caveat that both mark epistemic habits and ways of knowing cut through with competing investments and altering claims" (2009: 43).

In summary, norms are intra-actively produced and so in turn produce material ontological cuts. They do not do so as "tamed" mechanical forces, or a "vector of influence among separate events" (Barad 2007: 393). They enact (or foreclose) causal clusters. Furthermore, the assessment of meaning requires broader consideration than just linguistic content. As Barad argues, "intra-actions effect what is real and what's possible, as some things come to matter and others are excluded, as possibilities are opened up and others foreclosed" (2007: 393). If we imagine the world as entangled and emergent rather than inert, linear and flat, ethico-political endeavors take the shape of uncertain and situated engagements that must include careful assessment of the phenomena within which our agency intra-acts. Norms do not entail consequences as billiard balls on the billiard table. For Barad, in a way that is attuned to Foucault's archival approach, "statements and subjects emerge from a field of possibilities. This field of possibilities is non- static or singular but rather is a dynamic and contingent multiplicity" (Barad 2007: 147).

Intra-agential realism and ontologies of entanglements radically challenge substantialist views of ideas and meaning as well assumptions of linear relations of causality between norms and their effects. In an entangled ontology, "effect does not follow cause hand over fist, transferring the momentum of our actions from one individual to the next like the balls on a billiard table" (Barad 2007: 394). Instead,

> causality is an entangled affair: it is a matter of cutting things together and apart (within and as part of phenomena). It is *not* about momentum-transfer among individual events or beings. The future is not the end point of a set of branching chain reactions; it is a cascade experiment.
>
> (2007: 394)

These engagements, in turn, effect "what is real and possible" (2007: 393).

The murkiness of practice and possibilities for validating action

> Empiricist and scientific realists have each tried to connect these larger intralinguistic systems to something extralinguistic; theoretical holists have tried to incorporate experience and references to objects as intralingusitic or intratheoretical. A better alternative to both approaches is to think of linguistic performances as inextricable from larger patterns of practice that are not themselves understood on the model of a language or theory.
>
> (Rouse 2002: 268)

In Barad's words, "rejecting the metaphysics of individualism that serves as the foundation for traditional approaches to ethics, agential realism proposes an alternative meta/physics that entails a reworking of the notion of causality and agency" (2007: 393). Viewing international norms as intra-active entanglements paves the way for conducting inquiries that do not assume normative transparency and stability but rather explore norms' shifting interconnections, illuminate transformations of discourses of international order and study how statements are differently appropriated politically so as to form languages for justification of hegemonic practices and for their contestation. Such inquiries explore how existing practices are re-couched and reframed into new languages of operation, how new objects are constituted as the targets for intervention, and how normative formations are appropriated and hybridized in different political contexts. They also include the exploration of means-to-end approaches and of the actors and professional habits and administrative arrangements through which normative claims are translated in practice. A handful of scholars have explored the practical and murky dimensions of international norms. While not engaging in ontological explorations, these scholars have highlighted, in different ways, the central ontological relevance of contexts and professional epistemes, the non-linearity of causality between aspirations and their consequences, and the morphogenetic effects of the circulation of emotions in shaping ideas and politics.

Alan Kuperman for instance, has argued that norms of humanitarian intervention or the R2P often had perverse consequences. Thus during the Balkan Wars, political entrepreneurs escalated violence deliberately in order to entice such intervention (Kuperman 2008). In analyzing international norms regarding torture and their interpretation by the Bush administration, Anthony Lang (2009) challenged assumptions about linear relations of causality between normativity and its effects and suggested that the functioning of any norm be assessed in the context of the practices where they are deployed. In Lang's words,

> While we assume that rules will prohibit torture, what rules actually do is create a world in which torture is possible . . . what we imagine the rules can do for us- restrain violence and make the world more peaceful- is not what the rules actually do.
>
> (2009: 8)

Instead of assuming that rules will achieve the results they formally prescribe (i.e. eliminate torture), we should explore "what social and political context supports the practice of torture in the current war on terror" (Lang 2009: 9). Oliver Richmond (2011) and Roger Mac Ginty (2011) have critically addressed the possibility of treating discourses that legitimize and guide international intervention as a coherent script. The "liberal peace," for example, constitutes a hybrid discursive formation that simultaneously encompasses universal normative claims, postcolonial trajectories and bottom-up aspirations for emancipation. In my own work, I have shown that international intervention validates as universally valid practices that are historically and geographically rooted upon processes of state building in classical Europe and may not work well where the same conditions do not obtain (Zanotti 2011).

In the meantime, David Kennedy (2004, 2006) has critically scrutinized the growing imbrication of legal language in the practice of war and peacekeeping. "Rules of engagement" in war, as well as the prescriptions of what he calls the human rights scholars' and practitioners' "invisible college," together constitute a rhetoric of legitimization of "our" war as morally right and law-abiding, as opposed to the "unlawful" and "unethical" wars of others. For instance, the anodyne rhetoric of *jus in bellum* intends to provide standardized criteria for determining the acceptable number of civilian casualties (conveniently called collateral damage). In doing so, it also produces the effect of appeasing the consciousness of those who conduct war by diverting responsibility for civilian killings. Kennedy argues that universal human rights discourses and the practices they elicit have too often avoided careful consideration for the effects and trade-offs they produce and for the political and distributive consequences they entail. Furthermore, political choices regarding human rights are not simply the result of abstract processes of deliberation driven by anodyne principles and reason (as Habermas 1986 would have it). Instead, they are shaped and implemented in the context of the habits and epistemic orientations of specific professions. These professions (i.e. the military, politicians, IOs, human rights lawyers, NGOs, private businesses, etc.) all share a similar "legal language," but interpret and deploy it in very different ways and with different means and goals. Thus, contra idealist positions, international normativity is not the anodyne offspring of reason and human progress, but a *praxis* filtered and mediated by the professional episteme, interests and habits of its creators and implementers.

Differently from scholars who start from ideas and identities to account for political and social phenomena, Andrew Ross (2013) accounts for the emergence and formation of ideas and identities starting from processes that take place in the practice of social life. Ross challenges explanations of ethical and political movements that portray them as the result of rational processes and identities fully formed in the minds of subjects. He questions "the traditional assumptions that the intentional autonomous individual lies at the heart of human agency" (Ross 2013: 9) as well as the position, shared by analytic philosophers and cognitivists alike, that "emotions come in tidy, individually wrapped packages" (Ross 2013: 18). Instead, "shared emotions emerge from lived social interactions rather than from abstract cultural identities" and are not "pre-existing objects of political manipulation" (Ross 2013: 8). In relying upon neuroscience and on the pragmatist tradition, Ross regards the body "as less a property of a person than a malleable interface between coordinated concentrations of energy" (2013: 27). Ross's explanation of social dynamics focuses on contagion – i.e. the way emotions are transmitted and circulate. The effects of contagion do not follow linear relations of causality but are morphogenetic. They may not show any coordination or coherence or reproduce existing patterns. While Ross does not use the vocabulary of intra-agential agency, his research starts from intra-activity instead of entities and so implicitly embraces *practice ontology*. Circulation continuously contributes to the opening and foreclosing of possibilities of materialization of political energy. In this framework, the explanation of social and political phenomena moves away from the centrality of the rational subject or substantialist understandings of identities and ideas as mass forces "already there," and focuses instead on iterative, non-linear and morphogenetic processes of social interaction that cannot be fully modeled theoretically, but only be traced empirically.

In embracing a central concern for practice, Jack Amoureux and Brent Steele (2014) questioned the validity of rule-based behavior as the framework for justifying action and instead advocated the relevance of carefully understanding the appropriate contexts for the application of particular rules and norms. The evaluation of political choices needs not to be limited to *intentions*, but must rely upon a *competent* assessment of the means through which any given action will be carried out and of how a situation would look like as a result. Ethics is more about the ability of diagnosing what is at stake in practice and making good (yet still uncertain) bets on the best courses of action than about adjudicating in the abstract what the right guidelines for action may be across time, place, and space. Thus, for instance "if Just War, as both thought and practice, fails to deal with the political, it will ring hollow as an ethical guide for foreign policy, as it already does for many, particularly among the 'unintended' objects of its violence" (Amoureux and Steele 2014: 68). Insightfully, in embracing Hanna Arendt and Aristotle's virtue ethics, Amoureux (2016) has argued,

> The meaning of rules (or other "universals") is never readily apparent because the circumstances of each situation for evaluation and action vary. Thus, the

> specific form of the good fluctuates across context and must always be defined by the agent (*phronimos*) who deliberates and acts on those deliberations, and who prioritizes *particulars over general and abstract thoughts* . . . For Aristotle and Arendt, then, ethics is not formulating, learning and applying rules to every situation, but drawing on them judiciously and contingently-only when they are useful.
>
> (2016: 111, emphasis added)

Amoureux also advocates ethical reflexivity as a remedy to the shortcomings of bureaucratic thinking.[3] In a similar vein, Brent Steele (2011) shifted the center of ethical assessment from intention (or, I argue, universal presuppositions) to context. As a consequence, Steele (2010a) advocates "pragmatist humility" for politicians and scholars alike, warning against the dangers embedded in universal prescriptions. Following apparently benign norms and rules may indeed lead to unethical consequences. A case in point for Steele is "the Bush administration's use of democratic peace theory to justify Operation Iraqi Freedom" (2010b: 197). Steele, then, invites scholars and practitioners to assume responsibility for the concepts they adopt, and in particular to stay away from unverified panaceas or solutions to all problems. Politics, for Steele, requires the ability to move strategically – that is, the ability to seize opportunities for transformation available in specific situations and to adjust accordingly one's tactics of resistance as the practices of power shift. Humility, prudence, judgment and creativity emerge as central moral and intellectual virtues, joined with the ability to embrace uncertainty that characterize human existence.

An ethics without substantialist foundations is grounded on a specific *attitude* and *method* that privileges contextual accounts of justification. Validating ethics upon abstract criteria is flawed because of the dangers of self-appeasement and, indeed, "incompetence." From a non-subtantialist and non-foundationalist perspective, what counts as a solution to any given problem cannot be found in a set of prescriptions based upon the validity of any universal criterion for adjudicating good intentions, but in approaches that help us understand what is the case in and therefore provide "a way of understanding the possible ways of addressing . . . problems" (Festenstein 2009: 146). Answering the question *cui bono*, including considerations of means to end and of what kind of effects any given action may produce, becomes central in this perspective.

Conclusions

> Words are also deeds, of which one must bear the consequences. They seem to have no weight and matter . . . but they are in reality complex and powerful mechanisms, the use of which implies (and should imply) responsibility.
>
> (Gianrico Carofiglio 2010, translation mine)

An intra-agential ontological imaginary affirms the relevance of positions that in different ways have questioned substantialist conceptualizations of norms and have emphasized the centrality of practical entanglements both for constituting meaning and adjudicating the validity of abstract prescriptions. In an entangled ontology, practices are morphogenetic and agency is performative. As Barad argues, "The very nature and possibilities for change are reworked" in intra-agential processes (2007: 393). Furthermore, emergence

> is dependent not merely on the non linearity of relations but on their intra-active nature . . . Events and things do not occupy particular positions in space and time; rather space, time, and matter are iteratively produced and performed.
>
> (2007: 393)

Norms are not transparent, meaning only takes shape relationally as part of material entanglements and ideas do not function as masses impressing push and pull forces on other masses. Ideas are parts of apparatuses the configurations of which need to be explored in order to assess their meaning and the way they may have a casual role within the entanglements of which they are part. The chain of events that norms may trigger is dependent upon the clusters of conditions that obtain in any given situation and the means we adopt to achieve any given end.

An intra-agential ethos entails assuming radical responsibility for the materializations of matter we contribute to make actual. Justifications of ethical and political choices that rely mainly upon following norms, abstractions or intentions are prone to lead to ethically dangerous and politically disastrous positions. *Ceteris paribus* (i.e. the same) conditions rarely obtain and abstractions likely do not provide a valid benchmark upon which to base the certitude of the goodness of our choices.

Thus in an intra-active agential perspective, decision making would not be adjudicated based upon a debate on "the right foundation" for such decisions, or a categorical imperative valid across times and spaces. If we embrace an entangled ontological imaginary, *practice* is the horizon where ontological cuts are operated, knowledge acquired and ethics adjudicated. Norms are just one of the trajectories of practices. Ethical decisions should be driven by careful considerations of the entanglements of the situation at hand, of who bears the cost for any given choice and what kind of inclusions/exclusions would result from the apparatuses we deploy in carrying out our political initiatives. In this ontological imaginary, no question regarding *what* can be answered without answering the question of *how*. In an entangled ontological imaginary, the means we adopt to reach certain ends are integral parts of the causal clusters that obtain in specific situations, and so are of paramount importance for adjudicating the validity of any ethico-political choice. In fact, in this imaginary there is no clear distinction among material and ideal forces, as they all belong in entangled intra-active causal clusters. In Barad's words "ethics is therefore not about right response to a radically exteriorized other, but about the responsibility and accountability for the lively relationalities of becoming of which we are part" (2007: 393). Ontologies of entanglement raise the bar for the criteria we use to validate action. Radical assumption of responsibility drastically limits what is acceptable as "unintended consequences." In adjudication action, careful diagnostics of what is at stake and what could likely happen need to take primacy over abstract claims, norms and aspiration. On the other hand, ontologies of entanglement also broaden the possibilities of our agency. We never escape the space of ethics, with every micropolitical engagement having consequences for the developments it contributes to bring about.

Notes

1 I am not implying here that the United Nations as an institution bears sole or even primary responsibility for these massacres. In fact, the political pressure of member states played the critical role in both cases. My argument here is about embracing appeasing justifications. The United Nations has often been used as a conveyer of such justifications by member states, who in this way relinquished the political responsibility these humanitarian disasters.

2 My discussion of Foucault and Stoler expands upon Zanotti 2016.

3 In building upon Foucault, Arendt and Giddens, Amoureux defines ethical reflexivity as "the dialectic, dialogic, and affective navigation of thought and action coupled with a critical ontology of the self, wherein we investigate our subjectivity and the potential for its transformation as a response to difference, relationship, and epistemological uncertainty" (Amoureux 2016: 107).

Bibliography

Amoureux, Jack L. 2016. *A Practice of Ethics for Global Politics: Ethical Reflexivity*. London and New York: Routledge.

Amoureux, Jack L., and Brent J. Steele. 2014. "Competence and Just War." *International Relations* 28.1: 67–87.

Barad, Karen. 2007. *Meeting the Universe Half Way: Quantum Physics and the Entanglement of Matter and Meaning*. Durham and London: Duke University Press.

Carofiglio, Gianrico. 2010. *La Manomissione Delle Parole*. Torino: BUR.

Dreyfus, Hubert, and Paul Rabinov. 1982. *Beyond Structuralism and Hermeneutics*. Chicago: University of Chicago Press.

Festenstein, Matthew. 2009. "National Identity, Political Trust, and the Public Realm." *Critical Review of Social and Political Philosophy* 12.2: 279–296.

Finnemore, Martha. 1996. "Constructing Norms of Humanitarian Intervention." In *The Culture of National Security: Norms and Identity in World Politics*, ed. Peter J. Katzestein, 153–185. New York: Columbia University Press.

Foucault, Michel. 1972. *The Order of Things: Archaeology of Knowledge*. New York: Vintage.

Guehénno, Jean Marie. 2001. "The Impact of Globalization on Strategy." In *Turbulent Peace: The Challenges of Managing International Conflict*, eds. Chester A. Crocker, Fen Osler Hampson and Pamela Aall, 83–95. Washington, DC: United States Institute for Peace.

Habermas, Jurgen. 1986. *Moral Consciousness and Communicative Ethics*. Cambridge: MIT Press.

Kaldor, Mary. 2003. "The Idea of Global Civil Society." *International Affairs* 79.3: 583–593.

Kant, Immanuel. 2016. *Groundwork of the Metaphysics of Morals*. Dancing Unicorn Book. (Kindle edition)

Kennedy, David. 2004. *The Dark Sides of Virtue: Reassessing International Humanitarianism*. Princeton, NJ: Princeton University Press.

———. 2006. *Of War and Law*. Princeton, NJ: Princeton University Press.
Kuperman, Alan J. 2008. "The Moral Hazard of Humanitarian Intervention: Lessons From the Balkans." *International Studies Quarterly* 52.1: 49–80.
Lang, Anthony F. 2009. *Punishment, Justice and International Relations: Ethics and Order After the Cold War*. London and New York: Routledge.
Mac Ginty, Roger, and Andrew J. Williams. 2011. *Conflict and Development*. London and New York: Routledge.
Onuf, Nicholas. 2009. "Structure, What Structure?" *International Relations* 23.2: 183–199.
Putnam, Hilary. 2004. *Ethics Without Ontology*. Cambridge, MA and London: Harvard University Press.
Richmond, Oliver P. 2011. *A Post-Liberal Peace*. London and New York: Routledge.
Ross, Andrew A.G. 2013. *Mixed Emotions: Beyond Fear and Hatred in International Affairs*. Chicago: University of Chicago Press.
Rouse, Joseph. 2002. *How Scientific Practices Matter: Reclaiming Philosophical Naturalism*. Chicago: University of Chicago Press.
Shapcott, Richard. 2010. *International Ethics : A Critical Introduction*. New York: Polity.
Steele, Brent J. 2011. "Alternative Accountability After the 'Naughts.'" *Review of International Studies* 37, 2603–2625.
2010a. *Defacing Power: The Aesthetics of Insecurity in Global Politics*. Ann Arbor: University of Michigan Press.
———. 2010b. "Of 'Witch's Brew' and Scholarly Communities: The Dangers and Promise of Academic Parrhesia." *Cambridge Review of International Affairs* 23.1: 49–68.
Stoler, Ann Laura. 2002. *Carnal Knowledge and Imperial Power: Race and the Intimate in Colonial Rule*. Berkeley and Los Angeles: University of California Press.
———. 2009. *Along the Archival Grain: Epistemic Anxieties and Colonial Common Sense*. Princeton, NJ: Princeton University Press.
Tanesini, Alessandra. 1999. *An Introduction to Feminist Epistemologies*. New York: Wiley-Blackwell.
———. 2004. *Wittgenstein: A Feminist Interpretation*. Cambridge: Polity.
Zanotti, Laura. 2011. *Governing Disorder. UN Peace Operations, International Security, and Democratization in the Post-Cold War Era*. University Park, Pennsylvania: The Pennsylvania State University Press.
———. 2014. "The Danger of Following Rules: Reflections on 'Eichmann in Jerusalem'". *Spectra,* Vol.3, no.2.
———. 2016. "Constructivism, Archaeology, and Humanitarian Intervention: A Reflection on Method." In *The Ashgate Research Companion to Modern Theory, Modern Power*, World Politics: Critical Investigations, eds. Scott Nelson and Nevzat Soguk, 347–360. London: Ashgate.

6 Entangled IR

The relevance for practice

Substantialism, foundationalism and universalism are imbricated with conceptualizations of who we are and how we relate to the world; thus, they are extremely relevant for the way we theorize how as humans we intervene in it. As metaethical philosopher Peg O'Connor aptly puts it, "Assumptions will always frame not only what counts as an intelligible description of a problem, but also what *can* count as solution" (2008: emphasis in original).

Scholars from different orientations have advocated the abandonment of understandings of epistemology as "first philosophy" (Bauer and Brighi 2009; Flax 1993; Kratochwil 2010; Rorty 1979). While I do sympathize with the reasons for moving away from debates that consider epistemology as an exploration of the universally valid foundations of knowledge, I argue in this chapter that reflecting on what we consider valid knowledge is an ethically and politically relevant exercise. A reflection on epistemology does not need to focus, in line with foundationalist positions, on finding the grounds on which the criteria for validity of all knowledge can be established or support a representationalist understanding of knowledge as the rational subject's correct and truthful representations of entities "out there." This view of epistemology presupposes a substantialist ontology that imagines reality as endowed with fixed characteristics and causal properties waiting to be discovered. Wittgensteinianism feminist philosopher Alessandra Tanesini rejects three central tenets of philosophy of science – i.e. universalism, foundationalism and reflectivism:

> The first tenet is the belief that epistemology is first philosophy. The second is the belief that knowledge depends on foundations. The third is the belief that knowledge is best understood in terms of how subjects represent their environment.
>
> (1999: 6)

For Tanesini, epistemologies elaborated from Descartes on, have "consisted in attempts to formulate universal accounts of knowledge which ignore the social context within which knowledge is located" (1999: 17). Tanesini also rejected the ontological individualism of the Western philosophical tradition originating with Descartes and Locke. Both "take individual cognitive autonomy as a fundamental epistemic value. They both stress that achieving knowledge is an individual feat" (Tanesini 1999: 17). In fact, representationalism is grounded upon images of the subject as ontologically separate from external reality (Rouse 1996: 209 in Barad 2007: 49). Nicholas Onuf and Harry Gould (2009), drawing on Rorty, challenged representationalist theories of knowledge, and argued that knowing the properties of entities cannot be separated from understanding their relations: "We never know 'what something is' as distinct from knowing how something stands in relation to other things" (Rorty 1998 in Gould and Onuf 2009: 30).

Intra-agential realism highlights the importance of connections a step forward. Relationality is not only the pre-condition for achieving valid knowledge, but the very first ontological horizon within which the materialization of matter and the ontological closure of the world happen. As I have discussed earlier, for Barad and Niels Bohr, phenomena are ontologically prior to entities, and relations are ontologically prior to *relata*. Knowing and doing are therefore part of the same onto-epistemological endeavor and the debate on epistemology cannot be severed from the debate on ontology and ethics. Knowledge is a performative (ethical) engagement and it invoques issues of responsibility. In Barad's words,

> Values are integral to the nature of knowing and being. Objectivity is simultaneously an epistemological, ontological and axiological issue, and questions of responsibility and accountability lie at the core of scientific practice . . . Realism, then, is not about representations of an independent reality but about the *real consequences, interventions, creative possibilities, and responsibilities* of intra-acting within and as part of the world.
>
> (2007: 37, emphasis added)

For Barad/Bohr, the apparatuses through which we engage with and know the world

> are the local physical conditions that enable and constrains knowledge practices such as conceptualizing and measuring; they are productive of (and part of) the phenomena produced; they enact a local cut that produces "objects" of particular knowledge practices within the particular phenomena produced.
>
> (Barad 2007: 147)

In this framework, "concepts" and "things" "do not have determinate boundaries, properties or meanings apart from their intra-actions" (Barad 2007: 147). Ontology and epistemology are inseparable. By starting from entangled phenomena instead of entities, intra-agential realism challenges the ontological bedrocks of reflectivist epistemologies' (as well as critical realism's) conceptualizations of objectivity. Furthermore, differently from Wendt's view, who postulated consciousness all the way down, in an intra-agential perspective the mental and the material are not ontologically distinct, there is no hierarchy of being and ontology is partially open-ended (Barad 2007: 125). Knowledge is an ethical and political endeavor through which we play a role in enabling different materializations of matter. Science and ethics do not belong to different spheres of reality, but rather are part of the same enterprise of enabling or foreclosing a specific enfolding of what is. By looking at ontology and epistemology as part of apparatuses through which we open or foreclose possible materializations of matter, and in line with Foucault and Judith Butler, Barad understands knowledge as an entangled discursive and material performative practice.

Thus, for Barad,

> objectivity cannot be about producing undistorted representation from afar; objectivity is about being *accountable to the specific materializations of which we are part*. And this requires a methodology that is attentive to, and responsive/responsible to, the specificity of material entanglements in their agential becoming.
>
> (2007: 91, emphasis added)

Such a methodological approach, Barad argues,

> does not take the boundaries of any of the objects or subjects . . . for granted but rather investigates the material-discursive boundary making practices that produce "objects" and "subjects" and other differences out of, and in terms of, a changing relationality
>
> (2007: 93),

thus redefining the relations between epistemology, ontology and ethics.

In relying upon Tanesini and Foucault,[1] I suggest re-thinking knowledge as a tool. The assessment of the "goodness" of a tool includes considerations of its adequacy for the task it is designed to accomplish. In this vein, the validation of any theory would not be adjudicated with reference to its ability to explain all that exists through a few principles, or to predict very general trends and patterns, but rather in terms of its adequacy for the task to be performed. Furthermore, diagnostics of *how* different trajectories come to be entangled in a given practice, as E. H. Carr, Michel Foucault and Heikki Patomäki have maintained, are central for making good political decisions as well as to affirm the practical relevance of the discipline of IR. A central implication of IR embracing an ontology of entanglement is that the justification of ethical choices may not be based on abstractions and universal principles, aloof from the exploration of *how* they would be implemented and of the possible practical consequences they would entail. The *how*, in other words, cannot be severed from the *what* and must be made a central part of adjudication of ethical validity.

In the remainder of this chapter, I will address the positions of scholars whose political ethos shows family resemblances with an intra-agential position. Feminist theorists question the masculine bias embedded in conceptualizing knowledge merely as a reflection of reality undertaken by the "rational subject." Tanesini in particular uses the metaphor of the tool, which I embrace, to describe knowledge. Furthermore, Carr's constructions of realism and idealism, along with Friedrich

Kratochwil's understanding of what accounts for a practically relevant way of doing political science, are both attuned to an intra-agential ethos. Carr rejects causal determinism and regards knowledge as a politically relevant practice that may contribute to bringing about change. Similarly, Kratochwil rejects the possibility of finding a theoretical solution to the Cartesian doubt as well as the possibility of grounding sound political decision-making upon universal abstractions and simplified assumptions regarding relations of causality. While not engaging in ontological debates, these scholars have moved towards redefining the political and ethical relevance of IR in non-substantialist terms.

Using tools, producing knowledge

> A post epistemological interpretation of scientific knowledge takes scientific practices as the primary focus of interpretation, and recognizes that sciences are ongoing ways of dealing with the world practically and discursively.
>
> (Rouse 2002: 50)

As I have already argued, intra-agential realism invites us to re-imagine our human agency in the world beyond the strictures of structuralism and individualism and beyond the dichotomy of determinism and freedom. This ontological imaginary invites us to re-think how we relate to the world we live in, how we conceive of our subjectivity, how we know what we know of the world and, as a result, how we may act to change it. In the Western tradition from the Enlightenment onwards, the possibility of achieving valid knowledge has been connected with the idea of autonomy – i.e. detachment of the knowing subject from external influences and the objects of observation. Valid knowledge is imagined to be the result of separatedness – i.e. the ability to look at reality from a standpoint situated in a different spatial and temporal dimension, from where we can gaze upon the world and theorize. Ethics, following this imaginary, is validated as the result of the abstract ruminations of reasonable individuals. In both cases, emotions are to be shunned off, because they may obfuscate the clarity of our gaze and the anodyne considerations of reason.

Conceptualizations of knowledge as an individual enterprise are entangled with conceptualizations of the knowing subject as a rational monad separate from others and aloof from emotions. In the Kantian tradition, ethics is the expression of the rational subject's ability to grasp universal criteria of behavior. Posthumanist onto epistemologies challenge the notion of knowing subject as separated and detached from the world of becoming within which we are entangled as we recognize "thinking as one manifestation of the movement which we are part of" (Penttinen 2018: 80). Feminist theorists have argued that the obsession with objectivity and abstraction that has characterized Western sciences (both social and natural) reveals the masculine anxiety with loss of control, for which distance and separation are supposed to be the cure. In this vein, Evelyn Fox Keller (1985) pointed out that conceptualizations of the subject as an autonomous and emotionally detached monad reflect masculine anxiety with commingling. Furthermore, Tanesini (1999) argued that denying the importance of practical knowledge is tainted by gender bias, as practical activities are traditionally feminine.[2] I maintain the subordination of practical knowledge is also tainted with class prejudice. It vilifies the knowledge deriving from the practical, productive activities of people (male and female) who keep our lives going, such as plumbers, electricians, cooks, nannies, construction workers, in summary, the "working class." It affirms "academic rationality" as the model of how human beings know the world while falling short of recognizing that while only a limited number of people actually engage in theorizing, many use and create knowledge by building and using instruments for intervening in the world in order to solve (practical) problems. Practical knowledge is by and large the kind of knowledge of social groups that "do" but seldom get to "speak." It is the knowledge of those who, while using tools to keep life going, do not, however, craft the conceptual apparatus through which we represent human existence.

In arguing that the exclusion of practical knowledge is tainted with gender and class biases, I do not imply, as some feminist and Marxist scholars have, that "subjugated knowledge" is necessarily more "truthful" or "authentic" than the knowledge of those who are, by education or social class, "entitled to speak." Holding such a view again subtantializes a particular social group as having a better "consciousness" than others. Instead, I argue starting from practical knowledge is politically democratic because (methodologically) it brings to the forefront the *doing* rather than the *theorizing*. In an entangled ontology, how we know the world and how we relate to it are not the result of the separated, objective rationality of the free, detached, rational and un-emotional subject. Rather, knowing and doing are entangled practices through which we encounter what is and at the same time contribute to *shaping*, but not *determining*, its forms of materialization.

Michel Foucault (1994, 1977) has also shown that knowledge is not the anodyne process of abstraction of the unbiased mind observing what exists and achieving cumulative degrees of "objectivity," but is instead imbricated with historically situated social practices and ways of exerting power. This does not mean that knowledge is superstructural or instrumental to power. Instead, it means that its production is imbricated with, and cannot be separated from, intra-active entanglements that in Barad's ontological imaginary include the non-human. For her,

> knowing is not an ideational affair, or a capacity that is the exclusive birthright of the human. Knowing is a material practice, a specific engagement of the world where part of the world becomes differentially intelligible to another part of the world in its differentiated accountability to or for that of which it is part.
>
> (Barad 2007: 342)

While relying on a different philosophical tradition, Tanesini also embraces a practice-centered conceptualization of knowledge. She relies upon Martin

Heidegger's account of knowledge as derived from our doing and centered on the metaphor of "tool." In Tanesini's words,

> We are thus concerned with the kind of knowledge we manifest in our everyday dealings with the world. This knowledge is practical mastery. It involves our ability to use, respond to, and produce things. It is the sort of knowledge we manifest when we drive, build a table, or prepare a meal. These things which we use and produce are already invested with human values. They are socially constituted. Heidegger's favorite example of a socially constituted thing is the hammer. How do we distinguish a hammer from something else? Hammers have different colors, weight, dimensions. They are made of different materials. What all hammers have in common is what they are for.
>
> (1999: 12)

It is use that makes it possible to classify a hammer as such, not its physical features *per se*. A tool is constituted by its use and therefore its existence and the understanding of what is depends upon socially constituted practices: "equipment inherits its significance from the significance of human performances that involve it" (Tanesini 1999: 13). In this framework theories are a special case of practice, not the other way around. As Tanesini puts it, "science is eminently a practical activity that often involves the usage of instruments in laboratory" (1999: 91). Tanesini's position in fact emphasizes the importance of the apparatuses we put in place in order to know what to know.

Similarly to Tanesini, Ian Hacking (1983) rejects conceptualizing knowledge primarily as a process of abstraction and representation, and puts doing and tools at the center of his reflections on how we know what we know. For Hacking, knowledge is not an individual achievement; it involves many actors; it is not necessarily driven by the aspiration to theorize; it does not follow linear paths; it may not be cumulative; it results (primarily) from attempts to find practical solutions to (contingent) problems.

For Hacking, we acquire knowledge primarily by *intervening* in the world, not by *representing* it. We manipulate the world by using tools in the context of practices aimed at solving problems that interest us. These practices are multifarious and include, but cannot be reduced merely to, scientific experiments. For Hacking, tools are both heuristic and veridiction instruments that offer a way out of the impasse of representationalist theories of knowledge – i.e. the impossibility to account for the correspondence of mental representation to the object represented. Concepts are tools. As heuristic utensils, concepts can be used to create, measure and study phenomena. It is only when we are able to use concepts as tools to investigate something else that they lose their hypothetical status (Hacking 1983: 272).

Hacking argues,

> Experimental work provides the strongest evidence for scientific realism. This is not because we test hypotheses about entities. It is because entities that in principle cannot be 'observed' are regularly manipulated to produce

> a new phenomena and to investigate other aspects of nature. They are tools, instruments not for thinking but for doing.
>
> (1983: 262)

The electron here is an example of how using a concept as a tool provides veridiction of its validity:

> *We are completely convinced of the reality of electrons when we regularly set out to build – and often enough succeed in building- new kinds of device that use various well- understood causal properties of electrons to interfere in other more hypothetical parts of nature.*
>
> (1983: 265, emphasis in text)

If we start from tools as metaphors for understanding how we know what we know, knowledge is not imagined as a description of an objective reality "out there," nor as the result of the speculation of an individual mind aloof from "interference" and distorting factors, nor as mainly a process through which we discover regularities in nature. Instead, knowledge is very much a form of know-how and results from commingling and doing together with others. It is not the outcome of one individual's ability of correctly representing what is out there by separating himself/herself from the world, but of activities aimed at solving problems. These activities are mostly social and involve apparatuses made of people with different skills, and theory-imbedded material instruments. Hacking demonstrates how, for instance, experimental situations involve an array of figures with different expertise (from those who formulate hypotheses, to those who build the instruments that make their testing possible, to those who prepare the experiments, etc.). Knowing, in this perspective, is a conceptual, practical and material entanglement. It is the result of processes that are socially constituted, performed and economically supported (or not). It is "for a purpose," garnered through intervening in the world – i.e. *manipulating* what exists rather than *representing* it.

Embracing the metaphor of the tool challenges conceptualizations of science as unitary, based upon abstract rationality, and validated based upon how much of the world it can explain. Tools are indeed task-specific. We cannot eat with a hammer, and it would be difficult to plant a nail with a fork. Tools produce effects (or fail to do so) but do not create universally valid models of reality. They are also not adequate for all of the tasks we need to accomplish, regardless of circumstances.

Debating the relevance of IR theories for practice and for political decision making

> Critical reflections upon knowledge claims are always both moral/political and epistemic.
>
> (Rouse 2002: 158)

Intra-agential realism's ontological imaginary sustains and supports the centrality of *practice* for generating knowledge as well as for producing ontological closures – i.e. materializations of matter. Because of its focus on non-linear causality and its affirmation of the entanglement of ontology and epistemology, intra-agential realism has important bearings on the long-standing debate regarding the relevance of IR for practice. Entangled ontologies challenge the divide between idealism and materialism and between constructivism and realism. These divides are based upon the separation of ontology-epistemology and material-ideational, imagined as belonging to different spheres of being.

In the introduction to his seminal 1986 book covering the debates between neorealism and its critics, Robert Kehoane defined one of the goals of the volume as an inquiry on the practical relevance of IR.[3] More recently the debate on the relevance of IR for political practice has been revived in prominent journals in the discipline. Stefano Guzzini (2013) rejects positions that identify IR with "practical knowledge" (i.e. the knowledge produced by practitioners such as diplomats and statesman) because that may reduce theorizing to empirical generalizations and preservation of the *status quo*. Theory, Guzzini argues, has a constitutive function. It is not simply "the result of knowledge, but also the condition for its possibility . . . Theorizing must cover both aspects and the fact that not all knowledge is empirically determined" (Guzzini 2013: 531). Theory does not precede or proceed from inquiry; it is embedded within it. Fruitful theorizing in IR needs to take the "constitutive function of theories seriously and . . . put concepts and their analysis at the center-stage for our scientific communication" (Guzzini 2013: 535). Thus theorizing does not limit itself to a description or a diagnostic of the *status quo*. It is indeed a creative and always unfinished process of rewriting the discipline's dictionary.

Here I embrace Guzzini's understanding of inquiry as a reflection on the constitutive status of theory. Indeed, in embracing intra-agential realism, I take steps towards rewriting a few words of the vocabulary of political agency in non-substantialist and non-foundationalist ways. However, differently from Guzzini, who regards practical knowledge as the IR practitioners' description or justification of what is, I consider practical knowledge as central for re-thinking how we relate to the world both as inquirers and political subjects and for reconceptualizing international political agency and ethics more broadly. I regard practical knowledge not simply as a description of the *status quo*. Instead, as an intra-agential activity, knowledge embraces the imbrication of practice and theorizing supported by Guzzini.

Ontologies of entanglement affirm a performative understanding of knowledge as an endeavor by which we pragmatically interact with the world and enable different materializations of matter. This ontological starting point is critically important for which forms of inquiry in IR are privileged as a good grounds for sound ethical and political decisions. In an intra-agential framework, knowledge results from apparatuses that are part of the entangled phenomena they aim to explore. If the apparatus is the (onto-epistemological) space where ontological closure happens and human agency is part of said apparatus, we can only make valid ethical and political decisions by providing an as-thorough-as-possible account of how the apparatus is set up, of the ontological cuts it performs and the inclusion/exclusions it operates as well as of the materializations of matter it enables. The ground for sound political agency is therefore based upon the possibility of understanding the relations that obtain in the specific entanglements of phenomena and apparatuses of which we are part, which we contribute to, and for which we must assume responsibility. More than offering predictions or universal prescriptions, science must be able to make "good bets" about what is the case and the course of action to be taken. In this framework, forms of inquiry and disciplinary domains that do not rely upon substantialism and mechanistic causal models are not forms of "lesser" knowledge. In an intra-actively shaped world, politically and ethically useful theorizing must explore how specific clusters of causes come together, how the apparatuses we deploy to study such clusters are assembled and what kind of practical effects our knowledge engagements produce.[4]

More than seven decades ago, E. H. Carr ([1946] 2011) published the second edition of *The Twenty Years' Crisis* (first published in 1939), in which he questioned the relevance of abstract theorizations for political and ethical decisions. Carr did not explicitly engage in ontological discussions. However, his position on the relevance of IR for practice is attuned to an intra-agential-realist ontological imaginary. Carr's understanding of causality in the social world is non-deterministic, embracing the ethical importance of ways of inquiry and their political salience. As a practitioner turned academic, Carr was more concerned with the outcomes of political processes than with the elegance of theorizations or their ability to explain a wide range of phenomena. He warned against the shortcomings of addressing political problems based upon the opposite abstractions of utopianism and realism. While utopianism ignores "what is in contemplation of what should be," realism deduces "what should be from what was and what is" ([1946] 2011: 12). In Carr's words, "the antithesis of utopia and reality can in some aspects be identified with the antithesis between Free Will and Determinism" ([1946] 2011: 12). While utopianism is voluntaristic because it aspires to substituting utopia for reality "by an act of will" ([1946] 2011: 12), realism is casually deterministic because it assumes that the future is the outcome of immutable laws of history that humans can discover but upon which they cannot intervene. Thus neither of these positions offers good grounds for making ethical decisions or engage politically.

All in all, for Carr, nineteenth century liberalism was based on the Kantian idea that "reason could determine what were the universally valid moral laws; and the assumption was made that, once these laws were determined, human beings would conform to them just as matter conformed to the physical laws of nature" ([1946] 2011: 25). Of course, the laws of nature Carr had in mind were Newton's. Carr questioned Woodrow Wilson's utopianism for the assumption that aspirational statements could in fact be translated into reality without careful consideration of "how and why" ([1946] 2011: 8). In doing so, Carr pointed to the centrality of praxis for ethico-political decision making. Carr also questioned the validity of assumptions about *ceteris paribus* conditions in the social world. For instance, in establishing the League of Nations, Wilson's political thought was based "on certain *a priori* rational principles which had only to be applied in other contexts to produce similar results" ([1946] 2011: 29). However, Carr observes, while rationalism can create a utopia, it cannot make it real ([1946] 2011). The League of Nations' failure to prevent the break out of World War II testifies to the fact that the assumption that "if men [sic] reason right about international politics they will also act rightly" does not obtain in politics ([1946] 2011: 39). In critiquing also utopian socialists, such as Saint Simon, Charles Fourier and Robert Owen, Carr argued,

> These men . . . simply made unverified assumptions about human behavior and, on the strength of these, drew up visionary schemes of ideal communities in which men of all classes would live together in amity . . . For all of them, as Engels remarked "socialism is the expression of absolute truth, reason and justice and needs only to be discovered in order to conquer all the world in virtue of its own power."
>
> ([1946] 2011, 8)

Contra the limitations of both utopianism and realism, Carr makes the case for a way of doing political science that recognizes the interdependence of theory and practice. For Carr, political processes are the result of this interdependence and cannot be described as a succession of laws or as the outcomes of aspirations:

> The political process does not consist, as the realist believes, purely in a succession of phenomena governed by mechanical laws of causation; nor does it consist, as the utopian believes, purely in the application to practice of certain theoretical truths evolved out of their inner consciousness by wise and far seeing people. Political science must be based on a recognition of the interdependence of theory and practice, which can be attained only through a combination of utopia and reality.
>
> ([1946] 2011: 14)

Appropriate theorizing in social sciences is not measured by "parsimony" - i.e. by the ability to explain with a very few assumptions a very wide range of phenomena as positivist as well as neorealist such as Kenneth Waltz would have it. It relies instead on an attitude of humility and on the ability of distinguishing aspirational statements from "analysis." This attitude is central to producing "good science": "no science deserves the name until it has acquired sufficient humility not to consider itself omnipotent, and to distinguish analysis from what is from aspiration from what should be." ([1946] 2011: 9). Carr advocates a way of conducting political science, which he calls "mature thought" that combines "purpose with observation and analysis" ([1946] 2011: 10). He counters this position to "immature thought," mainly purposive and utopian, and to the thought of old age, "which rejects purpose all together" ([1946] 2011: 10). Carr in fact embraced the morphogenetic power of ideas and judgments and the imbrication of the science and ethics. Thus, for Carr, "political judgment helps to modify the facts on which it is passed. Political thought is in itself a form of political action" ([1946] 2011: 6).

Inquiries in social science are not detached from but inextricably entangled with purpose. Political judgment contributes to "modify[ing] the fact on which it passed" ([1946] 2011: 6).

In a similar vein, Kratochwil (2010) identified the preference with broad abstractions and overarching theorizations as one of the main problematic aspects of the discipline of IR. Kratochwil embraces a pragmatist anti-foundationalist position, one that "does not begin with objects or things (ontology), or with reason and method (epistemology), but with 'acting' (*prattein*), thereby preventing some false starts" (2010: 20).[5] Rather than assessing a theory's validity based upon its generality and capacity to encompass a wide range of phenomena, we should do exactly the opposite: "instead of relying on certainty and universal validity gained through abstraction and controlled experiments, we know that completeness and attentiveness to detail, rather than to generality, matter" (2010: 20). Indeed, ethical and political choices are always made in conditions of partial uncertainty. It is exactly because it takes seriously the "always preliminary character of knowledge" that a pragmatic approach is likely to provide us with instruments to follow a course of action that is a "good bet" in contingent circumstances. In this framework, a theory's veridiction does not rest upon how much of the world out there can be made to fit into a model, or upon how many outcomes a theory may be able to predict. The cure for the Cartesian doubt (i.e. doubting the totality of our knowledge claims) cannot be found by aspiring to "absolute certainty," but by accepting and embracing uncertainty. Indeed, Jacques Derrida (1992) argued ethics and political engagements alike are rooted upon the undecidability of meaning. In making ethical decisions, we exceed what can be calculated or delimited by law, while remaining aware that our critique is never waged from an external standpoint of absolute knowledge, but is inevitably imbricated in the very foundations we criticize.

While not embracing this language, Kratochwil views theories as tools. Useful theories should not provide universal solutions to all human problems, but help us in making choices in contingent conditions of uncertainty (i.e. "get by" in the world), and to generate questions that were not previously on the table (i.e. creatively imagine alternative possibilities to what is). International politics requires focusing on diagnostics, "appraisal" and "judgment," instead of abstractions. Uncertainty is imbricated with human being in the world. *Pace* versions of constructivism that reify and substantialize norms as "(enabling) causes" of behavior (Finnemore 1996), for Kratochwil norms are not transparent and self-contained, and cannot be imagined as efficient causes. Instead, the understanding of rules is complex and always defined by "what is the case in the context of a social understanding" (Kratochwil 2010: 93).

Kratochwil's emphasis on uncertainty is rooted on an embrace of causality as entangled, complex and non-linear along the lines of what has been proposed by quantum ontological imaginaries. Events should be understood as the result of a cluster of conditions coming together under specific circumstances rather than deriving from linear cause-effect relations. These clusters of conditions may be described ex-post facto but cannot necessarily be abstractly modeled, as we have seen in Chapter 2. Kratochwil's understanding of causality demands a conceptualization of knowledge as an endeavor that embraces contingency, offers roadmaps to navigate them and devises new possibilities for making sense of the world we live in. It also fosters an ethics that is not justified based on what is "universally right" but is instead practiced by embracing uncertainty and by assuming responsibility for choices that take into account what is at stake in a given situation. Universal normativity is flawed not only because the meaning of norms is non-transparent. Uncertainty pertains not only to the interpretation of norms but also to their applicability in specific situations. This position is based upon the recognition that the same clusters of causes do not obtain across circumstances and that most of the time the information we possess in this regard is limited. In this framework, our place as agents is not patterned on the model of "sovereignty," or on the image of a subject endowed with power, able to ordain effects by triggering linear chains of causality. Agency is indeed uncertain and path-dependent. It is rooted on the ability to appraise and diagnose what is the case and to make "good bets" with incomplete information in complex situations.

In the conclusions of his "Tartu Lecture" (2007), Kratochwil summarizes a few points that are quite relevant for my argument. A pragmatic starting point fosters a revision of ideas of knowledge as a representation of what is. For Kratochwil, as stated before, theories are valuable when they enable us to ask questions that were not previously asked, and to help us "to get by" in the world. While asking new questions has to do with creativity, which Connolly (2013) considers a political virtue of central importance for transforming what is, the ability to get by in the world points at the need for carefully assessing what obtains in the situations we engage as actors. It is indeed a practical skill more similar to know-how than to rule following for which we need to be equipped with tools that are adequate for the task we need to accomplish.

Kratochwil advocates letting go of notions of truth as anchored "either in things themselves (as in classical ontology) or in reason itself (as in the foundationalist interpretation of the Kantian project)" (2008: 13). However, embracing uncertainty for Kratochwil does not equate to embracing "anything goes" positions – i.e. absolute skepticism. Absolute skepticism is indeed the result of "fruitless meta theoretical traps" and conceiving of knowledge as deriving from "private ruminations of actors." Instead, Kratochwil sees the task of theorizing as a diagnostic of "what is the case" contextually and in practice. The validation of a theory depends upon its capacity of providing tools to make "good bets" while creatively transforming what is. In this framework, ways of inquiry and disciplinary domains that do not rely upon substantialism and mechanistic causal models may offer good decision-making tools. In an intra-actively shaped world, politically and ethically useful theorizing must explore how specific clusters of causes come together, how the apparatuses we deploy to study such clusters are assembled and what kind of practical effects our engagements produce. "*Cui bono*" and "*how*" are central questions in assessing ethical engagements.

Conclusions

In an entangled ontology that does not portray the world as a homogenous space suitable to descriptions through parsimonious vectors of push and pull, inquiries that explore the causal clusters that obtain in specific situations offer a more plausible ground for adjudicating the ethical and political validity of any given choice than research programs that aspire to explaining all that happens, or offer prescriptions for action based upon abstract principles. Validating ethical choices based upon abstract universal normativity, in fact *the very aspiration to universality*, obfuscates the complex clusters of causes that shape practical entanglements and may lead to ethically bad choices. In this framework, practically useful knowledge looks more like a tool for engaging the world than an abstract explanation of all that happens in it. Tools are not universally good or bad. They are more or less apt to solve specific practical issues. If we conceive knowledge as part of entangled process of intervening in the world (i.e. Barad's and Foucault's apparatuses) and think of concepts and the activity of theorizing as tools for generating ways of engaging the world and fixing some problems, knowledge is a form of political agency and a way of practicing ethics. I have argued the metaphor of the tool offers an alternative to extant understandings of knowledge as a reflection upon the world resulting from the rationality of separated subjects. We gain knowledge by intervening in the world for a purpose, through socially instituted practices. In doing so, we relate to others that may have something at stake in the same practices. As we have seen before, practical purpose is what helps us understand what "things" are for. At the same time, we know what "things" are like if we can use them as tools for intervening in what is.

Looking at theorizing as a tool shows family resemblances with Kratochwil's understanding of the role of theory in IR: a way to deal with the specific situations that occur, and to generate questions that were not on the table previously. It also addresses Guzzini's concern about flattening theorizing to a description of the *status quo*. If conceived as a special case of practical knowledge and as a tool, theorizing is provisional and, indeed, constitutive and transformative. In an entangled ontology, knowledge is not a detached, anodyne activity that reflects reality while leaving it untouched. It is an ethico-political engagement that produces ontological cuts and therefore requisites assumption of responsibility. Tools do something. They intervene in what is to modify it.

In an intra-agential ethos, options for changing what is are not limited to regaining a pristine freedom from all constraints or bringing about an immanent ideal social order that can be planned according to aspirational prescriptions. They take the shape of multifarious and contingent struggles that are constituted within the entanglements that obtain and at the same time exceed and transform those entanglements. This approach nurtures a radical skepticism about identifying universally valid solutions to political problems. Power interacts in complex ways within heterogeneous political spaces and within these spaces it is appropriated, hybridized, re-described, hijacked and tinkered with. International ethics needs to embrace uncertainty rather than (universal) normative prescriptions that, while reassuring, may not be relevant for what is the case under the circumstances and may provide appeasing prescriptions while producing aberrant "unintended consequences." Indeed "it is precisely because there is no recipe for liberation that epistemic evaluation is of fundamental importance" (Tanesini 1999: 244).

We should not take epistemologies we adopt lightly. As Carr and Cox argued several decades ago, theorizing is always for a purpose. Some theories favor the reproduction of the status quo, while others aim at showing that some of the (social) arrangements we consider ontological necessities, are in fact the result of historical contingency. In line with E. H. Carr ethos, if we move away from the search for universal truths and norms and privilege instead ways of inquiry that help us assessing what is the case in specific situations, our ethical action will likely be driven by prudent and modest claims and careful assessments of practical entanglements. In an intra-agential framework, ethics and political agency are practices to be reinvented in context and practiced with radical assumption of responsibility in mind. In the following chapter, following Foucault, I will explore possibilities for devising an ethos that does not find its validation upon universal foundations and is not confined to abstract aspirations of actualizing an absolutely good and immanent social order, but upon an *attitude* of constant and uncertain critique and creativity.

Notes

1 In fact, Foucault suggests using his books "as a tool-box which others can dig in to find a tool with which they can make good use, in whatever manner they wish, in their own area" (Foucault 1970–75, 523 in Shapiro 2017 131).

2 This section builds upon Zanotti 2015.

3 In Keohane's words "the enterprise represented in this volume – abstract discussion of theoretical issues in international relations – [is] relevant to the practical task of interpreting the world and seeking to change it? Does the theory of international relations have implications for practice?" (Keohane 1986: 2).

4 In a way, intra-agential ontological imaginaries support interdisciplinary inquiries.

5 The role of practical knowledge in rewriting IR's (ethical) vocabulary has been the object of some degree of scholarly attention. Pragmatism in particular has been shown to offer some openings in this direction (Bauer and Brighi 2009). The book collects contributions by numerous authors, some of them based upon articles that have appeared in a special issue of *Millennium: Journal of International Studies. 2002.* 31.3. The *Millennium* issue as well as Bauer and Brighi's book, testify to the fact that there are remarkable differences among scholars who claim to embrace a pragmatist perspective. An in-depth discussion of these differences is beyond the scope of this chapter. For the purpose of my argument, I embrace Friedrich Kratochwil's version of a pragmatist perspective in IR.

Bibliography

Barad, Karen. 2007. *Meeting the Universe Half Way: Quantum Physics and the Entanglement of Matter and Meaning*. Durham and London: Duke University Press.

Bauer, Harry, and Elisabetta Brighi (eds.). 2009. *Pragmatism in International Relations*. London and New York: Routledge.

Carr, Edward H. [1946] 2011. *The Twenty Years' Crisis, 1919–1939: An Introduction to the Study of International Relations*. London and New York: Palgrave Macmillan.

Connolly, William. 2013. *The Fragility of Things: Self-Organizing Processes, Neoliberal Fantasies, and Democratic Activism*. Durham and London: Duke University Press.

Derrida, Jaques. 1992. "Force of Law: The 'Mystical Foundation of Authority.'" In *Deconstruction and the Possibility of Justice*, eds. Drucilla Cornell et al., 3–67. London and New York: Routledge.

Finnemore, Martha. 1996. "Constructing Norms of Humanitarian Intervention." In *The Culture of National Security: Norms and Identity in World Politics*, ed. Peter J. Katzestein, 153–185. New York: Columbia University Press.

Flax, Jane. 1993. "Multiples: On the Contemporary Politics of Subjectivity." *Human Studies* 16.1–2: 33–49.

Foucault, Michel. 1970–1975. *Dits et Ecrits, Vol. II*. Paris: Gallimard.

———. 1977. *Discipline and Punish*. New York: Pantheon Books.

——. 1994. *The Order of Things*. New York: Vintage.

Gould, Harry D., and Onuf Nicholas. 2009. "Pragmatism, Legal Realism and Constructivism." In *Pragmatism in International Relations*, eds. Harry Bauer and Elisabetta Brighi, 26–44. London and New York: Routledge.

Guzzini, Stefano, and Anna Leander (eds.). 2006. *Constructivism and International Relations: Alexander Wendt and His Critics*. Abingdon: Routledge.

Guzzini, Stefano. 2013. "The Ends of International Relations Theory: Stages of Reflexivity and Modes of Theorizing." *European Journal of International Relations* 19.3: 521–541

Hacking, Ian. 1983. *Representing and Intervening: Introductory Topics in the Philosophy of Natural Science*. Cambridge: Cambridge University Press.

Keller, Evelyn Fox. 1985. *Reflections on Gender and Science*. New Haven: Yale University Press.

Keohane, Robert. 1986. *Neorealism and Its Critics*. New York: Columbia University Press.

Kratochwil, Friedrich. 2007. "Of False Promises and Good Bets. A Plea for a Pragmatic Approach to Theory Building (the Tartu Lecture)." *Journal of International Relations and Development* 10.1: 1–15.

———. 2008. "Constructivism: What It Is (Not) and How It Matters." In *Approaches and Methodologies in the Social Sciences: A Pluralist Perspective*, eds. Donatella Della Porta and Michael Keating, 80–98. Cambridge: Cambridge University Press.

———. 2010. *The Puzzles of Politics: Inquiries Into the Genesis and Transformation of International Relations*. Abingdon: Routledge.

O'Connor, Peg. 2008. *Morality and Our Complicated Form of Life: Feminist Wittgensteinian Metaethic*. University Park, PA: Penn State University Press.

Penttinen, Elina. 2018. "Potential of Posthumanist Onto-Epistemology for the Study of International Relations." In *Posthuman Dialogues in International Relations*, eds. Cudworth Erika, Stephen Hobden and Emilian Kavalski, 2–88. London and New York: Routledge.

Rorty, Richard. 1979. *Philosophy and the Mirror of Nature*. Princeton, NJ: Princeton University Press.

———. 1998. *Achieving Our Country: Leftist Thought in Twentieth Century America. Cambridge*, MA: Harvard University Press.

Rouse, Joseph. 1996. *Engaging Science: How to Understand Its Practices Philosophically*. Ithaca: Cornell University Press.

———. 2002. *How Scientific Practices Matter: Reclaiming Philosophical Naturalism*. Chicago: University of Chicago Press.

Shapiro, Michael J. 2017. "Foucault and Method." In *Foucault and the Modern International: Sciences and Legacies in the Studies of World Politics*, ed. Philippe Bonditti (with Didier Bigo and Fredéric Gros), 115–134. London and New York: Palgrave Macmillan.

Tanesini, Alessandra. 1999. *An Introduction to Feminist Epistemologies*. Malden, Massachusetts: Blackwell Publishers.

Zanotti, Laura. 2015. "Questioning Universalism, Devising an Ethics Without Foundations: An Exploration of International Relations Ontologies and Epistemologies." *Journal of International Political Theory* 11.3: 277–295. (First published online October 28, 2014)

7 Imagining an intra-agential ethos

In a quantum ontological imaginary uncertainty is not the *limit*, but the very *condition of possibility* for ethical action. In a universe of complex entanglements where matter matters, assumptions regarding the human capacity for controlling and planning for complex chains of events come under question. In this onto-epistemological horizon, both universal normativity and plans to bring about an immanent alternative social order offer inadequate guidelines for exercising political agency. In an intra-agential framework, humans are not *above* the world, but *of* the world. As such, we do not have the power to re-shape what exists to fit our plans. Yet through our everyday practices of being in the world, we shape specific materializations of matter. An intra-agential ontological imaginary relies upon the following trajectories: an entangled notion of subjectivity and, for that matter, of everything; non-linear relations of causality; the affirmation of the ontological primacy of phenomena (where praxis and theories are entangled); the morphogenetic properties of what is; and the ontological (and hence ethical) relevance of the way how we inhabit the world. Intra-agential realism redefines materialism as a position beginning with the ontological primacy of phenomena and, in doing so, it reconfigures the notion of mind as well as matter. For Barad, the world reveals itself to us in its continuous enfolding. Not only are the laws that govern the social non-causally deterministic but also the laws that govern the universe. Barad neither draws a clear line between matter and non-matter nor posits a hierarchy of being where consciousness and the human comes first.

Intra-agential realism rejects the hubris of individualism as well as the causal determinism of versions of realism and structuralism. It embraces structuralism's attention to forces that shape possibilities for agency and politics beyond the individual's will. At the same time, it denies such forces deterministic, inescapable or immutable qualities. In this regard, an intra-agential ethos is attuned to Margaret Archer's (1998) position on the morphogenetic, yet non-deterministic, transformative possibilities of agency. From an intra-agential perspective, practices are not the residue of abstractions. Rather, they are the primary ontological referent, the entangled phenomena where we intra-act with each other and the non-human and so enable possibilities for materialization of matter.

An entangled ontological imaginary begs a redefinition of ethos. Instead of embracing, as in the Kantian tradition, the potential universal validity of any given choice as the criterion for adjudication, it suggests justifying action based upon careful assessment of what obtains in specific situations; it advocates a radical assumption of responsibility for the practical entanglements our actions entail; it affirms creativity and contestation as ways of bringing about alternative forms of materialization of matter. While nobody can direct and plan for the totality of events abstract principles aim at bringing about, even small engagements may open or foreclose possibilities for different enfoldings of what is. However, performativity is not an attribute of human agency only, but also of the non-human. And while we cannot plan everything, we must carefully assess the entanglements of the situation where we exert our agency and the ontological cuts the apparatuses we deploy entail. In this vein, instead of being the yardsticks by which we measure the moral validity of our choices, detachment and universal prescriptions become suspiciously associated with self-appeasement and with denying responsibility for the consequences of our acts.

In the pages that follow, I engage with the work of scholars who devised conceptualizations of ethics centered on practice, uncertainty and the radical assumption of responsibility. In different ways, the authors I address here pave the way for reconceptualizing possibilities for political agency and for validating ethics that start from the assumption of our entanglement with the world rather than upon the assumption of separateness. My selection does not have any aspiration to completeness.[1] My aim is to detect family resemblances among ways of thinking about ethics and agency that, while not necessarily focusing on ontological debates, embrace non-substantialist starting points. I engage with scholars who are widely read in IR, such as William Connolly, and with authors such as feminist, Wittgensteinian, and metaethical philosophers Peg O' Connor and Alessandra Tanesini, who are rather unknown in the discipline. I also re-engage with Foucault to argue that his political ethos is centered upon a radical rejection of substantialism. I argue that by re-imagining how we inhabit the world ontologies of entanglement affirm these positions and uphold their ethical potential as an alternative to prescription ethics. An entangled ontology affirms the possibility of a political ethos that is not grounded upon substantialist assumptions regarding the characteristics of the subject nor of the world. It makes ethics possible in the context of the subject's deconstruction and inherent uncertainty of the results to come.

Our felted being: inhabiting a house on the cliff

Feminist metaethical philosopher Peg O'Connor (2008) affirms a radical interconnection between epistemology, ontology and agency. O'Connor relies on Ludwig Wittgenstein instead of quantum physics. Nevertheless, her ontological starting points regarding our status in the world as agents are attuned to Barad's intra-agential realism. In rejecting the dualism of nature/normativity, she devises a non-substantialist formulation of ethics that avoids the straightjacket of Cartesian doubt, which (similarly to Kratochwil and Barad) she considers a "bad" starting point that inevitably leads to a dead end. Universalism and skepticism alike are indeed the result of substantialist assumptions that posit normativity and nature as separate. This assumption fundamentally misreads the "world out there," agency and normativity.[2] For O'Connor, the shortcomings of both realist and anti-realist approaches, committed as they both are to the nature/normativity dualism, resides in their shared inability to provide a "standard of correctness" – i.e. a credible elaboration of the linchpin between the knowing subject and the world out there:

> Surface conventionalism's failure is the companion to realism's failure: it imputes too much to human agency as opposed to or at the expenses of the world. Where realism misconstrues the role of humans in causal relations, surface conventionalism has a tendency to underestimate and misunderstand the formative, defining, and shaping power of the world. The physical world is real, actual, and something in which we live as material objects ourselves. . . . Conventions are not established by mere stipulation or verbal agreements but rather by *practices over time*.
>
> (2008: 53, emphasis added)

Central to her metaethical project is "creating a moral epistemology" founded on an understanding of our position in the world as "felted" (2008: 5). O'Connor's argument regarding how we connect with the world ontologically, epistemologically and ethically are centered upon two metaphors: the "felt" and "the house on the cliff." Felting, O'Connor says, is the process by which wool fibers are transformed into a "dense tangled mat, in which the individual fibers can no longer be distinguished" (2008: 61). O'Connor's choice of the image of the "felt" to portray how we relate to the world deeply resonates with the notion of entanglement. Matter is not flat, inert nor "out there." Rather, it constitutes the dimension within which we are constituted and from which we are inseparable. In this vein, O'Connor rejects atomistic understandings of the subject, knowledge and ethical assertions alike. Context is necessary for all meaningful claims and the felted world is the site for verifying the validity and applicability of norms. "In the absence of this context, there can never be rules of correctness in any domain of inquiry" (2008: 63). This statement clarifies the imbrication of theories with what we do in the world and what kind of "form of life" we share with others. "Forms of life," for O' Connor, are "sayings and doings . . . combined with the multiplicity of language-games, combined with the facts or givens of nature. . . . These enmeshments are our ways of living" (2008: 77).

The house on the cliff provides a metaphor of how we can go about re-imagining the grounding of our moral life based not upon the foundations of stable universal principles, but upon careful appraisals of what conditions obtain and upon the ability to adapt and adjust to what is the case here and now. The house on the cliff is a house in Bordeaux designed by Balamond and Koolhaas. It has no foundations, but it stands because of the relations among its parts and to its environment. In O'Connor words,

> This house shows that stability is a matter of balanced relationships among a whole host of factors, and that stability comes with a constant recognition of

> limitations and locations. . . . Stability is not simply a matter of immobility but also flexibility; just consider the importance of movement in a tall building or bridge. Stability is not a given but rather an achievement of balance and tension . . . in terms of examining the groundings of moral life . . . I am looking at some of the factors that can provide stability so long as they are in balance with one another.
>
> (2008: 15)

Stability is contingent and may require different strategies in different circumstances. It is not attained once and forever but it is the result of a continuous engagement with shifting conditions. It is deeply relational because it can only be attained through a combination of different elements. In tune with her Wittgensteinian inspiration, O'Connor rejects notions of normativity as context-independent, instead embracing a notion of ethics as deeply rooted upon careful assessments of what is at stake in the specific situation one engages with. O'Connor warns against validating ethical choices through universal prescriptions. Prescriptions and norms are inevitably based upon (substantialist) assumptions that "groundings of our moral lives are organized in a certain way" (2008: xii). Ethical imperatives are not universal, and ethical choices cannot be severed from specific ways of life we share with others. For O' Connor,

> with respect to moral principles, concepts, and rules, these are not responsible to reality (understood in a realist sense) in term of correspondence but rather responsible to a felted reality in terms of their meaning, uses, and roles in our lives.
>
> (2008: 156)

Similarly to Foucault (whom I will address next), O'Connor emphasizes the radical relevance of ethical practices – i.e. ways of life. Positions assuming that ethics can be derived from universal laws are for O'Connor ridden with danger because they divert attention from our responsibility to others. Indeed, in O'Connor's words,

> Hiding behind abstract rules makes it much easier not to see the pain and suffering of others and not to see ourselves, in whatever way, as like them. It also makes it easier to feel more allegiance to the rules rather than to the people.
>
> (2008: 167)

O'Connor offers a pathway for a reconceptualization of ethics that is directly relevant for addressing perplexities surrounding the effects of norms and rules produced by the human rights regime and more generally for a critical assessment of the role of International Organizations.[3] O'Connor suggests prudence and skepticism regarding universalist claims to possess solutions to all evils that affect humanity. However, rejecting prescriptive ethics as a valid starting point for justification for action does not lead to ethical nihilism. Actually, some of the worst evils may indeed derive by embracing institutionalized "rules" (Onuf

2009). In a "stabilist" rather than a "foundationalist" conceptualization of ethics, it is not possible to determine what the right ethical action should looks like once and forever. Nevertheless, it is possible to suggest an attitude and method through which we may devise a context-dependent valid ethical behavior. The house on the cliff exemplifies a way of conceptualizing ethics as a practice that does not rely on foundations but upon continuously adjusted engagements with the complex causal clusters within which we have agency.

Differently from O'Connor, Connolly (2013) explicitly relies upon an ontology of entanglements to validate micropolitics and to criticize the stifling effects on political agency of prevalent IR imaginaries that portray reality as divided into "levels" of analysis. Connolly's ontology is flat. Interconnections straddle "levels," and systems are organized neither by stable laws nor by one mighty principle. Thus the effects of our political action may not be confined, as in long-standing IR debates, to the "levels" within which such changes are contained. Connolly consequently rejects the dualism of human/non-human that portrays the first as being characterized by freedom and the other as being constrained by determinism:

> [The Newtonian world] must *appear to us* to be governed by mechanical laws while we must also *postulate* a human power of freedom that escapes those determinations as it also possesses almost magical power to act back upon bodily processes to guide behavior.
>
> (2013: 159)

Differently from mechanical physics imaginary, natural laws for Connolly are not impositional but immanent – i.e. they allow for degrees of liberty and variance. Furthermore, "the universe consists of entangled active elements rather than discrete particles" (2013: 153). In this ontological imaginary, microscopic phenomena may have relevant (and unforeseen) effects on macroscopic processes (2013: 153). While Kant's regulative reason presupposes a two-world metaphysics (the super sensible and the sensible), a flat ontology (which Connolly calls "immanent naturalism") challenges "Kantian, reductionist, and teleological models of human embodiment" (2002: 60). Ethics is not validated by divine or transcendental command or a juridical source. Instead, Connolly's ethos rejects "both a command model of morality set in a juridical rendering of the transcendental field and a teleological image of ethics set in a divine order of things" (2002: 86). In echoing Derrida, Connolly maintains that ethics exceeds codes and that codes of law may very well lead to ethically undesirable behaviors such as "simplification, cruelty and violence" (2002: 106). As I will show in the next chapter (following Arendt), an extreme example of the inadequacy of codes of law as a valid foundation for ethics is Alfred Eichmann's justification of his role as the logistician of the Holocaust as an act of "following the rules" (Arendt 1964).

Reflexivity and creativity are for Connolly key political virtues. In line with posthumanist perspectives, creativity is not simply an attribute of human agents or subjects but it also concerns "nature" and non-human self-organizing processes which generate conditions that were not there before (Connoly 2013: 157). Furthermore, creativity is never aloof from what already exists. It is "always a conditioned creativity in which that which is created involves enabling and constraining relations of ingression and concrescence between actual entities" (2013: 158). Because of his embrace of an ontology of entanglements, Connolly, similarly to Foucault, expresses reservations towards political ethos that confines political agency to revolutionary reversals of "the system." For Connolly,

> the point today is not to wait for a revolution that overthrows the whole system. The "system" . . . is replete with too many loose ends, uneven hedges, dicey intersection with nonhuman forces and uncertain trajectories to make such a wholesale project plausible. Besides, things are too urgent and too many people on the ground are suffering too much now.
>
> (2013: 42)

The justification of ethico-political endeavors, then, must be based upon "legitimate contestability of presumptions," not on the certainty of foundations (Connolly 2002: 112). On this ground, Connolly suggests that it is possible to imagine a brand of cosmopolitanism based on the recognition of plurality and contestation in Kant's regulative ideas, instead of upon an "innate duty" or apodeictic recognition of universals that are already there.[4] Embracing contestation, Connolly argue, shelters against the *hubris* inherent to universality. This attitude is especially important in an interconnected world that operates at an increasing speed. For Connolly, if we embrace it, acceleration "sets a condition of possibility for achievements that democrat pluralists prize" (2002: 143). By exposing all of us to difference and shrinking physical distance, acceleration demands modesty and openness. In fact, unless we embrace the challenges acceleration and interconnections pose with such an attitude, acceleration may entice tendencies opposite those inherent to democracy and pluralism – i.e. fundamentalism.

Fundamentalism is the nostalgia towards certitude and foundations, and it finds its roots in one's refusal to embrace or accept the pluralism fostered within and by a fast-moving world. Thus fundamentalism is "the shape the desire for a slow, centered world takes when its temporal conditions of possibility are absent" (2002: 180). In summary, the aspiration towards finding solid and immutable foundations for ethics or to bring about an immanent alternative social order may lead to very unethical outcomes. Connolly's ethos affirms the contestability of representations and advocates relinquishing hubris in favor of practicing micropolitical initiatives that may lead to broader transformations. In a time of increasing political radicalization, this position is central for outlining a politics of care within a network of modest, multiple engagements. Positions that embrace our being entangled with the world value uncertainty as the horizon for ethical choices and conceptualize political engagements as performative but not omnipotent. This ethos fosters engagement in the absence of certainty.

Notwithstanding these important contributions, I argue intra-agential ethos goes beyond reflexivity and creativity as a key political virtues, and it emphasizes radical assumption of responsibility. Reflexivity differs from intra-agential agency. While the first focuses on representations and their contestations, the latter focuses on the ontological primacy and ethical relevance of phenomena that include the human and the non-human. In doing so, Barad emphasizes not only imagination and creativity, but very importantly the need for prudence and radical assumption of responsibility for the material apparatuses we set in place and the effects of inclusion/exclusion these apparatuses entail. In an entangled ontological imaginary, ethics is not an affair of "the mind," but a practical way of life and conduct.

Reading Foucault in an intra-agential perspective: re-imagining the ethos of modernity

While Barad criticized Foucault for not taking the non-human into consideration, as we have seen, Barad's intra-agential realism is actually deeply rooted in Foucault's conceptual tools. Like Barad, Foucault affirms practices (Barad's phenomena) and apparatuses as ontologically primary and central to manifesting forms of materialization of matter. This non-substantialist starting point establishes important family resemblances between Foucault's and Barad's political ethos.

Like Barad, Foucault does not begin his inquiries from entities but from phenomena. He advocates conducting social inquiries as if universals did not exist - i.e. exploring how specific practical entanglements turned into social entities. Social entities (what Foucault calls "universals" or "truths") take shape as the result of ontological cuts that happen contingently in the practices within which we deploy specific apparatuses. The central commitment of Foucault's ethos is a quest for possibilities of challenging what is and exploring how substances come together as a result of contingent processes. Political contestation for Foucault is precisely about questioning assumptions that portray *historical contingencies* as *entities*.

As we have seen in Chapter 3, Barad embraces the Foucauldian concept of apparatus as the practical entanglement where ontological closure takes place intra-actively. For Foucault, apparatuses are the material embodiments of power – i.e. uneven and unequal social practices. They include, like the Panopticon or the clinic, physical constructs and ways of organizing space. They are constitutive of what social entities, including subjects, are. Conversely, power is not an abstraction or an organizing principle of the whole. Power can only be understood in its contingent articulations. In turn, freedom is not an ontological endowment of humans, but rather a practice of challenging what is taken as being the case. As we have seen in Chapter 4, this radically non-substantialist reconceptualization of power and subjects is central to shaping Foucault's political ethos. If power and subjects are imagined as entangled rather than separate, the liberal notion of freedom, as well as the Marxist conceptualization of the relations of subject and power as characterized by oppression, come under question. In fact, for Foucault, the relation between power and subjects is not a relation of externality but a constitutive one. Power is neither a juridical entity nor even an economic order. It is the assemblage of uneven and unequal entanglements embodied in apparatuses that produce ontological cuts. It includes the knowledge practices embedded in material configurations of space and the instruments through which society is organized and we shape ourselves as subjects. Foucault's conceptualization of power highlights the relevance of administrative arrangements, of means to end, as well as the situated and contingent, yet sticky, character of ways of living together. Thus, as I have argued in Chapter 2, differently from prevalent "governmentality" readings, Foucault's ethos is not centered upon a condemnation of the mighty, nefarious and totalizing mechanisms of power. These readings of Foucault once again substantialize power and subjects as entities standing in relation of externality.

In "What Is Enlightenment" (in Rabinow 1984) a piece rather under-read in IR and yet central to understanding the non-substantialist roots of Foucault's ethos, Foucault engages directly with the response Immanuel Kant gave to the same question in the *Berlinische Monatschrift* in 1784. For him, Kant's response is still relevant because of the outline of the *attitude* of modernity, instead of the prescription to obey social norms and customs. Foucault emphasizes the fact that we should move away from regarding the Enlightenment as a "theme" to embrace or reject. In his words, "We must escape from the historical and moral confusionism that mixes the *theme of humanism with the question of enlightenment*" (1984: 45, emphasis added). In Foucault's words,

> The thread that may connect us to the Enlightenment is not faithfulness to doctrinal elements, but rather the *permanent reactivation of an attitude* – that is of a philosophical ethos that could be described as a *permanent critique* of our historical era.
>
> (ibid 42, emphasis added)

What defines modernity therefore is not the theme of humanism, but rather "*the principle of a critique* and permanent creation of ourselves in our autonomy" (1984: 44, emphasis added). Kant's central contribution to the ethos of modernity is not his quest for "knowing what limits knowledge has to renounce transgressing" (1984: 45). The relevance of Kant's ethos is his *method*. It is a certain type of philosophical interrogation that "simultaneously problematizes man's [sic] relation to the present, man's [sic] historical mode of being, and the constitution of the self as an autonomous subject" (1984: 42). In other words, Kant's continued relevance is found in his *problematization* of the subject, a critical attitude that is concerned with identifying possible transgressions of what is assumed to be immutable, not in the doctrinal elements of his philosophy.

In this vein, for Foucault the central aspiration regarding the ethos of modernity is not to discover the final answer to *what* questions. Foucault's ethos is instead centered upon challenging substantialist assumptions about what exist by exploring *how* social entities came to be what they are. The ethos of modernity is formulated as a commitment to explore three "how" questions, along three trajectories:

how, as subjects, we are constituted along "the axis of knowledge, the axis of power, the axis of ethics" (1984: 48). Such a quest identifies the contingency in what has been portrayed as a necessity and, in doing so, it allows for practical possibilities of contestation and transformation. Archeology and genealogy are the methodological approaches upon which Foucault's political ethos relies. Foucault delineates his reservations towards structuralism and ethical universalism by affirming as the central trajectory of his political project as the search for *singularities*. The following excerpt is central in this regard and worthwhile quoting extensively:

> Criticism is no longer going to be practiced in the search for formal structures with universal value, but rather as a historical investigation into the events that have led to constitute ourselves and to recognize ourselves as subjects of what we are doing, thinking, saying. In that sense, this criticism is not transcendental, and its goal is not that of making a metaphysics possible: it is genealogical in its design and archeological in its method. Archeological -and not transcendental- in the sense that it will not seek to identify the universal structures of all knowledge or of all possible moral action, but will seek to treat the instances of discourse that articulate what we think, say, and do as so many historical events. And this critique will be genealogical in the sense that it will not deduce from the form of what we are what it is impossible for us to do and to know; but it will separate out, from the contingency that has made us what we are, the possibility of no longer being, doing, or thinking what we are, do, or think.
>
> (1984: 46)

While for Foucault the outward trajectory of modern ethos is an attitude of relentless questioning, the inward trajectory is oriented towards accepting one's finitude along with a commitment to a continuous elaboration of the self. Foucault's ethos is framed as a practical test of our limits not an ambition to establish an alternative metaphysic of the subject or an attempt to answer once and for all the Cartesian doubt.[5] Freedom, the pillar of Western political thought that shaped the liberal and, to some extent the Marxist debate on power and the political more generally, is in fact not an ontological attribute of humans, but the result of relentless work that requires creativity, constant engagement and the ability to deal with the conditions that are handed to us. Differently from the liberal understanding, freedom is not an ontological entitlement of the subject inevitably threatened by power. Differently from Marxism, freedom is not necessarily crushed by the structure of international capitalism. For Foucault, freedom is the result of a method of inquiry and a way of life. It is an *achievement*, not a starting point. The following excerpt elucidates Foucault's position in this regard:

> The point in brief is to transform the critique conducted in the form of necessary limitation into a practical critique that takes the form of a possible transgression. This entails an obvious consequence: that criticism . . . is not

> seeking to make possible a metaphysics that has finally become a science; it is seeking to give new impetus, as far and wide as possible, to the *unfinished work of freedom*.
>
> (1984: 46)

The process of constructing oneself as a free subject is necessarily contingent, complex, provisional and situated and is the demands a continuous *work* of the self on itself. There is no prescriptive or teleological aspiration that can guarantee the success of such project of freedom. In mobilizing Baudelaire's *flanêur*, Foucault argues that as a relation to the self, modernity is a "tied to an indispensable asceticism. To be modern is to accept oneself as one in the flux of the passing moments; it is to take oneself as object of a complex and difficult elaboration" (1984: 41). Thus our impatience for liberty takes the form of the *labor* of multiple inquiries. (1984).

In this framework, ethical justification does not rely upon substantialist starting points that posit a set of given attributes of the subject upon which to ground universally valid ways of adjudicating action. Instead, the central trajectory of Foucault's ethos is the constant critique of such starting points. In his insightful exploration of Foucault's position regarding human rights, Ben Golder (2015) argued that Foucault's position with regard to human rights is directly linked to an ethos centered on discovering possibilities for things being different from what they are. Foucault, Golder argues, uses rights not as a grand theory, but as a political resource to be deployed pragmatically and tactically. In other words, Foucault's position with regard to human rights is deeply rooted in his non-substantialist starting points and upon an ontological imaginary that sees the world as an entanglement of complex and heterogenous assemblages within which we have agency. His ethos is firmly positioned in the field of practice and is rooted within, not made impossible by, the deconstruction of aspirations to universality.

For Foucault, freedom and political agency are attitudes of existence at the borderline. Freedom is not an empty dream nor a game of all or nothing, but a practical and situation-specific experiment in pushing the limits that are given to us. It is the job of "grasping the point where change is possible and desirable, and to determine the *precise form* this change should take" (1984: 46, emphasis added). Foucault sees political agency as engaging in "specific transformations . . . in a certain number of areas," transformations that should rely upon accurate assessment not only of the opportunity for change, but also of its potential practical effects. Thus one must be particularly weary of "programs for a new man that the worst political systems have repeated throughout the twentieth century" (1984: 47). Ethical political critique should perform diagnoses "precisely" as well as

> turn away from all projects that claim to be global or radical. In fact, we know from experience that the claim to escape from the system of contemporary reality so as to produce the overall program of an other society, of an other way of thinking, another culture, another vision of the world has led only to the return of the most dangerous traditions.
>
> (1984: 46)

In summary, Foucault's ethos challenges positions that aspire at bringing about a totalizing alternative social order, the features of which may be planned in advance, or, alternatively, that embrace the resignation to accept the *status quo* as the only possible and plausible arrangement of social relations. As Patomäki and Connolly, following Foucault, have also argued, totalitarianism and political violence loom as the dangers of political projects that claim to bring an immanent good as opposed to whatever the designated existing evil is. Foucault's response to the Marxist/structuralist question regarding political agency (i.e. "if we limit ourselves to this type of always partial and local inquiry or test, do we not run the risk of letting ourselves be determined by more general structures of which we may well not be conscious, and over which we may have no control?" (1984: 47) is exemplary of his rejection of totalizing solutions based upon universal abstractions and aspirations. His arguments reiterate his deeply non-substantialist and practice-oriented position:

> We have to give up hope of ever acceding to a point of view that could give us access to any complete and definite knowledge of what may constitute our historical limits. And from this point of view the theoretical and practical experience that we have our limits and of the possibility of moving beyond them is always limited and determined; thus we are always in the position of beginning again.
>
> (1984: 47)

Foucault's ethos includes both a commitment to modesty and a commitment to starting again in the face of failure. A non-substantialist ethos concerns assuming the risk of continuously walking a fine line and remaining politically engaged, while embracing the radically provisional nature of life and the hard work it takes to become decent human beings, all while questioning what appears in society as natural and obvious. Foucault's ethos is a practice, a way of life. It is not a theory or a series of already-developed prescriptions, but "a practical critique that takes the form of possible transgressions" (1984: 46). In his own words, it is

> a way of relating to contemporary reality; a voluntary choice made by certain people . . . a way of thinking and feeling; a way too, of acting and behaving that at one end and the same time marks a relation of belonging and presents itself as a task.
>
> (1984: 39)

Knowledge is a central trajectory of Foucault's ethos. As we have seen, both for Foucault and for Barad, knowledge is not reflective but performative. Therefore, ways of inquiry are forms of political agency. In *The Government of Self and Others*, Foucault reflects on philosophy as a practice of knowledge, simultaneously a "practice of the self" and a political endeavor. In commenting on ancient Greek philosophy, Foucault argued "The reality of philosophy is its practice" (Foucault 2010: 242) Such practice, however, is not aimed at abstract theorizing. Instead, it is an activity of the "self on self." What is at stake here is not *logos* – i.e. the quest for an abstract and universal truth, but the cultivation of a *particular kind of character*. In his words,

> Philosophy finds its reality in the *practice* of philosophy understood as a set of practices through which the subject has a relationship to itself, and works on itself. The reality of philosophy is this work of self on self.
>
> (2010: 242)

Philosophical life is a testimony of the truth – in fact a performance of it. Further,

> through the type of life one leads, the set of choices one makes, the things one renounces and those one accepts, how one dresses, how one speaks, etcetera, the philosophical life should be from start to finish the manifestation of this truth.
>
> (2010: 333–334)

This understanding shifts the goals of philosophical activity from abstract reasoning to performativity. In exploring the role of philosophy in ancient Greece Foucault argues that throughout antiquity philosophy was lived as the "free questioning of men's conduct by a truth-telling which accepts the risk of danger to itself" (2010: 346). As a form of life, "philosophy . . . is also a sort of both private and public office of critical advice." (2010: 345). *Parrēsia*, or the constant calling to task those who have social power, is an integral part of philosophical life. Foucault draws on his reflection on the ancient Greeks to devise a role for modern philosophy, which should function as an interrogation of "illusion, deception and trickery" (2010: 354). As a political activity, philosophy does not necessary need to be *prescriptive* of a particular a model of behavior or society. The philosopher exercises political agency by rendering testimony of a way of life and by interrogating what is taken for granted, rather than by finding overarching truths or prescribing universal laws of behavior.

In other words, philosophy should not,

> want to say what must be done in the realm of politics and how one should govern . . . It would be wrong to say what is true or false in the realm of science. And it would equally be wrong to want to give itself the mission of liberation or disalienation of the subject itself. It is not for philosophy to say what should be done in politics. It has to exist in a permanent and restive exteriority with regard to politics, and it is in this that it is real . . . It has to constantly practice its criticism with regard to deception, trickery, and illusion, and it is in this that it plays the dialectical game of its own truth.
>
> (2010: 354)

Foucault's political ethos is centered upon a radical non-substantialism – i.e. the performative character of everything. As we have seen, knowledge does not privilege the analysis of constant causal relations among entities, but rather the exploration of *how*, specifically, entities came to being. In addition, ethical and political decisions do not rely upon the assumption that some prescriptions hold true across situations and that we can plan chains of event in such a way as to trigger effects envisaged by simplifying planning rationalities. If ontological cuts happen in practices, attempts at oversimplification inevitably overlook the morphogenetic properties of practices and the relevance of entangled causal clusters. Valid ways of making decisions must be rooted upon careful diagnostic of contingencies, embracing uncertainty, asking questions of *how* and assuming responsibility for consequences. In this ontological horizon, ethics is nurtured by attitudes of curiosity and questioning the necessity of what is as well as of prudence for the kind of effects our agency may trigger.

Together, Barad's intra-agential realism and the Foucauldian ethos stem from a similar non-substantialist root. Instead of starting with assumptions of entities or overarching laws that regulate "the system" (however defined), an intra-agential ethos is based upon the exploration of *specific materializations of matter* and of the ontological cuts political agency entails. These considerations are deeply practical and must take into account the phenomena within which we have agency. Such phenomena are ontologically flat and complex. There is no hierarchy between *cogito*, consciousness and matter. Practices are the phenomena that constitute who we are, and in turn are constituted but not directed by our being in the world. Barad's ethos affirms and brings a step forward a Foucauldian ethos of practice. In fact, Barad's emphasis on our ontological entanglement with the non-human and her redefinition of materialism affirms more forcefully the centrality of responsibility. We are entangled being and we never step out of ethics. We are indeed radically responsible for the ontological closures we open or foreclose with our ways of life.

Conclusions

So far, I have explored how ethics can be affirmed if we start from non-substantialist ontological positions. I have also argued that a non-substantialist ontological imaginary affirms the political potential for deconstruction. I have addressed the work of scholars who questioned foundationalist and substantialist accounts of who we are, how we know what we know and explored positions that reconfigure knowledge as *praxis* and so embrace a non-substantialist understanding of political agency.

Foucault did not concern himself directly with ontological questions. However, he defended an intellectual and political project that challenges what is taken for granted, rather than attempting to identify an overarching principle for explaining all that happens in society. Foucault's political ethos does not aspire to guaranteeing an "appropriate" outcome of political engagements. Instead, his political and research project sought to unsettle certainties, participate in the "difficult displacement of forms of sensibility" and unveil the trickeries of those who have power (1991: 83). For O'Connor, options for changing what is are found in multifarious and contingent struggles that come as part of our being "felted" in the world and in the practical ability of engaging with forces that obtain in any given situation (2008). Both for Foucault and O'Connor political ethos, ways of life are central. For his part, Connolly relies upon an ontology of entanglement that grounds his understanding of reflexivity and creativity as political virtues as well as his position on the potentially transformative effects of micropolitics (2013).

All of these scholars share a notion of theory and praxis as profoundly enmeshed, a central interest in starting from doing rather than theorizing and a mistrust for privileging "substances" and "universals" over phenomena. These conceptualizations support prudent engagements and relentless interrogation of the extant orders, without imposing the stifling effects of a unifying *logos* to the diversity of human practices or reductionist interpretation of all that happens in society in deference to a few organizing principles. As Barder and Levine argue, given the failure of the promises of liberalism in the '90s, "Western reason and moral progress can no longer be conceived as the lubricants of a perpetual motion machine leading to a specific *telos*" (Barder and Levine 2012: 603, emphasis in original).

By questioning substantialist representations, possibilities for political agency are reframed in a way that focuses on relations and contingent processes of (trans) formation as well as responsibility. In a non-substantialist framework, options for changing what is are not limited to regaining a pristine freedom from all constraints or an immanent ideal social order. It is found instead in multifarious and contingent struggles that are constituted within the "felted world" and at the same time exceed and transform it. As O'Connor puts it, ethics is a practice of inhabiting a house on the cliff, whose stability does not depend on hard foundations but instead on our ability to keep it together by adjusting the relations among its elements and with its environment. This approach nurtures a radical skepticism about identifying abstract and universally valid solutions to complex political problems. In an entangled universe, questions of *how* i.e. consideration for the means to ends of any given action and the specific conditions of implementation of aspirational endeavors must be integral part of ethical decision making.

An intra-agential, non-substantialist ethos empowers us because our agency is relevant for bringing about specific materializations of matter. It also invites us to modesty, because we do not determine such materializations according to linear relations of causality. Furthermore, it requires radical assumption of responsibility because our way of knowing, acting and, more broadly, living our lives, has ontologically relevant consequences. Such an ethos radically questions advocating "following rules" as a valid justification for action (or the lack thereof) and challenges bureaucratic reasoning as harboring the potential for ethical disasters.

An ethics without foundations embraces uncertainty. There is no assurance that any political choice will lead to desirable outcomes. Ethics is about assuming responsibility for getting out of traced paths while carefully assessing the likely consequences of our actions. Norms that claim to possess validity regardless of context may indeed be based upon hubris and a myth of *potentia* and separateness that reflects extant relations of power more than rationality and "truth." International political ethics must embrace uncertainty rather than (universal) normative prescriptions that, while reassuring, may not be relevant for "what is the case under the circumstances" and may provide appeasing justifications for action while producing aberrant "unintended consequences."

This chapter concludes my theoretical elaboration of an ethos based upon an entangled ontological imaginary. In the following two chapters, I will explore practices that exemplify different ways of justifying ethical choices. While no practice can exhaustively portray all aspects of my argument, the next chapters exemplify how justification for actions based upon abstract norms have legitimized ineffective standardized initiatives in international peacekeeping and offered the background for justifying questionable policies and morally repugnant actions while diverting responsibilities for their effects. In addition, I will show how a commitment to challenging accepted truths, to the clear assessment of practical entanglement and to the exercise of prudent practical solidarity has driven the work of a medical doctor who made quite a difference in poor people's access to health care in Haiti and elsewhere.

Notes

1 For an extensive assessment of practice studies in IR, see Solomon and Steele 2017.
2 O'Connor's dissatisfaction with both realism and conventionalism resonates with Carr's predicament with both realism and idealism as positions which on the one hand exaggerate the deterministic power of the *status quo* and on the other, overstate the transformative power of ideas. Carr does not elaborate on our ontological status in the world to make his argument. However, his conceptualization of theories as tools for understanding what conditions and possibilities for action exist, as well as his emphasis on careful assessments of what obtains in a given historical situation shows family resemblances with O'Connor's conceptualization of a "stabilist" ethics.
3 As we have seen, David Kennedy (2004) has critically addressed the human rights profession's (what he calls "the invisible college") preference for upholding abstract norms rather than being concerned with the real lives of people.
4 Nicola Abbagnano in Dizionario di Filosofia defines "apodeictic" as necessary. Kant defined "apodeictic" as the judgments determined *a priori* through the laws of reason, and so, are logically necessary.
5 Thus "the critical ontology of ourselves has to be considered not, certainly, as a theory, a doctrine, nor even as permanent body of knowledge that is accumulating; it has to conceived as an attitude, an ethos, a philosophical life in which the critique of what we are is one and at the same time the historical analysis of the limits that are imposed on us and an experiment with the possibility of going beyond them" (Foucault 1984: 13.)

Bibliography

Abbagnano, Nicola. 2013. *Dizionario di Filosofia*. Torino: UTET [first published 1961]
Archer, Margaret. 1998. "Realism and Morphogenesis." In *Critical Realism: Essential Readings*, eds. Archer et al., 356–381. London and New York: Routledge.
Arendt, Hannah. 1964. *Eichmann in Jerusalem: A Report on the Banality of Evil*. New York: Viking Press.
Barad, Karen. 2007. *Meeting the Universe Half Way: Quantum Physics and the Entanglement of Matter and Meaning*. Durham and London: Duke University Press.
Barder, Alexander, and Daniel J. Levine. 2012. " 'The World Is Too Much With Us': Reification and the Depoliticization of Via Media Constructivist IR." *Millennium: Journal of International Studies* 40.3: 585–604.

Carr, Edward H. [1946] 2011. *The Twenty Years' Crisis, 1919–1939: An Introduction to the Study of International Relations*. London and New York: Palgrave Macmillan.

Connolly, William. 2002. *Neuropolitics: Thinking, Culture, Speed*. Minneapolis: University of Minnesota Press.

———. 2013. *The Fragility of Things: Self-Organizing Processes, Neoliberal Fantasies, and Democratic Activism*. Durham and London: Duke University Press.

Foucault, Michel. 1984. "What Is Enlightenment?" In *The Foucault Reader*, ed. Paul Rabinow, 32–50. New York: Pantheon Books.

———. 1991. "Questions of Method." In *The Foucault Effect: Studies in Governmentality*, eds. G. Burchell, C. Gordon and P. Miller, 73–86. Chicago: University of Chicago Press.

———. 1998. "Return to History." In *Aesthetics, Method and Epistemology*, eds. Faubion James and Paul Rabinow, 419–432. New York: New Press.

Foucault, Michel, (with Frédéric Gros, François Ewald, Alessandro Fontana, and Graham Burchell). 2010. *The Government of Self and Others: Lectures at the Collège de France 1982-1983*. Houndmills, Basingstoke, Hampshire: Palgrave Macmillan.

Golder, Ben. 2015. *Foucault and the Politics of Rights*. Stanford: Stanford University Press.

Kennedy, David. 2004. *The Dark Sides of Virtue: Reassessing International Humanitarianism*. Princeton, NJ: Princeton University Press.

O'Connor, Peg. 2008. *Morality and Our Complicated Form of Life: Feminist Wittgensteinian Metaethics*. University Park, PA: Penn State University Press.

Onuf, Nicholas. 2009. "Structure, What Structure?" *International Relations* 23.2: 183–199.

Solomon, Ty, and Brent J. Steele. 2017. "Micro-Moves in International Relations Theory." *European Journal of International Relations* 23.2: 267–291.

Tanesini, Alessandra. 2004. *Wittgenstein: A Feminist Interpretation*. Cambridge: Polity.

8 Relying on abstractions, relinquishing responsibility

Rwanda, Srebrenica, Haiti, Syria and other disasters

In previous chapters, I have argued that substantialist ontological imaginaries, which portray the world as a Newtonian space populated by already formed entities existing within linear relations of causality, support justification of action based upon abstract universal norms. Contrary to this view, Jacques Derrida (1992) argued that ethics is about making decisions in conditions of undecidability, in situations where abstract normativity does not suffice to provide good guidelines for making decisions. I have concluded the theoretical section of this book by arguing that this way of justifying ethics has relevant implications for international politics. In this chapter, I will exemplify the shortcomings of justifying international intervention and political actions (or lack thereof) based upon abstract norms and without a careful assessment of the conditions that obtain in the specific entangled situation of intervention and of the means emplyed to achieve apsirational ends.

Bureaucratic reasoning is central for a critical scrutiny of the relationships among ethics, abstract and universal normativity, and rule following.[1] As I have shown in Chapter 5, norms are not necessarily transparent in their meaning, nor do they stand in relations of linear causality with the actions they prescribe[2]. Thus, as I have argued, the Bush administration's relabeling of torture as "harsh interrogation" and its accompanying attempts to define carefully the degree of pain admissible before questioning becomes torture are examples of the substitution of anodyne language and apparently precise technical guidelines to obscure the horror evoked by the word "torture," replacing it with images of bureaucratic efficiency aimed at attaining the benign goal of protecting America's national security (Lang 2009; Onuf 2009). Supposedly, rational and detached universal normative systems, such as those that aim at defining the number of civilian deaths that can be tolerated in war, also often end up diverting responsibility from those who conduct war while simultaneously assuaging their consciences regarding the injuries and deaths their choices inflict (Kennedy 2006). David Kennedy (2004) also observes that the universal human rights regime (what he refers to as "the invisible college") accords higher standing to abstract principles and legal frameworks than to careful consideration of the political and distributive consequences and trade-offs that efforts to protect human rights entail.

Universal norms and bureaucratic routines play a major role in prescribing and justifying UN peacekeeping interventions. The same norms and rules, however, can also offer grounds for appeasement. The massacres that occurred in Rwanda and Srebrenica in the 1990s provide examples of how UN peacekeepers permitted atrocities by uncritically following institutionalized rules, key examples of which include the principle of "impartiality," the stipulations of Security Council mandates ore peacekeeping operations' rules of engagement. By doing so, however, UN officials have fallen short of considering the entanglements of such rules in specific practices, and therefore adjudicated action with little consideration for the possible consequences of upholding norms in those specific situations.

The United Nations' failure to take action to prevent the Rwandan genocide testifies to the fact that bureaucratic reasoning that prescribes relevant actors to follow universal norms (i.e. the imperative to preserve impartiality) and rules of engagement (i.e. to not intervene to disarm any party of the conflict) set the justificatory framework for avoiding a careful assessment of what was at stake at the eve of the massacre and appeased consciences for not taking decisions accountable to the people in danger. The answer General Romeo Dallaire, the Canadian force commander of the UN mission in Rwanda, received from UN headquarters when he warned that large-scale killings were imminent and asked for authorization to take action to disarm the factions that were preparing them provides a chilling example of how UN headquarters' leaders devotion to "proper process" allowed the massacre to occur:

> I woke up and this cable came in, signed by Kofi Annan in his normal staff responsibilities that essentially said cease and desist. Conduct no such operations. It's out of your mandate. On top of that, in the proper process of a Chapter VI, you will inform the ex-belligerent of the shortcomings that we notice and make it quite clear that he's got to rectify these shortcomings within a very short time frame, or else we will be in a position to have to review the mission, and ultimately their commitment to the peace agreement.
> (Dallaire 2003)

The United Nations' report on Srebrenica (United Nations General Assembly 1999) provides further disturbing testimony outlining how bureaucratic reasoning failed to prevent atrocities and massacres. The UN headquarters' staff lack of response to requests for airstrikes by the Dutch peacekeepers in charge of protecting the Srebrenica "safe haven" on the approaching Serb forces in July 1995 provides testimony of how adherence to norms and rules such as "impartiality" and "rules of engagement" allowed member states and UN high ranking officials alike to relinquish responsibility for a situation where Ratko Mladic and his paramilitary troops, known as the Skorpions, were clearly able to prevail over the peacekeepers and carry out a genocidal act with impunity. In Srebrenica, the United Nations offered a "safe haven" to Muslim men, women and children. Nevertheless, notwithstanding this promise, the United Nations did not take all necessary action to protect the people who gathered within the United Nations compound because they were promised protection. As a result, when the Skorpions reached the UN compound basically undisturbed, the 100 Dutch peacekeepers in charge found themselves as having little alternative but to negotiate with them. Women were released, while 8,000 men and boys were taken away to be killed in the next few days in the surrounding woods. The adherence to abstract norms and institutionalized routines in lieu of assuming responsibility for the unfolding events and making it a priority to protect the life of people at risk permitted UN officials and the member states' politicians who exerted pressure on them to distance themselves from the humanity of those whom they let die. The senior officials at the UN Secretariat were of course not the only decision makers in these disasters. The analysis of the specific role of member states in influencing the UN Secretariat's decision-making process especially in the Rwandan crises has been well documented (Thakur 2017; OAU 2000; Mamdani 2001; Melvern 2000; Power 2003; Dallaire 2003) and must not be discounted. However, regardless of the attribution of the main responsibility for the massacres, the justification of action (or the lack thereof) in normative terms functioned to appease UN officials, politicians and the general public's consciousness, and provided a framework for relinquishing responsibility for the chain of events and consequences of international intervention and for unkept promises.

The protection of civilians has been advocated as the guiding principle for the UN's role in international security. It was used to justify a variety of international interventions such as the bombing of Kosovo and the invasions of Iraq, Libya and, more recently, airstrikes in Syria. The adoption of R2P under Kofi Annan clearly attempted to shift the focus of the United Nations' role from protecting the international order to protecting people. However, a number of states have complained that R2P fosters an interventionist agenda, and that those governments labeled as "rogue" – i.e., unable or unwilling to protect their citizens from an array of issues, ranging from political oppression, to violence, to extreme poverty – have therefore become potential targets for international action. In the eyes of its proponents at the International Commission on Intervention and State Sovereignty (2001) R2P was not primarily concerned with militarized intervention. In fact, R2P has three pillars: the responsibility to prevent, react and rebuild, with military intervention being seen as an extreme measure to be pursued only with Security Council authorization.

However, critics have highlighted that in the context of the extant distribution of international power, R2P has been advocated to legitimize the right to bomb and that the "responsibility" trajectory of R2P has been shunned in favor of militarized solutions to the problem of protecting vulnerable populations (Thakur 2016; Cunliffe 2008). Following R2P's adoption as the organizing principle guiding the United Nations' role in international security, member states have become *more* willing to weaken or set aside the principle of state sovereignty, but *less* inclined to do so with care, prudence and accountability to the interests of the populations affected by such choices. For instance, the Western preference to support those opposed to Syrian President Bashar al-Assad because of that government's abhorrent human rights record, without inquiring deeply from the outset into the exact character of the forces on the ground arrayed against his rule, created a favorable terrain for such previously unknown groups as Islamic State of Iraq and Syria (ISIS) and *al-Nusra* to capitalize on instability in the region. Military interventions (with or without UN approval) are often undertaken by states in the name of grand principles, without assuming full responsibility for rebuilding what they may destroy by their interventions or, often, even considering carefully the forces at play or the consequences that could arise from de-stabilizing the political status quo. "Acts of excommunication" in the name of poor moral behavior of state leaders may be led by a single state and its allies (as in the case of the United States under the Bush administration in 2003 in Iraq), or via UN resolutions as happened with Libya in 2011 and Syria in 2013 (Manca, Stephenson and Zanotti 2016).

In all of these cases protection of civilians was used to justify interventions against the regime targeted. In 2011, UN Security Council Resolution 1973 authorized a no-fly zone and "all necessary measures" (i.e., military action) to protect civilians in Libya (United Nations Security Council 2011). In 2013, the General Assembly approved a resolution condemning human rights violations in Syria that Saudi Arabia had drafted and urged the Security Council to take measures to end such abuses in Syria (UN General Assembly 2013). Prior to the passage of a Saudi-sponsored resolution concerning human rights violations in Syria in December, the General Assembly "strongly condemned the Syrian government's indiscriminate violence against civilian populations and welcomed the establishment of the National Coalition for Syrian Revolutionary and Opposition Forces as interlocutors needed for a political transition" (ibid). This measure in particular challenged the principle of non-interference in the internal affairs of states established by Article 2.7 of the UN Charter in favor of international interventionism to protect people from government-sanctioned violence, and all the while poorly assessing the actors and forces at play on the ground. During 2015, France and a U.S.-led coalition that included Bahrain, Italy, Jordan, Qatar, Saudi Arabia and the United Arab Emirates began to bomb targets controlled by the self-proclaimed ISIS within Syrian territory. Meanwhile, Iranian troops and Hezbollah fighters have reportedly engaged in a ground offensive against anti-Assad forces, with Russian air support. Russia's aid to the Syrian government has often worked at cross-purposes with the France-USA coalition, a fact that threatens to broaden the conflict. In addition, Israel has launched at least a dozen airstrikes on Syria and Lebanon since 2011 targeting what it considers to be terrorist weapons caches and arms-transport convoys (Harel 2017). As this book goes in press, a coalition of US, French and British forces has bombed targets in Syria in response to an alleged chemical attack on civilians in the Damascus suburb of Douma before the Organization for Prohibition of Chemical Weapons (OPCW) was able to conduct the necessary investigation to ascertain the nature and perpetrators of the attacks (Borger and Baumont, 2018). Such strikes were conducted without Security Council authorization, while the UN Secretary General António Guterres made a general call for respect of international law.

These interventions have not addressed meaningfully a situation that presently threatens international stability. In the meantime, the ongoing massive refugee flow from destabilized regions has sharpened the polarization of political debate in Europe and the United States. Given the humanitarian and refugee crisis that has ensued and the continuing conflict on the ground, the question arises whether member states should not exercise more prudence before withdrawing legitimacy through UN bodies from governments that fail to match internationally recognized standards concerning how they treat people within their territories, while acting militarily outside the framework on international law when they so decide. In other words, advocating the R2P while exercising it imprudently has created humanitarian catastrophes and encouraged the destabilization of entire regions, while likely increasing, not reducing, human rights violations and human suffering. The use of force for humanitarian reasons rarely factors in the cost and practical consequences of war, such as the destruction of infrastructure and human lives that comes with it, as well as the long-lasting effects of war and peacekeeping operations alike on the economies of target states (O'Connell 2011; Pugh 2008; Selby 2008; Studdard 2004). These practical effects are rarely central to decision-making processes or assessments of potential actions, and instead disregarded as "unintended consequences" (Ammitzboell 2007).

An intra-agential rather than a shallow normative-driven justification for action suggests that R2P should be exercised responsibly – i.e. following careful consideration of the interests and agendas of the various players involved in complex conflicts and following study of the means adopted to undertake action and of the potential exacerbation of conflict that may result. Solutions to political problems that rely on abstractions, planning rationalities and mechanistic models of the world tend to easily accept oversimplified solutions to complex, entangled problems where causation works in non-linear ways. Political decision making is mostly based upon starting points that assume that abstract aspirations may have linear causal influence over reality. Instead, an intra-agential ethos starts from the assumption that causality is complex and works in clusters, and that practices have morphogenetic properties. Practical entanglements are not simply the residue of abstractions and need to be explored carefully. In this framework, unintended consequences should be used very sparingly as justifications of bad consequences of political decisions.

It is not only abstract norms that have been used to justify action and relinquish responsibility for consequences. Since the 1990s, abstract standardized programs for establishing good governance have been seen as a key tool for stopping conflict, establishing peace and triggering development. As an example, in 2002 the General Assembly and the Economic and Social Council identified "state capacity deficits, weak political democratic institutions and inefficient and badly run public administrations" as the main causes for the problems of developing countries (Zanotti 2011: 51). In times of increasing complex interconnections, "good governance" is imagined as a universally valid program for decreasing risk of conflict and improving the predictability of a government's "dangerous" behavior. The dissemination throughout the world of institutions considered able to channel social demands is considered the universal recipe for solving political problems.

The UN rationale for building peace generally embraces the blueprint for what Foucault called "carceralization," whereby "delinquent" states are under constant scrutiny, subjected to coercion and correction through military intervention and expert advising. The performance of these states is monitored through standardized benchmarks based upon which international rewards and punishments are measured, not to mention administered. For instance in the case of Haiti, the assumption of linear relations of causality between institutional and social reforms did not take into consideration the specific entanglements that obtained in practice. There, the UN sponsored police, prison and judiciary reform efforts. However, the member states that supported police reform in Haiti did only marginally contribute to sustain its operating budget or the material tools needed by the police to perform its job, for instance cars, fuel, bullets, uniforms and so on. In the meantime, a more centralized and structured police force increased the backlog in the judiciary and prisons. A modern and effective judiciary requires a strong administrative apparatus, not simply training judges. It requires courts, clerks and extensive technological resources. And prison systems not only demand training correction officers. They require means to keep record of inmates, to separate convicted criminals from those awaiting trial, minors from adults, to feed prisoners, etc. In Haiti computers are scarce electricity erratic, and even paper and pens are not always a given. Prisons in Haiti are places where people are forgotten and die of disease or starvation in overcrowded cells. Thus, while the United Nations imagined itself to be building the Haitian state along a blueprint formally patterned along the lines of idealized Western models of government, it ended up constructing institutions that were economically and politically unsustainable. The establishment of costly institutions, combined with the lack of international financial support to the Haitian government contributed to the leverage of non-state actors with economic power (such as drug dealers), created trade-offs with alternative uses of resources, led to the proliferation of NGOs in the country and stifled instead of promoting viable state institutions and local economy (Zanotti 2011). Assumptions that reality can be driven by abstractions and standardized blueprints, the failure of assessing the practical entanglements of the Haitian reality and the lack of UN member states' assumption of responsibility for sustaining the institutional apparatus the intervention established, ended up setting the stage for failure.[3]

Not only are practical entanglements at play in specific places of deployment of international intervention often disregarded in assessing the duties and responsibility for international intervention. The ways in which the various professions and institutions that are delegated to accomplish certain jobs function are also only marginally studied. In an intra-agential ethos, the apparatuses deployed to intervene in the world are relevant for producing specific forms of materialization of matter and have morphogenetic properties in the practices where they operate. Amidst studies of international intervention that have only marginally addressed how the professions and the institutions delegated to carry out those interventions influence outcomes, the work of Severine Autesserre is a welcome exception. Autesserre assessed how peacekeeping mandates and aspirations are always mediated by thick, layered and complex institutional practices. She conducted an ethnography of "peaceland" (i.e. the space inhabited by peacekeepers) and highlighted the political relevance of peacekeepers' everyday "practices, habits and narratives" (Autesserre 2014: 29). For Autesserre, in analyzing peacekeeping we must embrace an "empirical shift" and conduct an in-depth examination of intervention processes that appreciate local realities which are often obfuscated by macrolevel definitions. In Autesserre's word, her analysis "questions the dominant macro-level approach, challenging its assumption that instructions from capitals and headquarters automatically translate into corresponding action in the field, and complements the micro-level approach that typically focuses on host populations" (25).

The realization that the relationship between planning rationalities, ideas, and the effect they produce is not governed by abstract laws but by complex and contingent entanglements is attuned to an intra-agential ontology and epistemology. If practices have morphogenetic properties, the effects of norms, intentions, aspirations and planning rationalities must be assessed within the entanglements of practice. Relations of causality especially in conflict and post-conflict zones are entangled and complex Therefore, the exploration of the features of the apparatuses we deploy to achieve any normative claim is central to making good ethical and political decisions.

The banality of evil

By re-thinking the way we fit in the world, entangled ontologies radically challenge the possibility of justifying ethics based upon the assumptions that the world is homogenous, simple and constituted by separated entities connected through linear relations of causality. An intra-agential ethos implies addressing the question of what kind of effects any given action may produce for particular people in specific circumstances and always assessing the means to end. It also necessitates the assumption of radical responsibility for the ontological cuts our actions entail and for the inclusions and exclusions such cuts put in place.

In her *Eichmann in Jerusalem: A Report on the Banality of Evil*, Hannah Arendt drew on reports she first prepared for the *New Yorker* of her direct observation of Adolf Eichmann's trial to describe "the strange interdependence of thoughtlessness and evil" in modern bureaucratic societies (1964). The Nazi criminal tried and executed in Israel in 1962, Arendt argued, was not an eager activist for the extermination of Jews. Instead, in Arendt's view Eichmann was a bureaucrat who privileged obedience to rules over thinking empathically about other human beings. In simplifying his role in the Holocaust as just "following rules" Eichmann did show, in Arendt's words, to possess the "horrible gift of consoling himself with clichés." He was not a "monster," just an average man in harmony with his world, embracing an ideology considered normal and socially acceptable. In commenting on Marcel Ophuls's documentary, "The Memory of Justice" that documents the Holocaust, French torturing of Algerian citizens and the American slaughters of Vietnamese civilians, Ian Buruma argues that for Ophuls, portraying the Nazis simply as monsters is a form of complacency. In fact, it makes it easier for ordinary citizens to distance themselves from their crimes. Insightfully, Buruma notices, "if only monsters were responsible for the holocaust and other mass murders, there would never be any need for the rest of us to look in the mirror" (2017: 45).

Arendt's work shows that justifying ethical choices on the ground of following rules can easily lead to very unethical outcomes and that grand political projects that relied on the faith on planning rationalities produced "political evils" (Barder and Mc Clurt 2010). For Arendt our capacity to act is always a double-edged sword and does not entail linear relations of causality. As Amoureux argues, for Arendt, "action follows more of a means-means rather than a means-end dynamic because once one strikes out into the world, others react to our action in ways that upset its goal- oriented trajectory" (Amoureux 2016: 66). By alerting her readers to the tremendous devastation that the banal evil always latent in bureaucratic thinking may produce, Arendt warns against thoughtlessly "following rules" and calls for an ethics of responsibility. Embracing an ethics of responsibility towards other human beings, which includes the careful assessment of the means to be deployed to achieve particular ends, as well as the possible consequences of our actions in specific circumstances, may offer a better way than following norms to avoid calamities in the future. Ironically, blatantly extreme evil may ultimately be less insidious than bureaucratized countenancing of evil. Radical evil does not "look like us." Its modalities of operation are not embedded in the ongoing rhythm of our everyday lives and it is therefore easy to spot. When hidden in the banality of accepted ideologies, normativity and bureaucratic prescriptions, however, evil becomes more difficult to detect and, perversely, perhaps even palatable and reassuring. Arendt's call to be aware of the too smug surety provided by "following rules" is critical. Eichmann's experience tells us about the dangers of such widely accepted ways of justifying action. Self-awareness and vigilance are critical to preventing such appeasement in the future.

Conclusions

The justification for the international use of force based upon normative statements, with no consideration of the practical entanglements within which interventions are deployed, nor of the morphogenetic processes such interventions trigger, is widely accepted and is easy political currency, while there is no specific attribution or assumption of responsibility for the crises such interventions trigger. This lack of assumption of responsibility is rooted upon standpoints that validate action based upon a series of prescriptions, and upon representations of the world as a homogenous space regulated by linear relations of causality and governable by planning rationalities. Because it does not privilege prescription over *praxis*, an intra-agential ethos does not offer a language of self-appeasement for unintended consequences and requisites responsibility for the entire chain of effects our decisions trigger. In an intra-agential ethos, *what* questions cannot be severed from the *how* because both trajectories are entangled in practices and as such have morphogenetic properties. Central for ethically and politically sound decision making is the ability to diagnose what is the case in specific times and places.

Ontological imaginaries that portray the world as entangled, open possibilities for re-imagining ethics as a practice where the justifiability of any act needs to be assessed in the context of the phenomena within which we exert our agency. Questions about means-to-the-end and practical consequences of our acts must be included in ethical adjudication.

As I have argued earlier, justifying action based upon abstractions relies on a substantialist ontologically imaginary. I have proposed a possible alternative that, by beginning with entanglements and practices, radically challenges this way of justifying choices and advocates putting responsibility, rather than bureaucratic reasoning and universal prescriptions, at the center of decision making. Humility, challenging accepted truths, careful analysis of the situation at hand, creativity and a radical assumption of responsibility are the main trajectories of an intra-agential ethos. In the next chapter, I will show how this ethos can be practiced through the example of a medical doctor who provides health care for the poor in Haiti and elsewhere in the world.

Notes

1 I have worked for many years at the UN Department of Peacekeeping Operations and taken part in international interventions justified by appeal to "universal norms" and operationalized through bureaucratic procedures. Therefore, I see such reflection as extremely important.
2 I have argued earlier that positions that see ideas' causality as permissive do not challenge the mechanical model, they just embrace a "tamed" version of it.
3 For an in depth exploration of the United Nations Peacekeeping Operation in Haiti see Zanotti, 2011.

Bibliography

Ammitzboell, Katarina. 2007. "Unintended Consequences of Peace Operations on the Host Economy From a People's Perspective." In *Unintended Consequences of Peacekeeping Operations*, eds. Chiyuki Aoi, Cedric de Coning and Ramesh Thakur, 69–89. Tokyo, New York and Paris: United Nations University Press.

Amoureux, Jacques. 2016. *A Practice of Ethics for Global Politics: Ethical Reflexivity*. London and New York: Palgrave Macmillan.

Arendt, Hannah. 1964. *Eichmann in Jerusalem: A Report on the Banality of Evil*. New York: Viking Press.

Autesserre, Severeine. 2014. *Peaceland: Conflict Resolution and the Everyday Politics of International Intervention*. New York: Cambridge.

Barder, A. D., and D. M. Mc Clurt. 2010. "Rethinking International History, Theory and the Event With Hannah Arendt." *Journal of International Political Thoery*, 6.2: 117–141.

Borger Julian and Peter Baumont. 2018. "Syria: US, UK and France launch strikes in response to chemical attack" *The Guardian*, April 14

Buruma, Ian. 2017. "Fools, Cowards or Criminals." *The New York Review of Books*. August 17, 45–47.

Cunliffe, Philip. 2008. "A Dangerous Duty. Power, Paternalism and the Dangerous 'duty of care.'" In *Critical Perspectives on the Responsibility to Protect: Interrogating Theories and Practices*, ed. Philip Cunliffe, 51–70. London and New York: Routledge.

Dallaire, Romeo. 2003. *Shake Hands With the Devil: The Failure of Humanity in Rwanda*. Toronto: Random House.

———. 2004. "Frontline." *PBS Interview*. www.pbs.org/wgbh/pages/frontline/shows/ghosts/interviews/dallaire.html.

Derrida, Jacques. 1992. "Force of Law: The 'Mystical Foundation of Authority.'"In *Deconstruction and the Possibility of Justice*, eds. Drucilla Cornell, Michel Rosenfeld and David Gray Carlson, 3–67. London and New York: Routledge.

Harel, Amos. 2017. "Israel Struck Syrian and Hezbollah Arms Convoys Nearly 100 Times in Five Years, Top General Says." *Ha'aretz*. August 17. www.haaretz.com/israel-news/1.807246. Accessed January 9, 2017.

International Commission on Intervention and State Sovereignty. 2001. *The Responsibility to Protect*. Ottawa, CA: International Development Research Centre.

Kennedy, David. 2004. *The Dark Sides of Virtue: Reassessing International Humanitarianism*. Princeton, NJ: Princeton University Press.

———. 2006. *Of War and Law*. Princeton, NJ: Princeton University Press.

Lang, Anthony F. Jr. 2009. "Introduction: Rules and International Security: Dilemmas of a New World Order." In *War, Torture and Terrorism: Rethinking the Rules of International Security*, eds. Anthony F. Lang Jr. and Amanda Russell Beattie, 1–22. London and New York: Routledge.

Mamdani, Mahmood. 2001. *When Victims Become Killers: Colonialism, Nativism and the Genocide in Rwanda*. Princeton, NJ: Princeton University Press.

Manca, Francesco, Max Stephenson Jr., and Laura Zanotti. 2016. "UN Invocations of the 'Responsibility to Protect,' State Sovereignty, and State Action." Academic Council on the UN System.

Melvern, Linda. 2000. *A People Betrayed. The Role of the West in Rwanda's Genocide*. London: Zed books.

OAU (Organization of the African Union). 2000. "Rwanda: The Preventable Genocide." Report of the OAU's International Panel of Eminent Personalities, Addis Ababa. May.

O'Connell, Mary Ellen. 2011. "Responsibility to Peace." In *Critical Perspectives on the Responsibility to Protect: Interrogating Theories and Practices*, ed. Philip Cunliffe, 71–83. London and New York: Routledge.

Onuf, Nicholas. 2009. "Rules for Torture?" In *War, Torture and Terrorism: Rethinking the Rules of International Security*, eds. Anthony F. Lang, Jr. and Amanda Russell Beattie, 25–38. London and New York: Routledge.

Patomäki, Heikki. 2002. *After International Relations: Critical Realism and the (Re)Construction of World Politics*. London and New York: Routledge.

Power, Samantha. 2003. *A Problem From Hell: America's and the Age of Genocide*. New York: Harper.

Pugh, Michael. 2008. "Employment, Labor Rights and Social Resistance." In *Whose Peace: Critical Perspectives on the Political Economy of Peacebuilding*, eds. Michael Pugh, Neil Cooper and Mandy Turner, 139–156. London and New York: Palgrave Macmillan.

Selby, Jan. 2008. "The Political Economy of Peace Processes." In *Whose Peace: Critical Perspectives on the Political Economy of Peacebuilding*, eds. Michael Pugh, Neil Cooper and Mandy Turner, 11–29. London and New York: Palgrave Macmillan.

Studdard, Kaysie. 2004. *War Economies in a Regional Context: Overcoming the Challenges of Transformation*. IPA Policy Report: International Peace Academy. New York: United Nations Press.

Thakur, Ramesh. 2016. "The Responsibility to Protect at 15." *International Affairs* 92.2: 415–434.

———. 2017. *The United Nations, Peace and Security: From Collective Security to the Responsibility to Protect*. Cambridge: Cambridge University Press.
United Nations General Assembly. 1999. "Report of the Secretary-General Pursuant to GA Resolution 53/35: The Fall of Srebrenica." A/54/549.
———. 2013. "The Situation in the Syrian Arab Republic." Resolution 67/262. June.
United Nations Security Council. 2011. S/Res/1973. March.
Zanotti, Laura. 2011. *Governing Disorder: UN Peace Operations, International Security, and Democraziation in the Post-Cold War Era*. University Park, PA: Penn State University Press.

9 Practicing responsibility and solidarity

Providing medical care to the poor

> We draw on the resources of the world's leading medical and academic institutions and on the lived experience of the world's poorest and sickest communities. At its root, our mission is both medical and moral. It is based on solidarity, rather than charity alone.
>
> (Partners in Health, 2018)

Partners in Health (PIH, or, in Kreol, *Zanmi Lasante*) was established in the 1980s with the goal of providing health care to poor Haitians in the *Plateau Centrale.* PIH was initially supported by a South Carolina Episcopal church group that was present in Cange since the 1970s to provide health and education resources to families that had been displaced by a dam built on the Artibonite River in 1956 by the Duvaliers as part of an international development project sponsored by USAID. Since then, PIH has become the primary provider of free health care in Haiti. They operate hospitals at 12 sites in two of the poorest regions of the country, the Central Plateau and the lower Artibonite, serving a total of 4.5 million people. In line with its philosophy of cooperating with local governments, after the earthquake that devastated Haiti in 2012, PIH opened the University Hospital of Mirebalais, a public facility and teaching hospital, aimed not only at assisting patients but at training doctors and health care providers. PIH has also expanded beyond Haiti to provide health care to poor people in the Navajo Nation, Liberia, Sierra Leone, Russia, Peru, Mexico, Leshoto, Rwanda and Malawi.[1]

What is intriguing about PIH is not only the success of the organization, but Paul Farmer and associates' distinctive ethos, centered on *practical solidarity.* I argue in particular that co-founder and chief strategist for PIH Paul Farmer's life, writings and work offer examples of how an intra-agential ethos can be practiced.

In the theoretical chapters of this book, I have argued ontological imaginaries are critical to shaping the way we believe we fit in the world and how we can make a difference in it. I have also argued that an entangled ontological imaginary supports an ethos centered on practices rather than abstractions. An entangled ethos begins with the assumption that the world is not governed by mechanistic relations of causality, since causes work in clusters in particular entanglements that obtain in specific situations. Hence, such entanglements are central to adjudicating action. Maybe more importantly, the ontological imaginary I have embraced and developed in this book describes a reality not divided into separate realms of mind and matter; hence ontology and epistemology are not separate endeavors. In line with Barad and Tanesini, I think of knowledge as a tool that produces morphogenetic effects. The way we address any knowledge issue is part of apparatuses through which we produce ontological cuts, inclusions and exclusions. Knowledge is a politically relevant form of intra- activity and it requisites assumption of responsibility. In this ethos, *how* questions cannot be overlooked when making decisions about aspirational goals, and the ethical value of any given action cannot be validated in the abstract as a universal prescription. What obtains in practice and how we can change it are central tasks for devising ethical behavior and for justifying political agency. While others have advocated practical solidarity as an alternative to international development or security intervention (Duffield 2007; Robinson 2011), Farmer's life and writings testify how practical solidarity may be enacted. As I will show in the pages that follow, Farmer's positions on knowledge, normativity, agency and responsibility echoes an intra-agential ethos.

While he does not use this exact conceptual vocabulary, Farmer's onto-epistemology embraces an entangled ontological imaginary, where knowledge is an integral part of his ethical commitment. Farmer begins with practice and context; he values causal entanglements over linear attributions of causality and puts taking responsibility for the effects of one's interventions on the intended recipients before abstract justifications for agency. A central trajectory of this form of inquiry and practice is the notion that diseases must be treated as bio-social phenomena – i.e. as the result of complex clusters of causes that are both social and biological. Furthermore, Farmer maintains that an interdisciplinary analysis is central to effective medical practice, that action and intervention must be accountable primarily to their recipients rather than to academic research agendas or donor programs, that attentive consideration to the constraints and needs of beneficiaries must be placed at the center of how to provide medical care and that, in the context of structural constraints, action must prioritize improving the life of real people *in practice*.

Paul Farmer's approach to caring for the poor starts with assessing the specificity and causal complexity of how people experience disease in situations of extreme poverty. Metaethical philosophers like Peg O'Connor (2008) argued that in order to make good ethical decisions, the voices of the ones who normally do not have a voice in deciding how to prioritize action must be included. Paul Farmer's work testifies to a way of adjudicating the validity of health care interventions in Haiti that starts from carefully listening to those voices. In the pages that follow, I will highlight how his position relates to the main themes of this project.

The ethical and political salience of entangled attributions of causality. Challenging substantialism and oversimplification as a practice of ethics.

Farmer embraces the ethical salience of epistemology and methodology. He questions accepted understandings of how infectious diseases spread not only as an epistemological problem but also as an ethico-political one. A critical reflection on epistemology is central to Farmer's commitment to practical solidarity. In his words,

> A subtle and flexible understanding of emerging infections would be grounded in critical and reflexive study of how our knowledge develops. Units of analysis and key terms would be scrutinized and regularly redefined. These processes would include regular rethinking not only of methodologies and study design but also of the *validity of causal inference*, and they would allow reflection on the limits of human knowledge.
>
> (1999: 39, emphasis added)

Farmer's reflection on epistemology challenges the substantialism embedded in dominant medical language, a language that represents the poor as a part of a separate world or even belonging to a different species. A case in point are explanatory frameworks that rely on race, space and borders as valid analytical categories for understanding disease transmission, such as labeling illnesses that disproportionally affect the poor as "tropical diseases." Instead, Farmer argues, "The groups at risk for these diseases are often bounded more by socioeconomic status than by latitude" (1999: 41). Spatialized explanations obfuscate complex local and non-local relations of causality and, in particular, relations of inequality, as relevant variables for understanding epidemics. In fact, an analysis of mortality differentials within national boundaries would show that "health conditions are often more tightly linked to local inequalities than to nationality" (Farmer 1999: 42). Similarly, he is critical of substantializing relations of inequality as "cultural differences." On the one hand these representations reflect racist assumptions, while on the other they function as justifications for relinquishing responsibility to provide medical care to poor people. For instance, Farmer criticizes positions that, based upon a supposed difference between American and African cultures, advocate against "imposing western standards of care" to HIV treatment. In reality, such positions offer appeasing justifications for the difference in the quality of care provided to Africans. Contra the ethical appeasement afforded by substantialized culturalist positions, Farmer advocates instead for equality of access to the fruits of modern science as the "only acceptable goal" (1999: 35). Farmer is similarly critical of racialized understandings of the presence of certain diseases (for instance, tuberculosis in ethnic minorities) that omits the material entanglements that explain these patterns.

Another example of substantialist public health vocabulary is categorizing certain people as "risk groups" or explanations of the higher mortality of the poor as a result of the individual's non-compliance. The Haiti AIDS epidemic has often been explained along moralizing and othering lines, that cast a stigma on the victims of that disease and base explanations of its diffusion upon individuals' "bad" behavior while not taking into account how their living conditions may limit their choices. By contrast, Farmer argues that to understand the rural Haitian AIDS epidemics, we must move beyond the concept of risk groups to consider a key entanglement – i.e. "the interplay between human agency and the powerful forces that constrain it, focusing especially on those activities that promote or retard the spread of HIV" (1999: 128).[2] Poverty radically limits one's options while abstract and homogenous assumptions of human ability to make "free choices" stigmatize those who do not "behave well" as guilty, thus offering appeasing reasons for relinquishing the responsibility for care.[3]

Similarly, Farmer challenges explanations of the Ebola outbreak as rooted in African cultural practices rather than being attributable to a lack of access to medical care. In Farmer's words,

> Ebola is more a symptom of a weak healthcare system than anything else. But until this diagnosis is agreed on, there's plenty of room for other, more exotic explanations. The palaver (as Liberians say) includes a lot of talk about the 'cultural beliefs and behaviours' said to propagate the outbreak. The list usually includes activities that are not really "behaviour," such as hunting and eating bush meat, taking part in strange funerary practices or the bizarre rituals of "secret societies" like the Poro or the Human Leopard Societies. An obsession with funerary rituals – the more lurid the better – was characteristic of anthropology from the late 19th century on.
>
> (2014: 39)

In summary, Farmer questions substantialist representations of the world that portray it as divided into different spaces that are unrelated to one another, that privilege mono-causal biological explanations of disease and that portray the poor as ontologically different from the non-poor. Not only are such explanations scientifically flawed but they also justify and support relinquishing the ethical and political responsibility to provide care. Farmer advocates for an ethos of radically assuming responsibility for reducing inequality, an ethos that challenges the medical profession's "rhetoric of immediacy," a discourse that only takes note of epidemics when they may affect the West and obfuscates the fact that poor people constantly endure the conditions that leads to those "emergencies." Thus a narrow view of science, one that embraces simplified and biologically deterministic views of causality, needs to be supplemented by interdisciplinary work that includes the social sciences. Only in this way can we "aspire to a sound analytical purchase on disease emergence, a prerequisite of effective control mechanisms" (Farmer 1999: 58). Epidemiology should not shelter behind " 'validated' methodologies while ignoring the larger forces and processes that determine why some people are sick while others are shielded from risk" (Farmer 1999: 281). Instead, "the lack of systemic and critical analysis permits these global ties to be obscured. And yet, new kinds of proximity make inequality, and the plagues that accompany it, very modern affairs" (1999). Such forms of inquiry are virtually non-existent in the medical field.

In summary, in a way that echoes Barad's intra-agential ethos, for Farmer attributions of causality are not simply issues of knowledge, but ethical issues as well. Explanations that isolate and privilege biological causes of disease are "immodest claims of causality" which obfuscate "disparity of risks and outcomes" (1999: 4). Such causal claims "are immodest because they distract attention from the prevalent social disorder that exacerbates biological disorders" (Farmer 1999: 4).

Immodest claims of causality, often adopted by academics and embraced by the international aid machinery are not only theoretically blind but also politically misleading. In this, Farmer echoes the intra-agential view that knowledge requisites issues of responsibility.

Against prevalent substantialist othering representations of Africans, Farmer's critical epistemology challenges cultural and biological determinism in favor of inquiries that explore *how* specific experiences of diseases take shape the way they do. The ways disease impacts people's lives are embedded in realities that are "biological in their expression but are largely socially determined" (Farmer 1999: 4). Diseases are bio-social phenomena – i.e. the result of *human* and *non-human entanglements*. Understanding disease entails linking the local to the global while simultaneously avoiding oversimplicfications. Contextualization is key to avoiding the shortcomings of disciplines that reduce causal complexity to biological determinism, assume that space is divided into containers and that places are basically homogenous (and thus causality operates in similar ways). As critical realists also have it, the causal forces that operate in specific places may not *be* local, but they do affect the local *differently*. Causes work in clusters, and clusters of local and non-local causes become entangled in the life of real people to shape how they experience disease and have access to care. These entanglements may be spatially and temporally remote, but still have a bearing on what, for instance, a young Haitian girl's experience of HIV looks like (Farmer 1999: 59–93). In fact, in this perspective, the notions of local and global blur into an onto-epistemology that sees the world radically (yet unequally) connected. Ways of inquiry that uncover and address how these entanglements come to being in the everyday life of people are a central trajectory of practical solidarity.

Farmer's analyses of disease in Haiti testify to this main ethical concern. Farmer notices a fundamental discrepancy in the views of scholarly journals and those who were committed to "radical changes in the conditions endured by the poor" (1999: 21). Instead of relying on abstract assertions, statistics and numbers, Farmer relies on the analysis of how clusters of causes come together to affect individuals' life. In fact, the choice to separate the practice of knowledge from the practice of solidarity is not only analytically wrong but also ethically flawed. "The divorce of research and analysis from pragmatic efforts to remediate inequalities of access is a tactical and moral error- it may be an error that constitutes, in and of itself, a human rights abuse" (Farmer 2005: 22). This pragmatic commitment is also reflected, as we will see next, in Farmer's position with regard to liberal human rights.

Questioning normative ethic and abstract rights, practicing solidarity in the context of structural constraints

Farmer takes distance from the liberal understanding of justifications for action that is centered on abstract normativity. In relying upon Jon Sobrino's liberation theology, he argues that liberal human rights discourses are often disconnected from reality. For Farmer, the ethical validity of any given action is not measured because it would, in principle, abide by norms that are recognized as universally valid. Rather, validity is assessed against its ability to make a real difference in the everyday lives of people.

In challenging assumptions that overemphasize normative statements' causal power to change reality, Farmer observes that the rise in public awareness and the recent proliferation of talks about human rights has not been accompanied by a reduction in human rights abuses. Farmer challenges the normative focus of the human rights profession – a focus more interested in upholding principled discourses of rights than in producing practical results. Abstract discourses of rights may in fact nurture ethically questionable approaches to alleviating rights violations. Against positions that justify ethics as abiding by norms and laws, Farmer points at the imbrication of laws and power. Following laws does not guarantee the manifestation of justice or reaching wise ethical decisions.

For him, "a narrow legal approach to health and human rights can obscure the nature of violations, thereby enfeebling our best response to them" (Farmer 2005: 217). A case in point is the human rights profession's reluctance "to cross the line from a rights activism of pure principles to one involving transfers of money, food and medicine betrays a failure . . . to address the urgent needs of the people we are trying to defend" (2005: 9). Paul Farmer's ethical commitment to correcting such situations underlines that human rights professionals should be driven by the central commitment to offer practical solidarity to the poor. In this framework, one should not ask

> whether an event or a process violates an existing rule . . . [but] whether that event or process has ill effects on a patient or a population; . . . [and] whether such events can be prevented or remediated. Shunning social and economic rights from consideration prevents the health care professional from having an impact on addressing the problem.
>
> (2005: 235)

Farmer's understanding of agency and structures is also attuned to an intra-agential ethos inasmuch as it emphasizes the relevance of the phenomena within which we perform actions and challenges individualist voluntarism and structuralist determinism alike. Farmer explicitly embraces Galtung's notion of structural violence as an alternative to liberal ways of addressing the problematique of human rights. Structural analysis, however, does not constitute an appeasing reason for relinquishing the commitment to alleviating human suffering in the name of seeking instead totalizing alternative social orders. His position on political movements that embrace grand plans to reverse everything as opposed to taking care of real needs expressed by real people is well-exemplified by Farmer's reaction to an event that took place in the first years of his activities as a health care practitioner in Peru, when the community pharmacy built by PIH to offer medication access to poor slums dwellers in Lima was blown up by Sendero Luminoso shortly after being completed. Farmer asserts,

> [Sendero's] motive was held to be as usual: if we *were reformers, patching up the wounds of the poor, we were, in Sendero's eyes, palliatives, delaying*

> *the necessary radical transformation of Peruvian society*. A couple of years earlier, a Sendero communiqué had ordered nongovernmental organizations out of Peru because "you give crumbs to the people to entertain them and fail to realize that the correct path is that of the people's war."
>
> (1999: 30, emphasis added)

Against Sendero's totalizing aspiration, PIH decided to continue its "modest attempts" to patch up the wounds. In response to the bombing, PIH decided to argue for "the remediation of inequalities of access, calling for the sort of pragmatic solidarity that the . . . poor had demanded" (Farmer 1999: 31).

In summary, in line with an intra-agential ethos, Farmer challenges liberal views of human rights and emphasizes instead taking action to remedy injustice. He also challenges totalizing aspirations of revolutionary movements that uphold the certainty of an alternative social order validated by the certainty of abstract aspirational views of how the world should be. In this, Farmer echoes Foucault's response to the totalizing aspirations of the Marxist thinkers of his time that we have seen in Chapter 7. Structural factors do not act as impediments to agency and the only alternative. Committing to radical responsibility is rooted upon a method of inquiry aimed at studying what is the case and upon asking *how* questions with regard to the remedies to be proposed. Farmer's answer to a question by Sanjay Gupta in an interview for CNN testifies to this ethos, method and commitment. When asked whether it was possible to make a difference in Haiti, a place that he depicted as one of the poorest and hardest places to live in the world, Farmer responded by stating that the right question to be asked is not *whether* something is possible but *how* to make it happen (CNN 2017).

Conclusions

While Farmer does not specifically use this language, his ethos embraces a view of the world as complex, entangled and heterogeneous. He also embraces an ethos that puts at its center the assumption of responsibility and challenging accepted ways of asserting scientific truths. Ways of knowing are parts of apparatuses through which we engage the world and hence produce ontological effects. Immodest claims of causality, Farmer argues, offer grounds for relinquishing responsibility for people who are left to die. If indeed we live in an entangled and unequal world, we cannot relinquish responsibility for what happens to "those people" in "those spaces out there" as in mechanistic, atomistic and substantialist ontological imaginaries.

Farmer's ethico-political position challenges assumptions of the world as made of separate containers and governed by linear relations of causality; he highlights the ethical shortcomings and appeasing effects of justifications for actions based upon abstract normativity, biological determinism and othering substantialism. His ethos echoes E. H. Carr's – i.e. being committed to a form of political agency that is deeply rooted in historical analysis and accepts the primary relevance of practical considerations in making decisions. While embracing Galtung's notion of structural violence Farmer also challenges structuralist positions regarding agency. Social change then is not to be conceived as deriving from abstract aspirations to bring about a pre-determined, alternative notion of justice and the certainty of a luminous future, but from attempting practical ways of addressing peoples' concerns that maybe start putting a dent on the structural violence that affects them. In this way, Farmer embraces the morphogenetic potential of modest, micropolitical endeavors. Such commitment relies upon a method of inquiry that aims at studying what is the case and asking *how* questions with regard to the remedies to be proposed. In line with Foucault, Farmer affirms the centrality of the ethico-political task of challenging accepted narratives. If the world is entangled, we cannot relinquish the responsibility for remediating situations that are in fact connected in complex ways with our own everyday lives, and are perpetuated through ontological imaginaries that portray the world as homogenous, flat and divided in containers. In an intra-agential framework, the apparatuses we deploy to engage the world produce ontological cuts and require radical assumptions of responsibility. Because we are of the world and not above it, we never escape such responsibility regardless of whether we have the power to direct, through relations of push and pull, how the world will respond to our engagement.

Notes

1 For a more extensive analysis of PIH, see Zanotti 2010 as well as Stephenson and Zanotti 2012. See also Paul Farmer's biography by Tracy Kidder (2003).

2 For instance, Farmer shows that, contra accepted explanations that linked it to traditional cultures, the HIV epidemic did not spread from the Haitian countryside to the capital Port au Prince, but instead from Port au Prince to rural areas, and was imported to Haiti mostly by sex tourists from North America (Farmer 1992).

3 Farmer (1999, 2005) documents how this happens by narrating real-life stories of his patients.

Bibliography

CNN. 2017. "Enacting Change in a 'Place Forgotten.'" Video. June. www.cnn.com/videos/world/2017/06/12/champions-for-change- dr-sanjay-gupta.cnn. Accessed January 2018.

Duffield, Mark R. 2007. *Development, Security and Unending War: Governing the World of Peoples*. Cambridge: Polity.

Farmer, Paul. 1992. *Aids and Accusation: Haiti and the Geography of Blame*. Berkeley and Los Angeles: University of California Press.

———. 1999. *Infections and Inequalities: The Modern Plagues*. Berkeley and Los Angeles: University of California Press.

———. 2005. *Pathologies of Power: Health, Human Rights and the New War on the Poor*. Berkley and Los Angeles: University of California Press.

———. 2014. "Diary," *London Review of Books* 36.20: 38–39.

Kidder, Tracy. 2003. *Mountains Beyond Mountains*. New York: Random House. Partners in Health, Mission. www.pih.org/pages/our-mission. Accessed January 2018.

O'Connor, Peg. 2008. *Morality and Our Complicated Form of Life: Feminist Wittgensteinian Metaethics*. University Park, PA: Penn State University Press.

Partners in Health. 2018. Available at https://www.pih.org/pages/our-mission. Accessed April 22, 2018.

Robinson, Fiona. 2011. *The Ethics of Care: A Feminist Approach to Human Security*. Philadelphia: Temple University Press.

Stephenson, Max Jr. and Laura Zanotti. 2012. "Providing Service and Building the State Amid a Cacophony of International Aid: Partners in Health, Haiti." In *Peacebuilding Through Community-Based NGOs: Paradoxes and Possibilities*, eds. Stephenson Max Jr. and Laura Zanotti, 17–32. Sterling, VA: Kumarian.

Zanotti, Laura. 2010. "Cacophonies of Aid, Failed State Building and NGOs in Haiti: Setting the Stage for Disaster, Envisioning the Future." *Third World Quarterly* 31.5: 755–771.

Conclusions (just briefly)

This book is a dialogue between quantum ontologies and IR prevalent subtantialist ontological imaginaries, and more specifically IR debates on ways of conducting inquiries, conceptualizations of causality and justification of agency. In relying in particular upon Barad, Foucault and critical realism, I have argued that an entangled ontological imaginary opens the way for re-imagining ethics along the lines of responsibility and praxis instead of universal normativity, voluntarism and structural determinism. I have argued that an intra-agential perspective affirms the ethical potential of deconstruction. It paves the way for a reconceptualization of political ethos that does not rely upon given characteristics of the subject or universal principles or aspirations, but is grounded instead upon responsible consideration of the entanglements that obtain, the apparatuses we deploy to address them and the outcomes deriving from our engagement with what exists. An intra-agential ethos invites to an attitude of caution and modesty, curiosity, and relentless attention to the transformative possibilities that may open up in the practices within which we intra-act. An intra-agential ethos also raises the bar for what qualifies as a justifiable ethical choice. Following norms and rules does not provide a sufficient validation for actions. Intra-agential agency affirms the centrality of how aspirational goals are implemented. If we start from a relational ontology, externalities are not "external" but are ontologically rooted in the world's entanglements. Therefore, instead of being the inevitable residual of ethically valid prescriptions (unintended) consequences and means to ends are central for assessing the validity of ethical and political choices.

While raising the bar for adjudicating ethical validity and putting practices at the center of such assessments, an intra-agential ethos broadens what counts as transformative political engagement. Because it discards the causal closure of both ontological individualism and some versions of structuralism, an intra-agential ethos does not limit political imagination to rejecting and reversing the totality of what exist in order to bring about an immanent alternative benevolent social order. Micropolitical engagements contribute to different materializations of matter. At the same time, because what exists is performative and not an inert mass, the possibility that planning rationalities based upon simplified assumptions regarding causality may provide useful tools for predicting and governing all chains of events necessary for the realization of any given aspiration comes under question. This consideration is central for suggesting prudence in uttering bombastic political statements that advocate total rejection of what exists, or simplified solutions to complex political problems. It also puts under scrutiny the political rationale of international interventions based upon simplified assumptions regarding the causal clusters that obtain in conflict zones, that overlook the morphogenetic properties of practices.

This book has dealt mainly with the implication of entangled ontological imaginaries for human agency. The relevance of Newtonian, quantum, network and complexity theories for re-thinking how agency, control and resistance are exerted in an interconnected world is the topic of burgeoning scholarly debates (Cudworth, Hobden and Kavalski 2018; Kavalski 2016; Salter 2015; Pentinnen 2018; Walters 2017). Re-thinking human agency may be relevant for further discussions of how human/non-human assemblages come to being in specific practices of (inter)national governance.

In an intra-agential framework, practices are the spaces where ontological cuts take place and cannot be imagined as the residuals of abstractions. We never step out of ethics, as our being in the world contributes to its unfolding. An intra-agential ethos speaks to how we may imagine living creatively and responsibly.

Bibliography

Cudworth, Erika, Stephen Hobden and Emilian Kavalski. 2018. *Posthuman Dialogues in International Relations*. London and New York: Routledge.

Kavalski, Emilian. 2016. "Inside/Outside and Around: Observing the Complexity of Global Life." In *World Politics at the Edge of Chaos: Reflections on Complexity and Global Life*. New York: SUNY.

Pentinnen, Elina. 2018. "Potential of Posthumanist Onto-Epistemologies for the Study of International Relations." In *Posthuman Dialogues in International Relations*, eds. Cudworth Erika, Stephen Hobden and Emilian Kavalski. London and New York: Routledge.

Salter, Mark B. 2015. "Introduction: Circuits and Motion." In *Making Things International Vol 1*, ed. Mark B. Salter, vii–xxii. Minneapolis: University of Minnesota Press.

Walters, Williams. 2017. "The Micropolitics of Power Redux." In *Foucault and the Modern International: Silences and Legacies for the Study of World Politics*, ed. Philippe Bonditti (with Didier Bigo and Fredéric Gros), 57–75. London and New York: Palgrave Macmillan.

Index